W9-BMN-744

ROUGHNECK NINE-ONE

ROUGHNECK NINE-ONE

The Extraordinary Story of a Special Forces A-team at War

Sgt. 1st Class FRANK ANTENORI, US Army (Retired),

and

HANS HALBERSTADT

 St. Martin's Griffin ⚏ New York

ROUGHNECK NINE-ONE. Copyright © 2006 by Sgt. 1st Class Frank Antenori, US Army (Retired), and Hans Halberstadt. All rights reserved. Printed in the United States of America. No part of this book may be used or reproduced in any manner whatsoever without written permission except in the case of brief quotations embodied in critical articles or reviews. For information, address St. Martin's Press, 175 Fifth Avenue, New York, N.Y. 10010.

www.stmartins.com

Design by Level C

Library of Congress Cataloging-in-Publication Data

Antenori, Frank.
  Roughneck Nine-One : the extraordinary story of a special forces A-team at war / Frank Antenori and Hans Halberstadt.
      p. cm.
  Includes index.
  ISBN-13: 978-0-312-35333-9
  ISBN-10: 0-312-35333-2
  1. Iraq War, 2003– 2. United States. Army. Special Forces. 3. Antenori, Frank.
4. Iraq War, 2003—Personal narratives, American. I. Title: Roughneck 9 1.
II. Halberstadt, Hans. III. Title.

DS79.76.A58 2006
956.7044'342—dc22

                                                                2006040811

First St. Martin's Griffin Edition: August 2007

10 9 8 7 6 5 4 3 2 1

To the men of the Special Forces Regiment, who, over the years, have given the full measure of devotion in the name of defending the United States of America and liberating the oppressed peoples of this world.

Greater love hath no man than this,
that a man lay down his life for his friends.

—John 15:13.

CONTENTS

ACKNOWLEDGMENTS

The authors wish to thank their many friends in the Special Forces community, living and dead, in uniform and out, who have in their way written this book with us. They are, in the tradition of the community, unknown soldiers except to those they trust, an exceedingly small congregation. We are both blessed to count Green Berets as our friends.

Above all, a special thanks to the men of ODAs 391, 392, and 044, without whose valiant and heroic performance on the field of battle during those few days in April of 2003 this book would not have been possible. You are true professionals in your craft and fine soldiers. *"De Oppresso Liber!"*

Frank Antenori: I wish to thank my parents, Carol and Frank Senior, for providing me with the solid foundation that prepared me for the dynamic life of a Special Forces soldier. In particular, I want to give a special thanks to my mom, who was forced to endure two decades of anxiety as she watched CNN and Fox News, knowing her son was most likely in the middle of the chaos she was watching on TV. Like I've always said, Mom, "Don't worry, I'm in good company, and I'll make it back in one piece."

To my wife, Lesley, who for fourteen years has endured months and months of deployments, running the household and practically raising our two sons, Frank III and Brodie, on her own. Like most Special Forces wives, she is one of the unsung heroes of the Special Forces community, and I thank her not only for what she has done to support me throughout my career, but for her service to our country as well, both in and out of uniform.

I'd also like to thank my coauthor, Hans, who spent countless hours converting my recollections and endless war stories into the book you're about to read. His experience as an accomplished author as well as a fellow combat veteran helped him understand the complexities involved in writing a book about Special Forces. Hans, I salute your patience as well as your dedication to this project.

Last but not least, I'd like to thank my late great-uncle Gino J. Merli, a true American patriot who set the ultimate example of selfless sacrifice for one's country. From the day you were born until the day you passed, you lived to embody the motto "Duty, Honor, Country." I only pray that I am able to pass on those values to others, much in the same way you have passed them on to me.

Hans Halberstadt wishes to salute his mentors and friends from the late, great 3rd Battalion, 12th Special Forces Group (Airborne)— Gerry Schumacher, Russ Mann, Rick Cardin, Jim Gaston, John Padgett, Jim Shields, Jamie Allen, and many others who would prefer their names not appear in print. He would also like to thank his wife, April, who has been (mostly) tolerant of her husband's excursions to deepest, darkest Fort Bragg and Central America, and who has sanitized this and many other manuscripts over the years.

AUTHORS' NOTE

This book is based on the recollections of Sgt. 1st Class Frank Antenori, a retired member of the US Army. Conversations with others are re-created from his memory. The authors have attempted to confirm the descriptions of actual events and conversations with the persons involved. Unfortunately, they were prohibited from talking with active duty personnel by Army policy.

An advanced copy of the unedited manuscript for this story was submitted to the US Army Special Operations Command (USASOC) for two reviews. The first of those reviews consisted of a security review to ensure no information contained within the book inadvertently discloses sensitive or classified information that could prove harmful to current and future operations. Additionally, content was reviewed to ensure that the content included nothing in violation of Army regulations, and it has been approved without changes.

However, the content of this book has not been approved or endorsed by the US Army or USASOC Public Affairs Office and is the sole opinion of the authors. Neither the Army nor USASOC in any way influenced the content of, contributed to, or supported the production of any portion of this book.

WARNING ORDER

On April 6, 2003, my Special Forces A-team, along with a few other Americans, encountered a vastly superior enemy force at a remote, strategically essential crossroads near the little village of Debecka, Iraq.

Our force consisted of just over two dozen Army Green Berets, three Air Force controllers, and two Military Intelligence sergeants who volunteered to join us as drivers.

Equipped only with eight Humvees and two SUVs for transportation, and armed only with carbines, a few heavy machine guns, and a few Mk19 grenade launchers, our force was lightly armed and highly vulnerable. We also had about a dozen of the Army's new Javelin anti-tank guided missiles. None of us had ever fired one, and, at that time, we were all highly skeptical of their advertised performance.

The initial enemy force we encountered included four T-55 main battle tanks, eight MTLB armored personnel carriers, plus about 150 soldiers carried in half a dozen big troop trucks. In addition, the enemy also had heavy artillery support on call and a reserve force of six more T-55 main battle tanks and twelve MTLB armored personnel carriers. Unlike some enemy units, this one was well trained, well equipped, and well commanded. Its soldiers and leaders were brave, resourceful, and imaginative—a foe worthy of respect.

When discovered, the enemy force had us well within the range of its tank guns and heavy weapons. They deployed skillfully and engaged us in perfect order, catching us totally by surprise. The battlefield was a wide-open stretch of terrain on the valley floor with no place for us to hide.

Any normal American light infantry unit that found itself outnumbered over five to one and outgunned by such a heavy armored force would have turned and run. They would have called for close air support and artillery to cover their withdrawal, and let somebody else do the fighting.

But Green Berets just don't operate like conventional units, and we don't like to run. Before the war began, my team made the decision that we would never run from a fight, and we didn't run from this one, despite the odds.

We fought just the way we had trained on the practice ranges and in the backwoods of Virginia and North Carolina. We stopped the enemy advance, and then we killed the enemy, one by one, until the handful of Iraqi survivors finally fled the battlefield. The thirty-one of us, lightly armed and equipped, took on an enemy armored task force and destroyed it.

At the end of the battle at least fifty of the enemy lay dead in and around the intersection. Two of the tanks had been destroyed, along with their crews. All eight of the armored personnel carriers were destroyed, along with their crews, and many of the infantry they had carried were dead on the ground. Four troop trucks were knocked out, their infantry killed or wounded. Without effective help from American aviation or artillery, our tiny force routed a vastly superior force and captured key terrain for our follow-on forces.

During this encounter, while we fought the enemy, hordes of news media made our job harder as well. They didn't just report; they got in our way and at times even tried to tell us what to do. The difficulties were compounded during the peak of the fight, when a US Navy F-14 dropped a 500-pound bomb into the middle of a group of supporting Kurdish Peshmerga fighters, killing and wounding dozens of our allies.

There have been many important battles by American units in recent years, and this remarkable fight was full of lessons that have been studied carefully in the months since it was fought. The fight validated many years of tactical innovations, many lessons learned from Grenada, Somalia, Panama, Lebanon, the First Gulf War, and Afghanistan. It validated the value of new weapons like the Javelin missile and the value of old weapons like the M2 machine gun. It also validated the tradition of bravery and leadership that has been cherished by the US Army for more than two hundred years.

Our fight at Debecka was a test of all the training, the doctrine, and the technology that have been invested in the American Special Operations Forces during the entire twenty years I have been a soldier, and the battle at Debecka showed we passed that test.

Almost every man was a hero. One leader, whom I'll refer to throughout as "Maj. X," however, behaved in a way that made many of us question his competence on the battlefield. Along with that, some of his actions appeared to many as a significant lapse of courage, causing most of us to lose respect for him as a combat leader that day. His weak leadership and indecisiveness in the face of the enemy prevented our victory from being complete.

I am Sgt. 1st Class Frank Antenori, US Army, Retired; I was the team sergeant for Operational Detachment Alpha-391 (ODA-391).

The story of this amazing battle has been told privately to generals, members of congress, and senior personnel in government and industry. Some small parts of the story have appeared in *The New York Times*, on CNN, and in other media, but until now the complete account of this battle has not been available to the American public. Regulations now permit me to tell the whole story of how my team trained for a battle and how we fought alongside another full team and half of another.

Our call sign was "Roughneck Nine-One," and this is what we did.

LAYING ON THE MISSION

Since 9/11, all Special Forces Groups have been operating in harm's way on the front lines of the Global War on Terror, mostly unnoticed by the media or the American public. The business of Special Forces soldiers is a deadly serious one and keeping it low key increases our effectiveness. Often we are the only Americans operating in a country, under austere conditions and with very little support from other elements of the US military. Unnoticed anonymity is normal business for us. Our battle at Debecka was unusual in several ways, the first is that we are able to tell you about it at all. If Debecka had been an ordinary Special Forces mission and an ordinary fight, nobody outside the "community" would have ever heard about it. Our unofficial motto is "the quiet professionals," and that means we do not talk much in public about who we are or what we do, and we especially do not normally tell the public about fights like this one.

In this case, though, the US Army and its Special Operations Command (USASOC) decided to make an exception to the tradition. They have already told some of this story and identified some of us by name. The Army made this story public soon after it happened, and for a good reason—it was a remarkable success on many levels.

But there was another reason. The commanders of the Special Operations community thought it was time to bring Special Operations into the twenty-first century. That involved transforming the Special Operations Command from one that once supported other theater combatant commanders to one that would become a combatant command itself. SOCOM would now be supported by other units and eventually become the lead combatant command for the Global War on Terror.

To support this transformation, information about recent successes, including many Special Forces operations in Afghanistan and Iraq, were approved for public release to the media. The result was several articles in the national media, including *The New York Times*. The stories were also featured at the Army's annual Association of the United States Army (AUSA) convention in Washington, D.C., where several Special Forces soldiers told their stories to the public.

Many of the actual names of the soldiers involved in those operations were included in those stories, and for that reason they will be used in this book. The news media were present during part of the battle. In some cases, reporters saw more action than they anticipated. CNN and the BBC captured large portions of our battle on video, preventing anyone from keeping the story quiet.

The Army and the news media have already told the story the way they thought it should be told, but they didn't tell the whole story. At the same time, the Army discourages its soldiers from publishing stories while in uniform. I retired in July 2004 after an Army career of twenty years, the last sixteen in Special Forces. Having lived through it, I can now tell the whole story of how one A-team prepared for war and fought in battle.

ROUGHNECK NINE-ONE

ONE

AMBUSH AT GARDEZ

Looking back on it, I got my job as team sergeant for Operational Detachment Alpha-391 (ODA-391) as the result of an enemy ambush. It was a bloody business, but the good guys, with one exception, all lived, and the bad guys, from what we could see, were killed or captured.

I was assigned to Charlie Company, 3rd Battalion, 3rd Special Forces Group, and I was the company medic at the time. We were operating out of a "safe house" near Gardez, Afghanistan. Along with the other guys on the B-team, I had the job of providing support for the A-teams running patrols and operations in the Shah-e Khot valley in the weeks following Operation Anaconda. Home for us all was a walled compound typical of the area, and inside were two ODAs from 3rd Group, one from 20th, and another from 5th Group; we had set the place up with a little mess hall, a tactical operations center (TOC), a supply room, and my clinic.

I was having breakfast when a small convoy left our compound early on the morning of April 8, 2002, heading downtown to buy supplies at the local market. There were about twenty local AMF (Afghan Military Forces) and a few Special Forces guys from ODA-395 along for the ride, all mounted in pickup trucks and Land Rovers. The AMF soldiers were from the Eastern Alliance, a faction led by Gen. Zia Lodin. In the lead was a four-door Toyota Hilux pickup truck with two AMF men in the front seat, two in the back, and another six or so in the bed of the vehicle. There were two or three of these trucks in the lead, the Land Rovers followed.

There was only one practical route into Gardez, and that was over a bridge crossing a dry streambed. It was an obvious choke point and an ideal ambush location. The enemy knew this, and so did we, and the convoy approached the location with caution.

As the driver of the lead vehicle rolled up to the bridge, he saw what appeared to be a taxicab broken down on the road, with another vehicle parked alongside, apparently trying to help with repairs. The driver of the first truck responded in typical Afghan fashion by beeping his horn, yelling, and gesturing at the drivers to clear the road. The cab driver shrugged and indicated by gesture that he couldn't move the taxi.

The AMF driver was somehow convinced that this was an innocent event, and that turned out to be a bad mistake. The cab driver ambled over as if to talk, and he must have been a good actor because he got as far as the driver-side window, then dropped the first of several hand grenades inside. Before it detonated, he tossed another in the back of the truck among the half-dozen AMF. About the same time that the first grenade detonated in the cab, two Taliban popped up from the side of the bridge and opened up with AKs (as the AK-47 assault rifle is called) from close range, spraying the whole convoy with machine gun fire. The blast from the grenade blew out the windows of the cab, showering the bridge with millions of tiny shards of glass and severely injuring the four men inside.

The lead actor in this little play, the apparent cab driver, must have known he would not survive, but he stood there on the bridge throwing grenades at all of our vehicles for a few seconds. The AMF troops riding in the second vehicle cut him down almost immediately, with dozens of bullets hitting him in the head and chest. Then the AMF troops hosed down his accomplice, who was standing near the taxi on the bridge. When the AMF focused their fire on the two Taliban at the side of the bridge, their overwhelming fire forced the Taliban to flee into Gardez. The unharmed AMF quickly dismounted and took chase after

them. On the bridge lay close to two dozen of their fellow AMF soldiers, wounded and dying.

Back in the safe house, we all heard the detonations of the grenades
and the chatter of the automatic weapons and knew something must
have gone wrong. Then the radios came alive: "Phoenix Nine-Zero,
Phoenix Nine-Zero, the AMF have been hit! AMF have been ambushed at the bridge and have taken casualties. No American casualties. We're going to assist the AMF."

I looked up from my breakfast and across the table at Jeff Hull, but
before I could get a word out, Jeff was making a beeline for the door.
We grabbed our weapons, body armor, and an aid bag, ran outside, and
jumped on ATVs. We were roaring out the front gate when Maj. Mike
Hopkins, my company commander, ran out and stopped us, yelling,
"Stop! Frank, Stop! I need you to set up a casualty collection point
here. I'm going down there to find out what's going on."

Of course the whole compound was in controlled chaos. Mike took
ODA-394, the quick-reaction force (QRF), and they roared off in their
Ground Mobility Vehicles (GMVs) to support Nine-Five and the
AMF.

After a quick look around, I discovered I was the only medic in the
compound. I told all the remaining guys to start collecting cots from
our hooches and setting them up in the courtyard. With their help, I
started setting up a little MASH operation. While the cots were being
collected, the first truck rolled in the gate.

Jeff Hull was on the truck. "Casualties, casualties!" he called, and I
ran over to begin dealing with the victims. In the back was the poor
soul who was in the front seat of that first vehicle, clearly already dead.
All the flesh on his left leg had been cleanly removed and the bone re-
vealed; he had a gaping hole in his side, and his right hand was gone.
The grenade had apparently detonated in his hand while he was leaning over, trying to pick it up to throw it back out of the window of the
pickup. "This guy is gone," I told Jeff. "Let's put him to the side and
make this the start of the dead pile."

Then I asked the interpreter to find out how many more were coming in. "Twenty!" he said.

"Holy cow!" I said. "If we get twenty more like this, we're in trouble!"

The next truck that pulled in was literally a meat wagon, with about half a dozen wounded in the back, some sitting up, others lying down. The guys started taking them down, and I got to work on the one who seemed to be the most seriously wounded. He already had that ashen gray look and was unconscious, but he still had a pulse. It was hard to tell who was bleeding and who wasn't because the bed of the truck was covered in blood, and it had gotten on all of them, so we started cutting their clothes off. One guy had a major chest wound; another had lots of grenade fragments peppering his torso and head. Some were conscious and screaming.

When medics assess wounded for injuries, part of the inspection we do is by touch, and while I was running my hand down along the back of his head, two of my fingers disappeared into a hole at the base of his skull just behind the right ear. I carefully turned his head over and saw this gaping hole, definitely a major injury, thinking, *This guy is toast—he will never make it.* Although I didn't expect he'd survive, I called over the company sergeant major, Gary Koenitzer, and told him, "Take some of this Curlex [an absorbent bandage material] and start working on the rest of this guy's wounds."

Chris Manuel, our company operations warrant officer, asked me what he could do to help. "Chris, get on the radio and get us some helicopters," I said. "We're going to need at least two medevac aircraft, possibly more." Chris and one of the company commo guys ran back to the TOC and put in the call to the JSOTF (Joint Special Operations Task Force headquarters) at Bagram Airbase for help.

Even though the other guys were not medics, they had all been through the Combat Lifesaver program and had plenty of medical training to deal with just this sort of mayhem. And even though most of them had never had a chance to put that training to work before, they all dove in and performed brilliantly—a perfect example of why we all cross-train on each other's skills. They were clearing airways and putting on dressings, and I didn't have to show any of them what to do.

This let me deal with the most seriously wounded, and there were enough of them to keep me busy. One was a guy with a huge shrapnel wound to his back about the size of my fist; it was centered in the vicinity of his kidney. The wound was bleeding badly, so I started shoving Curlex into the hole, then slapped a dressing on it and told one of the guys to hold pressure on it as I moved to the next guy.

Both medics from Nine-Five arrived with the next truckload of casualties, so now there were three SF medics to deal with the worst cases: Matt Duffy, Jason Adams, and myself. "Matt, you grab the guy with the chest wound; Jason, you work on the guy with the head injury; and I'll take the kidney wound."

"Frank, we've got some more serious ones coming in," one of them said. A few minutes later, two more medics showed up from the 20th Group team who had been out on patrol but had hustled back to the compound when they heard the shooting. That brought the total of SF medics to five—literally a miracle for the Afghan soldiers. Because of the high level of difficulty and the long duration of Special Forces medical training, SF medics are usually in short supply. Many times, teams would be forced to deploy with only one medic instead of the standard two. Teams usually operate on their own when deployed, and if they are unfortunate enough to face a mass casualty situation, there will probably be a single medic handling all the chaos of both triage and treatment. This large number of medics at the compound would be the first of many miracles our wounded allies would be fortunate enough to experience.

We now had thirteen seriously wounded. Five of them were in critical condition, and if they did not receive immediate surgical attention, they would soon die. In addition, there were some others who were lightly wounded and would have to wait.

Jason's head-wound patient suddenly became the top priority. He began to have a seizure as a result of the head injury. His jaw locked shut, and then he vomited. Within seconds, his breathing stopped. Jason was a rookie medic just out of the course, but he knew what to do: the soldier needed a cricothyroidotomy, or "cric" (pronounced cr-ike), as we call it. This involves cutting a small hole in the front of the neck and inserting a tube into the trachea (windpipe), a technique that Jason had never used on a human previously but that he used now with textbook precision. Immediately, the man began to breathe, and his life was, for the moment, saved. For the next thirty minutes, we all worked like demons to stabilize all the casualties while waiting for the medevac helicopters.

The AMF soldier with the kidney wound had lost so much blood that he no longer had a pulse. We rapidly infused a blood expander called Hespan, and within minutes his pulse returned.

The soldier with the large chest wound now had a special dressing with an air valve in it, preventing the air leaking from the injured lung from building up pressure that would cause the other lung to collapse—a lethal condition. Three of the worst injured were literally brought back from death.

A UH-60 Blackhawk arrived first, complete with a flight medic and our 3rd Group surgeon. They immediately took charge of the three worst as we loaded them into the rotating carousel aboard the UH-60 medevac. The crew chief then told us a CH-47 Chinook was right behind them.

The Chinook's timing was perfect. Just as we finished loading the most critical guys into the Blackhawk, it took off, making room for the huge Chinook. We quickly loaded the remaining casualties into the back of the Chinook, and within minutes it, too, was in the air, on its way back to the expert care of the FAST (Forward Area Surgical Team) located in Bagram. Within thirty minutes, the wounded Afghans would be receiving the best medical care in all of Afghanistan.

You might not think so, but these wounded AMF guys were really lucky. They were lucky that they had SF medics nearby who could easily handle their severe wounds. They were lucky that the Army's best surgeons from Womack Army Medical Center at Fort Bragg provided stabilizing emergency surgery. Finally, for our guy with the severe open head wound, the Spanish army had a field hospital set up at Bagram, with a neurosurgeon on duty. The Spanish doctors operated on the guy for eight hours, repairing the injury to his brain; he woke up three days later, and a week later he walked out of the hospital with a cane. He had been clinically dead on the battlefield, with no pulse at all, and a bunch of Spanish surgeons, SF medics, and others saved him.

The man with the kidney wound lived, too, much to our surprise. The Afghan soldier with the massive chest wound had a collapsed lung, but the surgeons fixed him up and released him from the hospital after only a few days.

With the exception of the two worst cases, the head wound and the kidney wound, all the other AMF soldiers were flown back to our compound only a week after the event. We saved every single one of them who had arrived at our compound alive. When the helicopter brought them back to Gardez, their company commander, Hoshkiar, was there to meet them with hugs and tears. He and his staff dismounted from their vehicles, allowing the recovering wounded to ride in comfort while he and his officers walked back to the compound.

After the helicopter lifted off, we all walked back together, with Hoshkiar walking alongside us. He had been told by the returning AMF soldiers that all of his men were doing well; even the two critically wounded men had survived and would recover. With tears in his eyes, he said to me, "Those men would never have lived had you not been here to care for them. I want to thank you for this." With that he hugged me. So on behalf of all the Americans who gave their best to save the lives of our Afghan brothers in arms, I hugged him back.

This is the sort of thing that puts the "Special" in Special Forces, and it was one of many experiences that cemented the bonds between all the Afghan soldiers in the AMF and us Americans.

Gary Koenitzer worked as hard as anybody else during this mass casualty event, but that didn't keep him from doing his job as our company sergeant major at the same time. That job involves, among other things, evaluating the duty performance, particularly in stressful situations, of his subordinate noncommissioned officers, of whom I was one. While Gary didn't say a lot about it at the time, he apparently approved of how I managed the mass casualty situation, as I would find out later, when we got back to the States.

ERIC WRIGHT TAKES COMMAND

It was also during our tour in Afghanistan that Eric Wright was given his opportunity to become part of ODA-391. Eric had been assigned to the company only a few weeks before we deployed to Afghanistan. There wasn't enough time to get Eric up to speed enough to take an

A-team into combat, so he was assigned as our company executive officer (XO). As the XO, Eric had to grow up extremely fast. He assumed responsibility for compiling the company's Statement of Requirements (SOR) and oversaw many of the preparations to deploy an SF company into combat. He also managed the logistics associated with the initial "launching" of the teams involved in Operation Anaconda. His performance did not go unnoticed either. About six weeks through our tour, just after the completion of Operation Anaconda, our commander, Maj. Mike Hopkins, decided it was a good time for Eric to take over ODA-391. Normally, the command of a team is a two-year slot—enough time for an officer to become proficient at leading a team before he moves on in his career. The previous commander had his two years and a bit more. The problem was that the team was deployed and conducting "real-world" combat operations.

Changing commanders while deployed to a combat theater is not normal. A deployed team conducting combat operations needs to be one perfectly integrated unit that functions automatically during a crisis. All the members of the old Three-Nine-One had trained up together, understood each other's virtues and vices, and knew they could depend on each other. Good teams who have worked together for a long time can communicate without words, like a football team after the ball is hiked.

Even so, Maj. Hopkins decided to move Eric in to replace Three-Nine-One's commander while the team was still deployed in Afghanistan and conducting combat operations near the Pakistani border. Commanding a team in combat helps to advance an officer's career, and Maj. Hopkins was doing Eric a well-deserved favor with this assignment. At that time none of us knew that we would be fighting in Iraq, and we did not know how much longer we would be in Afghanistan, so this move was a precautionary one. The previous commander had done a fine job, but he already had his "trigger time" on his OER (Officer Evaluation Report), and it was time for Capt. Wright to get his.

Maj. Hopkins was a great commander and made the move with the best of intentions, but it immediately created problems within the team. Their old commander knew the ropes and was a vital member of the detachment, while Eric was considered by the members of ODA-391 as an unknown and untried leader. The members of ODA-391 were not happy, but they soldiered on and completed their tour.

MELTDOWN OF ODA-391

ODA-391 returned to the States in the spring of 2002, cleaned their gear, and then fell apart as a team. Special Forces detachments have the same problems and issues as any kind of team—people work well together for a while and then need to move on, and that is what happened at this time. Soon after their return, the team sergeant and most of the senior members of the team applied for other assignments and left. Capt. Wright suddenly had a detachment with no team sergeant and only five guys remaining. You do not want to do a mission with just five guys.

To add insult to injury, ODA-391 was scheduled to deploy to Africa for a month to train members of the Botswana armed forces in close-quarters battle (CQB). It was during those first few weeks after we got back that Gary Koenitzer called Jeff Hull and me into his office without saying why.

"What's up, Sergeant Major?" I asked. As the company sergeant major Gary had to fill Nine-One's vacancies, and he had to find suitable people in a hurry. Gary, remembering the ambush at Gardez, along with the way Jeff and I worked together that day, decided to offer us the opportunity to go back to an A-team.

"As you guys know, a lot of guys on Nine-One are leaving the team to go to schools or up to the group staff. Frank, I was thinking you could be the team sergeant, and Jeff, you could be his assistant Ops sergeant. What do you think?" Gary asked.

"Hell, yes," we both said.

And that's how I found myself as team sergeant of the "Roughnecks" of ODA-391.

TWO

THE ROAD TO SPECIAL FORCES

Most books on Special Forces leave out the most interesting part of the story—the way twelve guys form a team that can work all sorts of miracles on and off the battlefield. Every team has its own unique character, the result of the personalities of the men on it. And, since every man in Special Forces has a strong personality, the chemistry of these teams can be intense. Ordinarily, we don't talk in public about ourselves as individuals or as members of a specific ODA, but that is another unique part of this particular story, and I am able to introduce you to most of the guys who fought at Debecka with me.

Since I will be telling the story, and since I was the team sergeant, let me introduce myself first.

Two men were especially influential in my life and led me to a career in Special Forces. One was my dad, Frank Senior, and the other was my great-uncle Gino Merli.

My uncle Gino received the Medal of Honor for valor during World War II. He lived four doors down the street from us. Normally he wouldn't really talk much about what the war had been like for him, but for some reason he would occasionally open up with my dad and me. Beginning at about age sixteen, when I started getting interested in the military, his stories really began to sink in. He had a room in the house with his memorabilia on the walls, including his Medal of Honor, and dozens of other medals in a lighted curio cabinet, along with photographs of him with presidents, celebrities, and other important people. It all fascinated me. At age sixteen, a young man starts looking around for a role model—and Uncle Gino was a perfect one for me.

He had been a machine gunner whose unit was attacked by a much larger force of Germans. Most of the guys in his unit were forced to withdraw, but not Gino and his assistant gunner. They stayed to provide covering fire. He stood his ground and slowed the attack before being overrun. His assistant was killed in the process and lay beside him. When the Germans finally swept over his position, he played dead till they went by, pursuing the rest of Gino's company. Then he got back behind his gun, spun it around, and started cutting them down again.

The Germans counterattacked and came back through Gino's position, and once again Uncle Gino played dead. He manned his gun throughout the night, surrounded by dozens of dead and dying German soldiers, until an American unit finally returned to the position, finding him still manning his machine gun. On the battlefield lay fifty-two dead German soldiers, nineteen within a few feet of his position. Gino passed away shortly after I returned from Afghanistan in May of 2002.

My dad was and still is a tough guy with a short fuse—a strong Italian personality with a love for the outdoors. He frequently had my brothers, my sister, and me out fishing, hunting, and camping. When I was a kid, he taught me all the basic "field craft" skills that many guys have to learn the hard way later, in the Q course. We hunted every Saturday during the season in the fall. It was often cold and miserable, but he insisted that I sit there, in the deer stand, without making noise, and that helped me develop the kind of physical and mental toughness required of a Special Forces soldier. I watched these two guys, and they taught me my values in life. They both refused to let anybody take advantage of them, to lie to them or to jerk them around. Both had phenomenal standards of physical courage and personal integrity, and both were intensely patriotic. My uncle in particular taught me about soldiering—about loyalty to the guys on your team and never letting them down, even at the risk of death. He and my dad taught me to never run from a fight.

While I was in high school, about 1983, I had dreams of going to Penn State and becoming an electrical engineer. My grades, however, were not good. My father knew about both my dreams and my grades. He sat me down one day and said, "I am not paying a dime for you to go to college. You are a C student at best. I'm not paying for Cs. If you were an A student, my attitude would be different. You want to go to college? Pay for it with your own damn money—get a job or join the Army; they'll give you money for college. If you want it, you go get it yourself."

So I went and talked to a recruiter and told him I wanted an MOS (military occupational specialty) that had a lot of technical training that would be useful when I finally was able to go to Penn State and fulfill that dream of becoming an engineer. The recruiter went through all the job descriptions and came up with something that seemed to match: 55 Golf, Nuclear Weapons Specialist. It sounded perfect, and I signed the enlistment contract. Since I was not yet eighteen, my parents' consent was required. When the recruiter came by the house to get my parents to sign the form, my dad practically jerked his arm off, dragging him to the dining room table to sign it.

Off I went to Basic Training at Fort McClellan, Alabama, which was the same place Uncle Gino had gone for his Basic Training during World War II. Then I was sent to Redstone Arsenal for the six-month Nuclear Weapons School. During this training a major from USSO-COM (United States Special Operations Command) spoke to us one day.

"I'm looking for some male volunteers for assignment to go to Fort Bragg, North Carolina, to help Special Forces A-teams with a classified program. I can't tell you any more than that."

Four of the class volunteered, and one was me. He took all four and told us that after graduation from the 55G School, we would be sent to Fort Benning, Georgia, for training as paratroopers, and then we would be assigned to Fort Bragg.

I went through the rest of training with illusions of grandeur—the myth of the Green Berets back then was phenomenal—and I was excited about actually working with these guys. We graduated, and off I went to Benning. Of the four volunteers, one never even showed up, getting scared even before he saw an airplane; the other two guys quit during the first week of Jump School. We had all been together for six months and had promised that we would all hang together and help each other get through the three weeks of airborne training. By the end of the first week, I was there all by myself.

I finished and was assigned to Fort Bragg. My job was to support a Special Forces A-team that had an interesting mission. During the height of the Cold War, Special Forces possessed a small nuclear bomb that fit in a rucksack. It was called SADM, or Small Atomic Demolition Munition, and was also known as the "backpack nuke." It was during this mission that I was first exposed to team life and was bitten by the bug that would lead to a long SF career.

In the following years, I would go through the Q course and be assigned to the 5th Special Forces Group (SFG). My first mission would be teaching Combat Lifesaver skills to Afghani Mujahadeen in 1989 and 1990. In August 1990 I deployed to Saudi Arabia for Desert Shield, which later became Desert Storm. From being in combat I gained a lot of experience and confidence that would later set me up for success in Iraq. After eight years, I was assigned to the Special Warfare Center (SWC, pronounced *swick*) as a Q course instructor. After four rewarding years teaching future Special Forces, SEAL, Ranger Medics, and Air Force Para-rescuemen, I was assigned to the 3rd Special Forces Group. It would be during this tour that I would find myself on the battlefields of Afghanistan and Iraq.

REBUILDING THE TEAM

The few guys left on the team did not welcome the news of my new position. I had, and have, a reputation for being an abrasive individual and drawing fire in the form of unwanted attention from the chain of command. I was already two years overdue for promotion to master sergeant, a promotion that would never happen because I had a letter of reprimand in my personnel file as a result of a "disagreement" with a certain two-star general. The guys that remained on Nine-One had already dealt with plenty of tension and discord, and could not have been pleased to hear a troublemaker would be their new team sergeant.

I reported to Three-Nine-One and introduced myself to the half-dozen enlisted loyalists, none of whom were happy. Capt. Wright, on the other hand, was glad to see me. He had been commanding Nine-One for a couple of months, and it had not been fun. At the end of that first day, after the other guys went home, Eric and I sat down for a long discussion of recent events.

He told me about all the friction and discord on the team, then said, "Frank, I don't mind what your leadership style is or how you run the team, just don't ever argue with me in front of the guys. As team sergeant, you run the team, but as team leader I command it. If you have a gripe or bitch, you and I can go off somewhere and sort it out in private." This, apparently, was not the way things had been done previously, and Eric was insistent that he and I present a united front to the world above and below us.

"No problem," I told him. "I will never argue with you in front of the team."

We agreed to back each other up no matter what, and that was the beginning of an outstanding relationship. Since both of us were from Pennsylvania, we both jokingly nicknamed this relationship the "PA Connection."

From my earlier time on the B-team, I had already worked with pretty much everyone in the company. I knew the guys who had remained on Three-Nine-One pretty well. One by one I sat down with each and told them I had a plan to rebuild Nine-One. I wanted to model the team after the ODA I had been on in 5th Group. ODA-571 was also a team equipped with GMVs, and the SOPs (Standard Operating Procedure) and our tactics would be similar. Most of all, ODA-571 was a team filled with guys who were definitely not risk-averse. They were a strong team that had the reputation for being cowboys, but also for coming through some tough missions with remarkable success.

MARTY MCKENNA, TEAM WARRANT OFFICER

The first guy I sat down with was Warrant Officer One Marty McKenna, the team's warrant officer. Marty and I had served together as sergeants in 3rd Battalion, 5th Group. I was in A Company, Marty in B Company. He understood where I was coming from, modeling Nine-One after the ODAs of the Third-of-the-Fifth. He also remembered the reputation of the ODA I was on back then and was a bit nervous about trying to repeat the experiment in 3rd Group.

Marty had also found his way to Special Forces by interacting with them while he was a calvary scout in Germany. During a REFORGER exercise (REturn of FORces to GERmany, a Cold War military exercise) Marty was assigned to set a Traffic Control Point to ensure his battalion made the correct turn to cross the only bridge for 10 kilometers that could support the weight of a tank. When he got to the bridge, the Dutch troops who had been guarding it assured him all was well, for they had been at their guard post for two days.

As Marty sent two of his men to the far side of the bridge to ensure the approaching tanks made the turn, he noticed an umpire for the exercise walking toward him. Behind the umpire, two men began marking the bridge with engineer's tape.

"Who's in charge?" the umpire asked. Marty answered and said he was just there to make sure his battalion stayed on route.

The umpire told him that a Special Forces team from 10th SFG had been under the bridge placing dummy C-4, and that the bridge was blown and he was dead. He told Marty to retrieve his men from the other side and that their new job was to ensure no one used the bridge.

Marty decided then and there that he was going to sign up for Special Forces and go to the Q course.

Marty had now been in Special Forces for ten years. After finishing his tour as a Q-course instructor, he put in a packet to become a Special Forces warrant officer. After training at Fort Rucker in the Warrant Officer Basic Course, Marty went through the Special Forces Warrant Officer Course at Fort Bragg. Then, in late 2000, he came to the team. He would be promoted to chief warrant officer two (CW2) just prior to our deployment to Iraq.

If I was the yang of the team, Marty was the ying. He was reserved and often methodical, a perfect counter to my outspoken impulsiveness. Many a time Marty would pull me aside and say, "Frank, are you *sure* we want to do that?"

That simple question probably saved my ass from getting fired dozens of times.

Marty was probably the most respected and definitely one of the most highly valued members of the team. Next to me, he was also the most experienced. Because he was a warrant officer, he exerted more influence on the company leadership than I ever could. For all these reasons, I viewed Marty as a priceless ally.

ANDY PEZZELLA, SENIOR COMMO GUY

Then I met with Staff Sgt. Andy Pezzella, at twenty-seven the youngest member of the team. At that time, he was also the least experienced. Andy had become Three-Nine-One's "commo" (communications) man after the senior commo specialist departed with the post-Afghan exodus. I first met Andy a year earlier when I was with another team, which had gone to Botswana on a mission that happened to coincide with Three-Nine-One's. That was Andy's first mission. In less than a year, he had gotten several missions under his belt, including a combat tour in Afghanistan.

A fellow Yankee, Andy was from upstate New York, an area I was familiar with from many fishing trips to the Finger Lakes as a kid with my dad. Andy also had a New York accent, something that stuck out in the deep South. He was the most physically fit member of the team, doing daily physical training with the team and also hitting the gym daily. Since he was single, Andy maintained a lifestyle that focused around his own interests. We had all been single once—some of us more than once—and at times we envied Andy's freedom.

KENNEY WILSON, ENGINEER AND DEMOLITIONS SPECIALIST

Staff Sgt. Kenney Wilson, the team's junior "demo" man, was my next meeting. I had known Kenney for two years. He was what you would call your typical "good ol' boy." Born in North Carolina, he was familiar with the local culture and could speak "North Carolinian," a trait that would come in handy down the road. One of the unique things about Ken was his name. Unlike most Kens who officially are named Kenneth, he spelled his name with an "-ey," as he constantly reminded me.

He was generally quiet and reserved.

Kenney seldom displayed anger, even in situations where most of us would explode. It would take a lot to get *him* pissed off, but he would openly offer his opinion, usually in a pithy fashion. Kenney would come to me from time to time to address issues he felt were important. Some of his opinions were even *about* the way I was doing things. I took his comments to heart and respected his candor. Ken and I developed a friendship and would later go deer hunting together. That friendship allowed Ken to tell me things without worrying about retaliation from me. This is the kind of trust that a team sergeant needs to be effective.

I wanted to ensure that the guys would come to me if they had issues with me, with their teammates, or with the way things were going with the team. I even held frequent "bitch sessions" with the guys, telling them they should immediately speak up if they saw something that did not sit right with them, or if they had a better idea. This environment of open bitch sessions was something I encouraged, as long as it was inside the team room and no outsiders were present.

At times these sessions got heated, but the guys always remained professional and never took any of the comments personally.

FRED DEROSA, SENIOR ENGINEER

The last person on my meeting list was Sgt. 1st Class Fred DeRosa. Fred was also a New Yorker from Brooklyn. He had both the banter and the personality of a stereotypical Brooklynite. Fred, also a demo man, was Kenney's senior. While Kenney tended to quietly voice his opinion, Fred would occasionally have outbursts from frustration, sometimes with poor timing. Otherwise Fred's strong personality fit in with what would become the new Nine-One.

This reorganized team was getting ready for an overseas deployment, and we were technically without a medic. While I was trained as a medic, I did not want the company leadership to see me primarily as a medic who happened to be acting as a team sergeant. I wanted it to be perfectly clear that I was the team sergeant and that, as with any team sergeant, my primary role was running the team, not providing for its medical needs. So when I went to Gary and asked for a medic, I found he had thought ahead and had already gone to the battalion command sergeant major to ask for the next medic available.

MIKE RAY, SENIOR MEDIC

That next medic was Mike Ray. Mike, although he was a sergeant first class, he was a "cherry," or new guy in the business. He had just graduated from the Q course and was a former student of mine. He had no team experience, other than what he had gleaned from his time in the Q course. He was, however, an experienced NCO.

Mike also possessed a strong personality. He was frequently outspoken—a perfect match for the rest of us. Mike was previously a parachute rigger by trade and was a fellow Gulf War veteran. Over the years he had developed a leadership style that prepared him for a future in Special Forces. Mike was a strong advocate for his soldiers, or "Joes" as he referred to them, constantly telling his officers to stay out of what was "NCO business."

Many officers in the conventional Army tended to micromanage their sergeants, but Mike refused to be controlled. This sometimes put him in conflict with his previous commanders, but strong personalities among sergeants are nothing new in Special Forces. Some of his previous commanders became intimidated by Mike's strong leadership style and began to make Mike feel "unwelcome" in his old unit. Mike saw the writing on the wall and decided to go to where he would be a bit more appreciated. As a medic, I appreciated Mike's presence more than anyone else. His presence as the senior medic on the team helped solidify my position as the team sergeant. Mike's introduction to team life was short. We only had a few weeks to get ready for a deployment, so Mike had to jump through his ass in order to get the team medically ready to go.

THREE

ADVENTURES IN BOTSWANA

Even though most of us had only been back from Afghanistan for a short time, ODA-391 was scheduled to deploy overseas again very soon. Third Group's area of responsibility includes Africa. We deploy there every year to conduct what was called a JCET (Joint Combined Exchange Training). We work with other armies, sharing our knowledge. One army is that of Botswana, a country in southern Africa with a small, but fairly competent, military. Since one of the fundamental missions of Special Forces is the training of indigenous personnel, this "Foreign Internal Defense," or FID, mission has benefits for the host nation and for us, too. But it is not always easy or fun to pack up the team and set up shop out in the bush. Sometimes the biggest problems are the ones we bring along with us, and that was the case with our deployment to Botswana in the summer of 2002.

These deployments have budgets to cover the costs of transportation, lodging, and all the related materials—ammunition, explosives, local vehicle rental, and building materials needed to construct targets. And, just as sometimes happens with civilian companies, we arrived in Botswana to discover that another team had spent all the

JCET money allocated to us. Suddenly ODA-391 had a crisis—a job to do without the money to do it.

I tore into the other team sergeant, the other team leader, and anybody else involved. Many team sergeants might not challenge the commander of another team, but I am not built that way. I already knew I would never be promoted again, so I stuck up for my team, and the team saw me do it. This crisis over the budget, and my reaction, turned out to be the beginning of the rebirth of the team. My team now knew I would go to bat for them, no matter what. The issue was finally resolved when the other team's company commander provided the funds from his company's Op Fund, allowing us to carry out our mission and enabling us to obtain the supplies we needed.

These FID deployments are good for the team. We get to know each other without either the pressures of a combat environment or the distractions of our home station.

Most of us had been to Africa many times, but some of the younger guys had never been out of Botswana. I had been to Kruger National Park in South Africa twice and had a great time, and I encouraged the guys to consider a short visit.

"Look, guys, we have got to go there," I told them. "Kruger is the best national park on the planet. Who knows when we're going to get back here?"

We had an additional week in the schedule, so we had time for the team to do a "cultural and environmental immersion." As we drove to Kruger National Park, the discussion turned to events in Iraq.

"Frank, do you think we're going to go back to the Gulf for round two?" Mike asked. At the conclusion of Desert Storm in May of 1991, I had heard exactly the same question.

I was riding in a Humvee with Will Williams, a close friend and the senior commo guy for our team, ODA-571. We were heading toward the Saudi Arabian border to King Khalid Military City (KKMC) where a USAF C-5 cargo aircraft would fly us back to Fort Campbell, Kentucky.

Will looked over at me and asked,

"So, Franco, how long before you figure we're back over here to finish this thing?" I laughed and responded, "Probably in five years, ten at the latest."

"Yep, I give it about the same time," Will commented. "No doubt we'll both be over here again."

I relayed that old conversation from 1991 to Mike and he started to laugh. He had the very same conversation with his guys as they left Saudi Arabia in 1991 as well. He and I both knew Saddam would never honor the cease-fire. Sure enough, Saddam expelled the weapons inspectors and was firing on our air force jets that patrolled the no-fly zones. We just couldn't understand why we hadn't called him on it yet by ending our cease-fire.

"Well, Mike, it's been over ten years, looks like we were wrong."

"Not wrong, Frank, just a little off on the timeline." Mike chipped in. "No way in hell are we going to go back over there without finishing it this next time."

"I'm with you, Mike, no way we're stopping next time." I predicted.

"I'm surprised it's taken this long. There's no doubt we'll be back over there sooner or later," I told him.

While looking at the African wildlife, we were all getting to know each other. Our most productive times were spent around the campfires at night. We told stories of our families and our military exploits and started talking about the team. After that trip, the morale of Nine-One went through the roof.

BACK TO BRAGG

We came back from Botswana to Bragg in August of 2002 with a very different view of ourselves as a team. Shortly after, Fred DeRosa asked to leave the team due to a family hardship. I tried to convince him to stay, but his mind was made up, and he was gone. This left the senior engineer slot open, and our team was back down to just seven guys.

BOBBY FARMER, JUNIOR ENGINEER

After our Africa trip, the word started to get out that Nine-One was becoming a good team. This attracted new talent, like Bobby Farmer. Bobby was from West Virginia, a hillbilly. He had a terrific attitude; he was a real hard-charger and became a spark plug for the team, initiating all kinds of improvements.

Bobby had a lot of experience with off-road driving, both with 4×4s and with quads (all terrain vehicles), and this know-how would come in quite handy. He had also been a conventional engineer in the 20th Engineer Brigade, located just down the street. This link provided access to additional material and connections that Bobby would also bring to the team. In addition, he had just graduated from the Q course, and he had a lot of good friends whom he thought we could use.

"Frank," Bobby would say, "I know a great guy who would be perfect for this team. . . ." And soon we had people asking to join Three-Nine-One.

JASON BROWN SIGNS UP

Team slots began to fill up. Jason Brown was the next to join. A weapons guy, he hailed from Okalahoma and truly was an Okie. He had a lot of trouble with spelling, often times writing words phonetically in "Okie Talk," quickly becoming the brunt of jokes on the team.

The new members made Andy Pezzella happy. Until now he'd been the cherry, but in a few weeks Andy became one of the more senior guys on the team.

There were some major changes in the company as well. Both Maj. Mike Hopkins and Sgt. Maj. Gary Koenitzer were due to rotate out. Their departure made way for an officer who I'll call Maj. X (as a courtesy to his family) and Sgt. Maj. Joe Ward. Maj. X had served as a team leader in Charlie Company before going off to an assignment at Fort Polk. Sgt. Maj. Ward was a "10th Grouper" and had recently gotten his promotion. Little did we know his political connection to the 10th Group would come in handy in the future. Joe was also an accomplished mortar man from his earlier days in Special Forces as a heavy weapons sergeant—another critical skill that would be called upon in our not too distant future.

FOUR

WARNING ORDER FOR IRAQ

O rdinarily, a detachment gets six months between deployments. The fall of 2002 was not an ordinary time, and soon after we got back from Botswana, we were told to begin preparation for deployment and combat operations.

When a US Army unit is notified that it will get a mission, this notification comes in the form of something called a "warning order." This order is typically very sketchy, with just the general outlines of the mission. The warning order is normally delivered verbally, face-to-face, by the commander.

A warning order gets everybody moving, preparing for a more specific requirement known as an "operation order." Once we got our warning order, we got busier. Eric now had the opportunity to oversee the train-up of his own detachment before taking them into combat. One of Eric's best attributes as an officer was that he had immense confidence in his warrant and NCOs, but most of all, he trusted us. Eric wasn't one of those officers who felt he had to be the fastest runner or the best shot on his team to prove his worthiness to lead. He was a quiet, confident guy who was easy to work for and was well liked by the men. Because of these attributes, we always did our best to set him up for success. Eric viewed himself as the "synergist," being able to bring everyone together with all the unique personalities we had on the team and providing the focus needed to obtain the maximum output. Eric gave me and Marty all the leeway we needed to rebuild the team and make us a cohesive unit. He tasked us to come up with the training plan to get everyone ready for combat.

Marty and I had a long talk one night in September after the other guys had finally gone home. We typically worked late—especially Marty, who was always the last to leave—because there is usually so much administrative work. This evening, soon after we got the warning order and guidance from Eric, we opened our beers and had a long talk about how we wanted the team to function.

"Frank," he said, "you and I are finally in a position where we can make a difference—we've always wanted to be part of a team that was doing great things. This is our chance."

"One of the things that really bothers me," Marty said, "is the guys in this business that are risk-averse. There are too many guys who are afraid to do anything without a note from Mommy."

"You don't have to worry about that with me, Marty," I told him. "I have always been willing to step outside the box when necessary."

Marty's job was to design a long-term plan to prepare the team for missions. My job was to execute that plan and supervise the other NCOs on the team. The ODA commander's role was to function like a CEO in a civilian company and to direct the responsibilities of his two primary subordinates.

The deployment process begins with a "mission letter" that lays out all the tasks that the ODA will be expected to perform if called upon. In peacetime, mission letters guide the general day-to-day training and usually orient a team toward one of the primary Special Forces missions. Our mission was Special Reconnaissance, both mounted and dismounted. Because a mission letter is all the direction you have, the commander needs to think ahead. By the time the team receives an OpOrder, it is too late to do much training. If the commander, the warrant officer, and the team sergeant have done their work, they already have a plan and are all ready to execute the mission.

Eric was great at this type of planning. Eric's role was to explain, in somewhat general terms, how he wanted us to execute the assigned operation. My role, and any team sergeant's role, is to order the weapons, the ammunition, and all the other gear required to execute the mission. Marty's role was to begin the scheduling process while I worked on the grocery list.

While we had no idea what specific missions we would execute in Iraq, I knew from combat deployments to the First Gulf War and to Afghanistan that it was likely to be an adventure and an excellent experience. I came out of Desert Storm with tremendous understanding that the new guys could never get in peacetime training operations. I was just a young staff sergeant at the time, but I commanded a company of 120 Kuwaiti soldiers in combat, one of the many Kuwaiti infantry companies led by Special Forces advisors that were involved in the final assault on Kuwait City. Most US Army captains never get to lead a company in combat, but each sergeant on that ODA had that chance. It was a tremendously useful experience, one that helped guide the rest of my career in SF. I learned that if you have your act together and you put your mind to a mission, you can accomplish tremendous things as a member of Special Forces.

The younger members of ODA-391 who had not been in combat were all probably wondering how they would perform when put to the test. Everybody wonders how he will react when that first bullet goes by his head and how he will respond when somebody nearby is badly wounded. That apprehension is natural, important, and impossible to actually answer outside of mortal combat. Before the First Gulf War, I had a great team sergeant who helped get me and the other guys on my team ready for that test. Now it was time for me and the other experienced guys to prepare the new guys just out of the Q course for their experience under fire.

Marty and I talked about all these things that night in the team room, over our bottles of beer. We determined that ODA-391 was going to be fully prepared to accomplish its missions. We decided it would be a team that could make a significant difference on the battlefield. We did not know it at the time, but making a difference was exactly what fate had in store for our team on a remote battlefield on the other side of the world.

"I'm going to develop a training program to get us all ready for this," Marty said. "It's going to cut into home life, and some of the guys may object."

"I'll support you 100 percent, Marty," I told him.

Very soon, Marty had us all out of the team rooms and offices and into the weeds, refreshing our tactical skills. First we went on foot patrols in Area J, behind the headquarters of the 82nd Airborne Division in the woods of Fort Bragg.

We loaded up with our rucksacks and rifles and then went out to practice SOPs all day long. At the end of the day, we dropped our rucks in the team room, drank a beer with the guys, and went home. Next morning, we did it all over again—the most simple and basic of dismounted patrolling techniques that every soldier learns in basic training. For us older guys, these SOP drills were things we had done a million times, and the training was somewhat tedious, but Marty had a bigger plan. Sharing just these basic skills was helping the team to bond—his plan was working.

Now the physical training (PT) level started picking up, too. Since I hate running and avoid it whenever possible, I emphasized road marching when there was a choice. This is one of the exercises that get soldiers into shape for combat. Eric stressed doing a graded PT test as well. In the Army, a PT test, more formally titled the Army Physical Fitness Test (APFT), is comprised of three separate events: push-ups, sit-ups, and a two-mile run, each worth 100 points. They are used as a basic measurement of a soldier's fitness level and are often used to gage a leader's performance as well, depending on if his men do well or poorly. Eric wasn't nervous about the team doing well on the PT test, but he knew good scores are sometimes looked at by a commander for selecting teams for high-profile missions. The PT really paid off with the team obtaining an overall average of 292 out of a possible 300, a score Eric was proud of but still wanted to try to improve it to 300.

All the other ODAs were preparing for deployment at this time, too, but we kept looking for ways to work our training into everyday events that other teams might have neglected. One event was to do SOPs under full rucks, driving the GMVs to and from ranges while practicing formations and performing "dead driver/dead gunner drills" along the way. Using his connections from the Special Operations Medical Training Center, Mike and I set up medical training for the team. We would take our IMBTRs (radios) everywhere we went, and Andy made sure everyone knew how to program the frequencies and install the crypto codes. Every time we came to a bridge, Kenney and Bobby would give a quick class on the way to crater the approaching road, and he would show us techniques for blasting the supports.

The senior members of the team made sure that every part of the training exercises became part of our preparation for actual combat. This all involved a lot of time and hard work, but the team continued to gel as they trained together. Marty and I both tried to make it as much fun as possible by kicking back during lunch and by having a beer at the end of the day with the whole group. By mid-September, we were masters of dismounted patrolling and ready to move on.

ATVS AND GMVS

Now we started training with our vehicles. Third Group and 5th Group, unlike some others, are equipped with specialized Humvees. We train to conduct mounted patrols as well as foot patrols. Our ODA had four of these vehicles, each a variant of the basic M998 model that the Army calls a High Mobility Multipurpose Wheeled Vehicle (HMMWV).

These were no ordinary HMMWVs. The standard 1¼-ton suspension systems were replaced by a heavier suspension that doubled the cargo capacity to 2½ tons, the same capacity that the large FMTV (Family of Medium Tactical Vehicles) Army trucks had. They also had some additions under the hood: a turbo-charged diesel engine, an additional transmission cooler, an oil cooler, and an extralarge radiator for operating in desert heat.

Adding an extra alternator to keep the batteries charged while we were running the DC to AC power inverter increased the power-generation capability. The power inverter came in handy because it produced standard household current. This enabled us to plug in the battery chargers for our IMBTR and SATCOM radios, freeing us from carrying a lot of batteries and allowing us more room for ammo. It also allowed us to bring along the electric coffee maker that is standard equipment for any A-team. Besides the Humvees, we had four all-terrain vehicles (ATVs) made by Polaris.

Bobby Farmer, being a young and motivated sergeant, was always looking for something to do. He loved riding ATVs and off-road motorcycles for fun in West Virginia, where he grew up. Now Bobby asked if he could be in charge of the ATVs. He had some ideas about how to modify them, and he asked for the authority as well as for some money for the accessories he had in mind. Well, it seemed like a reasonable idea, and the team had just received its first funding authorization for the deployment—about $150,000—so Marty and I told Bobby to go ahead and get his list together.

YOUR TAX DOLLARS AT WORK

Special Forces teams and other military units, too, purchase a lot of things they need on the open market, frequently with a credit card known as an IMPAC (International Merchant Purchase Authorization Card). Of course, there are the normal rules and accounting requirements, but when an ODA needs something, they often need it quickly. They cannot wait to put a request out for bid. Kenney Wilson carried our credit card around, and it had a $25,000 limit, with a $2,500 limit per single purchase.

Bobby and Kenney put together an order for auxiliary fuel tanks that nearly tripled the range of the ATVs. Then he added big basket racks that enclosed the whole rear of each ATV and added lots of storage capacity for more fuel and ammo. He ordered brackets for our M4 carbines and brackets for our GPS receivers, saddlebags, and other things that made each ATV much more capable. Bobby did a hell of a job on these ATVs, and when he was done, he had still other ideas.

"I want to order some parts to trick out our shotguns," he told us. "If we're going to be operating in an urban environment, the Mk19 and .50cal will be useless at close quarters. The gunners need small, short-barreled shotguns, not those long clumsy ones we have, and I know exactly the parts we need to convert them."

"Sure, Bobby, go ahead," we told him.

We could easily order weapons parts with just the group commander's endorsement, and we were sure he would approve of Bobby's idea. We wrote it up, submitted the request, and got permission to buy the gun parts. Throughout the train-up and prep, the support from all levels of Special Forces Command and USASOC was almost unbelievable.

With the approval letter in hand, Bobby called up the Mossberg company and told the order clerk exactly what he had in mind. He ordered a very short barrel of 14 inches and a small custom pistol grip without a buttstock at all. It had a bungee-style shoulder harness so that it fit under the armpit and lay at your side between your arm and your rib cage. Mossberg ordered four sets of them for us and made our order a high priority, and we had the shotgun parts very shortly. Once the battalion armorer installed the new parts onto the receivers of our old Mossberg 500s, the shotguns looked odd, like overgrown pistols—but Bobby's idea was right on target. We used them in combat just a few months later at Debecka as well as in Kirkuk and Mosul.

Jason Brown and Kenney took over equipping the Humvees. These Humvees had been stripped of a lot of accessories and body panels and had racks on the back, with a large extended bumper for water, fuel, ammunition, and MREs (Meals Ready to Eat). When they are all tricked out, with a full complement of radios, an air compressor, infrared driving lights, and a multitude of special weapons mounts, they become known as GMVs—Ground Mobility Vehicles.

Each GMV had a ring mount on the roof for either an M2 .50cal heavy machine gun or an Mk19 40mm grenade launcher. There was a second mount for an M240 medium machine gun, operated by the front-seat passenger. And there was a third mount on the back for either an M249 SAW light machine gun, an M240, or a Barrett .50cal sniper rifle for doing assaults. These GMVs had the fuel to go much farther than a conventional Humvee—600 miles compared to the usual 200. They carried enough other supplies to sustain the crew for up to ten days. All of those modifications paid off big later on the battlefield.

RICH TURNER AND GERRY KIRK JOIN THE TEAM

The battalion had been earmarked for deployment, and the personnel managers within the command were diverting almost every new arrival to the 3rd, 5th, and 10th SFGs so the groups would be fully manned by the time hostilities started. This meant we had a steady stream of recruits—some fresh young blood from the Q course as well as some old-timers who came in from instructor or staff jobs. We received two new faces to the team: Richard Turner and Gerry Kirk.

Rich was a commo guy who had just finished logging time in the battalion C&E (Communications and Electronics) shop. As a bonus, they let him go to Ranger School; we picked him up just after he graduated and made it back to Bragg. Rich was a promotable staff sergeant. This made him senior to Andy, bumping Andy back into the junior commo slot. Andy had no problem with this and was more than happy to sign millions of dollars of radios and crypto gear over to Rich.

Gerry was an old salt. Like Marty and me, he had spent a lot of time in the 5th Legion. Instead of doing a tour at the "schoolhouse," Gerry did time in the 96th Civil Affairs (CA). During peacetime the 96th usually conducts humanitarian missions. But during wartime they handle displaced civilians and refugees on the battlefield, keeping them out of the way of the warring factions. Special Forces–qualified soldiers were assigned to CA because SF is noted for having the needed cultural, political, and situational awareness skills.

Gerry was a MOS 18F (Military Occupational Specialty 18F, Special Forces Intel sergeant). Jeff Hull had not been formally trained in Intelligence but was filling the position as the assistant Operations and Intelligence sergeant because he was senior to the rest of the guys. Now that Gerry was on the team, Jeff would move to the senior weapons sergeant slot, bumping Jason down to junior weapons sergeant.

The team was getting full. We had a team leader, a warrant, a team sergeant, and an intel sergeant. We had Jeff and Jason at weapons, Kenney and Bobby at demo, Andy and Rich at commo, but only Mike in the medic slot. We were still missing a junior medic.

Since I was a medic, I was told that the other teams would get two medics before one would come our way. During my ten years on a team, I never saw a time when every team in the battalion had two medics, so I knew the chances of getting a junior medic for Mike were slim. With a team of eleven guys, we headed off to Fort Picket for the next phase of the train-up.

FIVE

FORT PICKETT, VIRGINIA

In the fall of 2002, our rebuilt ODA-391 got ready for a serious work-out. We shifted our training emphasis to include the tactical use of our Ground Mobility Vehicles (GMVs). Jason and Kenney were still modifying these vehicles, but we did not wait until completion to assign each guy to a specific GMV. No matter where we went, each of us rode in his assigned vehicle at the assigned position. Even if we were just going down to the wash rack to hose off the mud, each of us rode like we would on an actual mission. This meant, of course, that everybody took particular interest in his GMV, and everybody made small changes to customize it, like the placement of the racks for the ammunition cans. Personalizing each GMV produced a great sense of personal commitment to the vehicle, the team, and the mission.

Early in November, we hooked up the utility trailers to the GMVs, filled them with ammo and chow, and deployed to Fort Pickett, a facility that is normally used for the training of Reserve and National Guard units. Our home station, Fort Bragg, North Carolina, is huge and has facilities for many kinds of training. But it also has thousands of soldiers using all those ranges, all the time, as well as restrictions on just how each range may be used. The Army says that we "train the way we fight," but if we actually had to fight the way we train at Fort

Bragg, nobody would fire a shot until a range safety officer (RSO) told us it was okay.

Training at Fort Pickett was a wonderful change for our ODA. The garrison commander, an Army colonel, made sure that we were given a high priority for use of the installation's excellent ranges. We were also given a great deal of freedom of operation. The rules at Pickett were much different than those at Bragg, and that helped all the 3rd Group teams do much more realistic training.

For example, consider the problems associated with carrying ammunition and explosives. When you are deployed to combat, you are carrying thousands of rounds for all your weapons. You have demolition materials—C4, detonating cord, blasting caps—stored on your vehicle and grenades in your load-bearing vest. You walk around with a full ammunition magazine in the well of your carbine and a round in the chamber. None of this constant arming is tolerated at Bragg or any other stateside garrison, but we got close to it at Fort Pickett, and that helped us get into the combat mind-set of maneuvering "locked and cocked."

From sunrise till sunset and on into the night, we fired up all kinds of targets, using every type of weapon we owned. Pausing only for a lunch break at noon, we blasted away with the Mk19s and .50cal machine guns, our M4 carbines, and our M9 pistols. Our first priority was getting the weapons zeroed and making sure that each of us was officially qualified to fire the M2 and Mk19 as well as our M4s and pistols. Each of us had to fire the official qualification courses of fire for record, and then we were each "certified." You cannot go off to combat, even in Special Forces, without having all the paperwork properly completed.

DOT DRILLS AND COMPETITION

After certification, the fun began with "dot drills." We placed small dots on the targets and began the exercise with our rifles held at the "low ready" position. On command, we would bring the weapon up and fire two quick rounds. This engagement technique is called "double-tapping." We did this over and over, building muscle-memory:

if you do it enough, your body learns to accurately point the weapon exactly where you are looking, without the use of the sights, even in the dark.

We were starting to get a little bored and looked for a new challenge. One of the guys proposed setting up the targets at a variety of distances, requiring us to fire on the move, with obstacles placed here and there just to make it all the more challenging. This time, we would be scored on our time through the course as well as our hits on the targets. Just to make this a little more interesting, we decided to have everybody contribute a dollar every time the team did the drill, the winner taking the $11. Most of us are highly competitive, so this intensified the process considerably.

After the targets were set up, we designated the firing points in challenging ways, and you had to run from one to the next. For example, the first point was out in the open, the second from behind a vehicle, the third from the base of the range tower, and so forth, with a 10-meter dash from one to the next. We shot at 2-inch dots out to about 50 meters, and at head-sized balloons out to 400 meters.

Some of the younger guys started getting really serious about this shooting, Kenney, Bobby, and Jason especially. Both Marty and I had been to the SOT (Special Operations Techniques) School long ago, and so we were experienced shooters, but competition was raising the level of intensity, and the younger guys loved it.

Practice paid off big. It only took forty-five seconds to run through the stations of the course, and a shooter would go through three magazine changes, firing thirty rounds in the process. Ordinarily in an exercise like this you would expect to see bullet holes all over the paper, but when our targets were scored, you would see two little holes close together on each of the dots.

When we got tired of those drills, we got out the sniper rifles. Everybody became proficient at engaging targets out to 800 meters and beyond. Marty was also a graduate of the SOTIC (Special Operations Target Interdiction Course), and, again, he made an excellent trainer. All of us were shooting to a standard that was far higher than normal, and the informal competition among us had a lot to do with it.

TANK RANGES

After a week of shooting our carbines, it was time to work on our skills with the heavy weapons, the 40mm Mk19 grenade launcher and the .50cal heavy machine gun.

Now, the M2 heavy machine gun is a wonderful weapon. The basic design goes back to the First World War era. The gun we use today is not much different from the gun mounted on nearly every jeep and Sherman tank during the Second World War, almost sixty years ago. It is tremendously accurate, powerful, and devastating against both enemy personnel in the open and "thin-skinned" vehicles like trucks, and its projectiles will punch right through a masonry wall. The specs say it is effective to about 1,800 meters—about a mile—but your target needs to be cooperating if you are to score many hits at that distance. We did not know it at the time, but the M2 would play a major role in our combat operations in the future.

We started out by firing at the standard targets for qualification, and, once again, everybody got certified on the weapon. Then we went over to the firing ranges designed for use by the Abrams tanks. We had no practice ranges like these at Bragg. There were targets out to 5 kilometers, or 3 miles, targets that popped up, and targets that moved like a vehicle. The targets could be programmed so that you had to hit them multiple times before they would go down, adding to the realism. These ranges were awesome for us, a new experience.

Until this time we had been operating alone. Now we linked up with our sister team, ODA-392. Running the tank range requires a lot of manpower. It takes two guys in the tower controlling the range, a couple of guys distributing ammo, one operating the moving targets, and another recording scores. Having one team run the range allows the other to concentrate on shooting.

Trading off was a very efficient system. It was also an opportunity for us to get to know the guys on Nine-Two since we did not have much contact with them back at Bragg. As it turned out, we would have plenty of contact with them on the battlefield, but we did not know that then.

Once again the staff at Fort Pickett had provided us with exceptional facilities. One of the great things we could do here was to "live-fire" and maneuver, which were impossible at Fort Bragg. At Bragg you could never shoot if anyone was forward of your position. In combat, you have to be ready to fire over or past other members of your team. Maybe the range-control staff at Pickett thought the Special Forces community operated under different rules, since they were far more tolerant of our need for realistic training. We were grateful.

We began by driving the GMVs into one of the static firing positions and spending half a day shooting at pop-up targets without leaving that position. In the afternoon we started moving down the same lanes the tanks used for their engagements, and this was a really interesting exercise for us. We began by driving down to the middle of the range, 2,500 meters from the tower, firing at targets popping up on the 3,500-meter line just a kilometer away. We practiced maneuvering back in 500-meter bounds, just as if we were breaking contact.

The guys in the tower brought up closer targets as we fell back, simulating an enemy chasing us. We did this exercise as a team, with two vehicles maneuvering while the other two maintained a base of fire on the enemy "tanks." When our first pair got back about 500 meters, we began to apply suppressive fire on the enemy while the second pair of GMVs leapfrogged back under covering fire and took over the suppression. This made for exceptionally realistic training that would be used sooner than any of us expected.

Despite the freezing November cold and rain, the machine-gunners were having a blast. Now that everybody was comfortable with the routine, we began inventing oddball scenarios and scoring the results as we each manned the big guns. During one of these drills, Capt. Wright and I were in the tower, running the range, when we got into a discussion about our SOP (Standard Operating Procedures) if we encountered enemy vehicles out in the real world.

"Frank," he said, "what are we really going to do if we run into a lot of Iraqis over there?" It was an important question to consider. During the First Gulf War, ODA-525 had been forced to fight several hundred Iraqis after being compromised on an SR (special reconnaissance) mission deep inside Iraq. My friend Jimmy Weatherford was the radio operator on that team, as well as another bud, Bobby "Buzz-saw" De-Groff, so I had heard exactly how it had all gone down, and there was an important lesson in their performance in that battle.

In the opening hours of Operation Desert Storm, on 24 February 1991, eight members of ODA-525 were inserted 145 miles inside Iraq. Under cover of darkness, they moved into their assigned position just across Highway 7 from a village. They dug two "hides" in the side of an irrigation ditch, climbed in, and covered the holes with tarps. Each tarp had a hole for observation. Unfortunately some children discovered the site, peeped through the hole, and recognized the team as Americans. The team had just a few seconds to decide how to respond—kill the kids with their silenced pistol or MP5 submachine gun, or let them go.

They let them go. The kids ran back to their village and told the adults, and soon the local militia was swarming around the area. Before the militia arrived, team sergeant Charlie Hopkins radioed that Five-Two-Five's location was compromised and needed close air support. He moved his team to a better fighting position as they watched truckloads of enemy soldiers begin moving toward them.

The guys on Five-Two-Five were armed only with M16s. They were attacked by at least two hundred enemy soldiers with AK-47s and SKS rifles. But Jimmy, Buzz-saw, and the other guys knew how to shoot and could consistently hit to 400 meters and beyond. The Iraqis' AKs and SKS weapons were effective to only 200 meters, and then only when used by a trained soldier. ODA-525 started eating up the enemy troops at long range, one at a time, with carefully aimed fire.

The enemy soldiers tried to flank Five-Two-Five's position. Every time the enemy tried to move closer, the guy in front was immediately hit by one of the team. The rest of the Iraqis hit the ground for a few seconds until they got the courage to try again. Immediately the new point man would get shot. The team's accurate and disciplined fire quickly demoralized the enemy and halted their attack. This fight went on for a long time before close air support arrived and slaughtered the remaining attackers. Members of the 160th Special Operations Aviation Regiment (SOAR) finally extracted the team. Not a single member of ODA-525 was killed or wounded, and their performance had become one of the important lessons learned from the First Gulf War.

Eric asked, "Frank, what do you think we should do if we run into the same sort of situation, where we encounter a much larger force of enemy dismounts?"

The answer would depend on a couple of factors, one of which was firepower and the other mobility. As long as we had trucks of some sort, along with weapons, I thought we would be able to deal with dismounted infantry. Our recent shooting just demonstrated that.

"Eric, until enemy tanks show up, we are going to slug it out with them. I am not going to run from two hundred Iraqis," I told him. "The way our guys are shooting right now, they are going to pile the enemy up. If we come over a hill into an enemy battalion's rear area, I think we should shoot them up."

In reality, such a decision would be based on all sorts of factors and was not a procedure that could be written into the team's SOP. But Eric was not trying to outline an SOP. He was just trying to make sure we were on the same philosophical page about how to deal with likely events. Eric's concern was a reasonable one, and his decision was part of his process of commanding the team. Every team commander has some latitude to decide what he is going to do during an operation. Of course, he will always have a plan, but plans almost never get executed as written—you get dropped into an LZ (landing zone) 20 miles from the one you expected, for example, or the enemy force turns out to be a battalion instead of a platoon. We make plans and SOPs, but the genius of the American commander is his ability to adapt those plans to what is actually on the ground.

When he adapts, he issues what we call a FRAGO, or fragmentary-order, that modifies the original concept of the operation and its objectives to the tactical reality on the battlefield. US Army commanders are taught to have this flexibility. And Eric was thinking ahead to the battlefield and trying to make sure that he and his team were going to flex in the same direction, and he was worried about overconfidence.

"Eric, our guys have been shooting really well," I said, "and if we get into a larger force of infantry, I am *not* running! As long as we have enough ammo, I don't care if half the damn Iraqi army is out there, I am going to keep killing them until we get to the point where you think we are at risk of being killed or captured, and then you can break contact and pull us back. Till then, I think we ought to pile them up." From this conversation came a policy decision for our team—that we would stand fast whenever possible and never run from a fight unless we clearly could not win it. The policy turned into a sort of motto: "Nine-One Don't Run."

We shared this conversation with the rest of the team over beers later that night. The "we'll pile 'em up" concept really struck a positive cord with the team. Jason chimed in that adding Javelin missiles to our basic load would give us a strong antiarmor capability as well. Javelins, combined with the mobility of the GMVs and effective use of terrain, would provide us with the ability to engage tanks without having to withdraw. As it turned out, the two statements of: first of all "we're not running," and then "we're going to pile them up" spread like a germ through the team, infecting the guys with the confidence needed for a fight with a much bigger force. This also seemed to have an effect on the new guys, easing their doubts about performing under fire and putting them into the mindset that they were capable of handling such a situation if it should happen.

Every battle has a decisive point (place, time, event, or decision on the battlefield that led to victory), but our decisive point wasn't on the battlefield. We didn't know it, but it was at that point in time, on that cold, rainy, November night, that the battle at Debecka was won.

GETTING ACQUAINTED WITH ODA-392

Special Forces is a small community within the Army. You might think that members of two ODAs within the same battalion, in the same company, with their team rooms in the same building directly across the hall from each other, would work together often. You might think they would be well acquainted, personally and professionally, but that is often not the case. Each ODA tends to train as an individual unit and is traditionally somewhat isolated from the others. While we do occasionally bump into each other in the hallway and exchange hellos at functions, we usually tend to keep to our own team and stay out of the other teams' business. Until the trip to Fort Pickett, we did not really know the guys on Nine-Two very well at all. Now we were supporting them on the tank gunnery ranges, and they were supporting us, so our relationship began to change.

After each run down the lanes, we would all go downrange to inspect the targets. Guys from the detachment doing the shooting went down as well as the guys who were operating the targets. Naturally, we started comparing scores, and this raised the level of competition. It pitted one team against the other, and that was good for us both. Of course, there was the usual kidding back and forth, but at the same time we began to bond with the guys on Nine-Two.

Ken Thompson took over as team sergeant for Nine-Two when the previous guy was injured in Afghanistan. Ken had an attitude a lot like mine—he tolerated no bullshit from anybody and refused to play the political games that were still an important fact of life at this time. As a result, Ken got a reputation similar to the one I had—hardheaded, cold-hearted, abrasive. Neither Three-Nine-One nor Three-Nine-Two was a popular team with the more senior officers and NCOs, who object to subordinates like us who hoist the "bullshit flag" during meetings.

And Ken was not alone with that attitude about Nine-Two. The captain on that team, Matt Saunders, seemed to have a huge set of balls. Using what could only be described as "covert finesse," he constantly challenged those on the battalion staff as well as the company leadership, criticizing aspects of their planning and questioning some decisions. While this may seem a bit out of line from a conventional standpoint, it was a trait that was quite common in most Detachment Commanders, especially the well-seasoned ones in Charlie Company. He was especially competent and outspoken, and we really admired him.

Capt. Saunders went out of his way to support our team when we were taking flak from the rest of the battalion, which was often. When Ken stood up in one of our team-sergeant meetings to point out some sort of foolishness, I normally backed him up, and he did the same for me. Eric and Matt Saunders were doing the same in the team leaders' meetings. ODAs Three-Nine-One and Three-Nine-Two were forming multiple bonds in late 2002, out on the ranges at Fort Pickett and back at Fort Bragg, as the preparation for deployment continued. We were not popular, but we were having fun and "leaning forward."

The increasing closeness of our two teams had the somewhat unfortunate result of pulling Nine-Two down the political ladder to our level, which was at the bottom. Because of my personality, some of the history of the team, and a variety of other factors, ODA-391 was normally in the doghouse with the command. We were the black sheep of the company and, most likely, the battalion, but at least Nine-Two kept us company. ODAs Nine-Four and Nine-Five were the company commander's favorites, and we were the outcasts.

Up at Fort Pickett, however, politics was not an issue except over the weekend. That's when the whole company gathered to run through our covert resupply drills, and only then did we meet up with Maj. X and the rest of the company.

THE B-TEAM AT PICKETT

At this point, our plan for the invasion of Iraq directed us to prepare to infiltrate through Turkey, drive our GMVs through the Kurdish-controlled part of the country, then scout routes for American armor through the "Green Line" that was the effective border with the rest of the country. This plan meant that we'd be driving over 400 miles before the serious part of the mission even kicked off, and that meant we'd need a lot of logistic support from the company's B-team.

Our company was a tad different from some other SF companies. While we had a similar structure, we'd only be going to Iraq with four A-teams instead of six like most companies. One of the teams in the company, nicknamed "the Long Hair Team," would not be deploying. They had a special mission and were under the control of the EUCOM CINC (European Command Commander in Chief) and SOCOM directly. The other team was referred to as the "ghost team" since the decision to cut an ODA from each company to compensate for manning shortages, caused it to remain empty.

The B-team looks almost like the A-team, but it is commanded by the company commander who in this case was Maj. X. It includes a few specialists we don't have on the A-teams. One of these was a mechanic, Specialist Art Thompson, and another was a supply sergeant, Sgt. Felix Paterson, and although both were qualified parachutists, neither were "tabbed" Green Berets. That didn't keep them from being very hard-core soldiers, and they played crucial roles during training and combat. Besides supporting the ODAs during operations, the B-team was always available as reinforcements if anybody got into trouble.

SIX

BIRTH OF THE BLACK SHEEP

We returned from Fort Pickett and during December continued our preparation for deployment. We had been up there for twelve days, and when we got back, ODA-391 was a solid team forged by many factors—the shooting competitions, the miserable weather, the isolation from the petty BS at Bragg, the long conversations about our destiny, and the closer and closer prospect of a combat deployment. We ate and drank together, as a team. Everybody on the ODA had come to trust and admire everybody else on the team. The young guys proved that they were ready to learn from the old guys and that in the process they could teach the old guys a few new tricks about shooting. Gary Koenitzer's and Joe Ward's choice of recruits had been validated along with Eric's general leadership of the team. ODA-391 had fallen apart a few months earlier, and now it was tightly glued back together with a lot of new components. Despite all that, we knew we were still considered the nonconformists and the bad boys of the battalion.

SORs

The US Army doesn't let you go off to war before you spend a lot of time doing paperwork, and this is especially true for a Special Forces detachment. Besides all the SOPs and qualification records, the up-dated wills and inoculations, and all the other documents required by our company, battalion, and group and by the Army, we started to get documents with the word "SECRET" stamped on them. One of these was our Statement of Requirements, a report we call an SOR, which we had to fill out with the things we needed to complete our mission—a sort of wish list.

At this point, in late November 2002, we knew we'd be going to Iraq, we knew we'd be in the north, but we did not know exactly what we'd be told to do. We presumed that we would run into enemy "light-skinned" vehicles—trucks and lightly armored personnel carriers, and possibly some tanks; we'd been told to expect everything from reconning airfields to seizing them, from screening the flank of the 4th Infantry Division to paving the way with close air support all the way to Baghdad. We'd even been told we might be doing trafficability assessments of highways and bridges and soil density tests of the desert along the way. And with that in mind, Eric, Marty, and I got together and started filling out the SOR. All of us had written SORs before, and we quickly added 90 percent of what we needed based on previous missions. Now all we had to do was tweak the list for the specific demands of this mission.

The original plan called for us to go in during January or February, and we knew that this part of the world would be cold and wet, so our SOR included a lot of Gortex and other "comfort" gear to deal with the climate. As the list began to grow, Marty looked at it and said, "There's a lot of stuff on this list that will probably get disapproved, so we need to put some fluff in here that we can sacrifice when we do the SOR scrub and they tell us to get rid of something."

"You're right, Marty," I said. "When they tell us to cross off part of the list, we can say, 'Okay, we will give up the automatic tire inflator if we can keep the North Face fleece jackets.'"

Marty started adding in all sorts of extra stuff to use as bargaining chips, and there was a lot of it, all plausible but with some things that were really not essential. Then we went up to battalion headquarters for our SOR review.

"So you guys really need all this stuff?" the Group S-3 (Operations officer) and S-4 (supply officer) asked.

"Oh, yes, sir," we replied.

"Okay," they said. "Approved." We were surprised but knew the list had to be reviewed again at the group level. The S3 and S4 up there reviewed the list with little comment, and stamped the form "APPROVED." Marty and I said, "Thanks," but we were both thinking, *Holy cow!* The SOR now went up to USASOC, where it was considered again, approved again, and finally delivered to the Contracting Office, where it was approved again—without a single thing being eliminated.

This attitude really impressed all of us. The command wasn't encouraging waste; they were actually trying to support us 100 percent. We still had a budget that we couldn't exceed; all the SOR did was give us the approval to use the money allocated to us to buy those items on the list. We figured that since the leadership was gracious enough to give us everything we asked for, we shouldn't take advantage of their generosity.

The weeks that followed were busy ones for UPS and the FedEx Company, especially the office that delivered parcels to Fort Bragg. The trucks were in a holding pattern out in the parking lot, waiting for an opening so they could pull in and unload all the boxes with our address on it. And it wasn't only our ODA but all of them that had anticipated a pruning process that didn't happen; all the ODAs in the battalion had trucks unloading more or less constantly.

TEACHING ERIC SUBTLE WAYS TO SAY NO

At the same time we were trying to get control of all our new gear, we were also being told to spend a lot of time developing and writing SOPs. Some of this seemed to be the result of Maj. X's previous assignment at the Joint Readiness Training Center where he had been an evaluator and instructed every visiting unit to have a plan for each and every contingency, no matter how remote. The mind-set at the company level required you to have a primary, alternate, and contingency plan for anything that might go wrong on the battlefield; our command told us to have an SOP for changing the tire on your vehicle and all sorts of other petty activities, and instead of preparing for combat, we were told to write up all these documents, get them approved, and follow them religiously.

Marty fought Maj. X on many of these things. They'd meet in the hall, and Maj. X would give him a long list of petty things to do. Marty replied, "Yes, sir, I'll get to them as soon as we get these other things finished."

"Marty," Maj. X replied, "I am sensing some passive resistance here."

"*Passive,* sir?" Marty answered. "It isn't really passive, sir; it is just resistance."

I was more blunt. Maj. X said, "Frank, I need to have Nine-One write up SOPs for these events."

"Sir, talk to Capt. Wright about that—we don't have time to do that shit. If he wants to do that at night when he's at home, fine, but we have more important things to do to get this team ready to deploy."

Then, of course, the major would go off to talk to Capt. Wright, and like a good conventional officer, Eric came back and tried to get us to write the SOPs. It didn't work. Instead, we tried to teach Eric a more "unconventional" approach when it came to dealing with what seemed to be small potatoes to Eric but a big deal to the rest of us.

Eric was by no means a "yes-man." On many occasions Eric had made the trip down the hallway to Maj. X's office to confront him on some of the decisions and guidance the company was putting out. Unfortunately though, officers in the conventional Army are conditioned to "pick and choose" their battles. Most will step in and fight for their men or question what seems to be a potentially dangerous order, but when it comes to the "small stuff" they tend to give in for the sake of saving their political capital for what they see as a more important issue.

Eric was from the school of "let's fight hard for the major issues, not the small ones." Unfortunately, the SOP issue may have seemed petty, but putting any effort into complying with it would be a major distraction from preparing for deployment.

NCOs and warrant officers in Special Forces have an implied duty to help develop officers along their career journey. The battalion commanders, group commanders, and even the generals had a virtual "sidekick" with them practically their entire careers; their warrants, team sergeants, and sergeants major that helped keep them in "tune" with their men. The best commanders in Special Forces didn't get there without having some supportive NCOs along the way.

So we sat down with Eric and explained our point of view. "Eric, we've got a million things going on, the last thing we need is doing this time-consuming BS for the sake of just checking one of Maj. X's little blocks on his personal list," Marty and I offered. Next we told him that he did have to fight for the small stuff because of the snowball effect constantly giving in would create.

"Eric, you're just going to have to tell him 'No.' Give him some sort of rationale behind it, but you just have to tell him no or he will continue to bury us in the small stuff."

Captains have a real hard time using this word with majors and senior officers; they have been conditioned to always say, "Yes, sir," but we tried to train Eric to say no at the appropriate times, and it got to be a running joke around the team. Now, this is not to say we wanted the team or our team leader to be insubordinate or negative about everything that the commander proposed. It was only that there were times to remind the headquarters people that they should avoid micromanaging the teams as they prepared for war.

Of course SOPs are essential, but just for the events that need a standardized reaction. The last thing you want in combat is a guy who is trained to be a robot and can only act exactly the way he was programmed. So Eric took our advice and went back to Maj. X's office to tell him no. He was met by an even stronger directive from Maj. X.

"If you guys don't make time for getting these things written during normal work hours," Maj. X said, "I am going to have you come in on the weekend to do them." Eric came back with the news that our little idea had failed, that Maj. X was pissed and he still wanted the SOPs to be done. In a way, Eric was right about not fighting the little battles, but then we showed him there's more than one way to say "No."

"Okay—if he wants SOPs, he'll get SOPs," Marty said, and he fired up his computer. The result was a set of SOPs, but the actions Marty specified were as ridiculous as the situations that the SOPs were intended to address. For example, there was supposed to be an SOP saying what the team would do if we ran into an enemy checkpoint. "If we're traveling faster than 20mph," Marty wrote, "we will run over them. If we are traveling less than 20mph, we will get out and shoot them." How the team would actually behave in such a situation would depend on many other factors and might be resolved in many different ways, but since the commander wanted an SOP, Marty gave him an SOP for that and all the other situations on the list. It was a waste of time and a distraction and produced many useless documents, but as a result of Marty's writing it, we were able to spend our weekends with our families.

Of course, Maj. X was not pleased with the SOPs and came down to confront us on the issue. All of us gathered in the team room. He gave us a little pep talk, then got onto the topic of the SOPs.

"Standard operating procedures are important," he said, "and you guys don't seem to be taking them seriously. What will you do if you come over the crest of a hill and find a hundred Iraqis on the other side?"

"We're going to kill them," we said. All of us were responding to his questions, not just Eric, Marty, or me. We may have been outranked, but he was outnumbered.

"No, get serious—what would you really do?" he demanded.

"Sir, we are going to kill them. That is the guidance we got from Lt. Col. Binford while we are on this screening mission. He told us, 'Kill any enemy that you can, and if you can't kill them yourselves, lure them out in the desert and kill them with CAS [close air support].' Sir, we can clean up a hundred Iraqis in twenty minutes by ourselves."

"I don't think so," he said.

"Sir, small arms fired by Iraqis are not a threat to this ODA. Enemy dismounts are not a threat to this ODA. We will kill them. If we come over a hill and run into dismounted infantry that only have AKs and similar weapons, we are going to kill them, and we are not going to run. We will shoot the hell out of them and pile them up."

"Well, what are you going to do if you run into a tank platoon?" he demanded.

"Sir, we are going to kill them," Jason chimed in.

"So now you're going to kill *tanks*? With what?"

"With the Javelins, sir. We have been training on the Javelin simulator. We are going to kill them."

At this point the commander's eyes sort of glazed, and he didn't seem to know how to admonish his brash, unorthodox, misfit team that was relying on a missile that had never been used in battle. "I think you guys are out of control," he said.

"No, sir, we aren't. We are not going to run as long as we posses the means to defend ourselves. We are not going to run as long as we are able to kill the enemy. Sir, we are going to pile them up." And we were not alone in this attitude—it came from our group commander; his attitude was as aggressive as ours. As far as that goes, there already was an SOP that covered these contingencies: the US Army's own basic doctrine not to break contact with the enemy unless you encounter a force clearly superior to your own. It was our company commander who seemed to want us all to minimize risk.

Neither Maj. X nor those of us on the team left that meeting very confident or encouraged. Maj. X clearly had big doubts about us and thought we were dangerously overconfident, that we had pumped up our confidence at Pickett, that we were thinking beyond our "capability radius." We read him as being extremely risk-averse; he seemed to be telling us that an enemy force larger than two guys by the side of the road was the signal to break contact, run, and call for CAS. We thought this guidance conflicted with basic Army doctrine and with the guidance we had gotten from our battalion and group commanders, so we had big doubts about him, too. And nobody left the meeting expecting that, about four months later, ODA-391 and ODA-392 would come over a hill, bump into 150 Iraqi soldiers, four tanks, and eight personnel carriers, and stand and fight them all, exactly the way we promised.

SEVEN

FROM ZEROS TO HEROES IN JUST ONE NIGHT

In early December it must have been clear to Maj. X that he was not going to change our mind about how we planned to complete our missions, and it was clear to all of us that he was mad at us. He concluded that was why ODA-391 was routinely assigned the least essential, most difficult, and most unpleasant missions. We were the last to be considered on his "decision tree." He appeared to believe that we refused to play by his rules and that we would get ourselves killed as a consequence. Everybody now knew that we were the black sheep of the company.

As the time for departure trickled down to weeks, the whole company prepared to head out to the field for a rehearsal of our skills. Special Forces are tasked with many kinds of missions, one of which is called "special reconnaissance," but commonly referred to as SR, and being tasked with such a mission would be highly likely when we got to Iraq. Recon missions are tremendously challenging and dangerous, always requiring great stealth and good luck.

The Weapons of Mass Destruction (WMD) threat was still on the minds of everyone at this point, and we all anticipated operations against such facilities. Our teams were the natural theater assets to use against them, and much of our preparation was based on sur-veilling and assaulting suspected WMD facilities.

Our battalion commander, Lt. Col. Binford, had been given a little book of missions that he should be prepared to execute, and some of them were related to this WMD threat. The commander expected that we would be tasked with a mission called "sensitive site exploitation," or SSE, and his staff had a long list of these places, each circled on their maps. Once we screened the 4th Infantry Division in its advance to Baghdad, he thought we might be sent off to take down these sites, and so the whole battalion prepared to rehearse such a mission.

Special Forces units are masters of mission-preparation, both for exercises and in the real world, and it is a very important part of our business. We learn in the Q course how to gather information, sort it out, verify it, and distill it all into a plan, and these plans are often ex-tremely elaborate. They include photography from the air, satellites, and the ground; interviews with people who know the area; and any-thing available to help understand the ground and the people in the area where our people will operate. A plan can take days or weeks to build and can involve the efforts of dozens of people—sometimes in-cluding prisoners who have been snatched right out of the area and brought back for interrogation, as they were in Afghanistan.

Once that plan is complete, we have to show it to our commander in a formal presentation called a "brief-back." If the commander approves—and there is no guarantee that he will—we go back into "isolation," where we are insulated from the world by barbed wire. There we rehearse and practice the mission, refine it even further, and prepare to put the plan in motion. Only then, after approval to execute the mission has come from higher up, is the team "launched" on the mission according to the precise schedule specified in the plan.

Elaborate planning and preparation are necessary because SF mis-sions are often extremely important to American national security. They are also often executed covertly—they are successful only when no-body knows they were executed. And SF missions are typically high-risk, high-payoff operations in which failure means death or capture for the team as well as political problems for the National Command

Authority. So during December, 3rd Battalion, 3rd Special Forces Group began to work on a rehearsal of a WMD mission. In the Army, these rehearsals are called "field training exercises," but we just refer to them as FTXs.

Lt. Col. Binford told us, "I am going to have B Company do the 'door-kicking' and C Company do all the reconnaissance." This was no surprise to us since we had been told to anticipate the SR (Special Reconnaissance) mission as our specialty.

We had the use of an excellent training area near Fort Bragg in the Spring Lake area of North Carolina known as the Northern Training Area (NTA). This property had been owned by the Rockefeller family before being donated to the government, and it included an airstrip along with several buildings in a compound. The Army added some railroad cars and other features to improve the compound's similarity to likely targets, with the result that it was a great place for units like ours to practice our reconnaissance and door-kicking skills.

Our FTX was based on the concept that an enemy WMD facility was located at the compound on the old Rockefeller property. We were told that the place was heavily guarded and that production and administration activities were housed in the various buildings on the site. Our battalion was directed, as part of the exercise, to first gather information about the site, then assault it and capture it intact. Soldiers from another unit were assigned to patrol the site and to do their best to prevent anybody from getting close to the place.

Even in something like this, unit politics plays a role. Maj. X assigned each of his four ODAs an area of the compound, then told us to get past the security patrols and document as much of the activity on the place as possible. We were all required to get photographs of the buildings that would provide essential information for the assaulting teams. But, as usual, ODAs Nine-Four and Nine-Five were given the routes and locations most likely to be successful, while Nine-One and Nine-Two were told to take the virtually impossible routes and got stuck with "disadvantaged" terrain.

We looked at the map, and I thought to myself, *I can see where this is going—Nine-Four and Nine-Five will be put in positions where they have clear fields of view, while we have to go in through the woods and swamp. We are going to have to work through that muck and crawl up onto the target to even see it.* It seemed the other teams were being set up for success, and we were being set up for failure. All of us felt the same way about this FTX, but we also felt that we were going to do our best to outperform the other ODAs, in spite of the way the exercise was set up. When the time for insertion came, we headed for Spring Lake in our GMVs.

We soon reached the original infil point, turned off the paved road, turned off all lights, and put on the NODs (night observation devices). A few minutes later we occupied the MSS. Jeff Hull, Bobby Farmer, and I were one of the SR teams, while Kenney and Rich were the other, and it was our job to actually move up close enough to photograph the compound. Eric, Andy, and Gerry Kirk set up shop at the MSS, where they would command and control the two SR teams. Their job was to send digital photos back over the radio and stay in contact with the two teams, the B-team, and the forward observation base's S-3 (battalion Operations) shop.

Shortly after we arrived at the MSS, it was time to move up on the compound while it was still dark. We loaded up with our rucks, each weighing around 80 pounds, and moved off into the deep, dark swamp. Kenney and Rich moved off toward their observation position, while Bobby, Jeff, and I headed toward ours. Movement was extremely difficult, and the three of us fought our way through the thickets, getting struck in the face by branches and making a tremendous amount of noise as we sloshed through the freezing water and muck.

With all the noise we're making, we are going to get caught, sure as hell, I thought, *while by now Nine-Five is probably already at their hide site at the far end of the runway, with eyes on target and already taking surveillance photos.* We were still a long way from the runway, deep in a ravine, and with a steep hill to climb before getting into position. It was time for drastic measures.

"Let's pull out of the swamp," I told the other guys, "and walk in the woods at the edge of the road. At the rate we are going, we are never going to reach our objective by the direct route by daylight." They both agreed. Since Bobby had the AN-PAS 13 thermal sight on his weapon, I told him to take point and keep an eye out for anything coming down the road.

After about twenty minutes, Bobby hand-signaled, *Freeze*. For a second, I thought someone was coming as I watched Bobby peer through the thermal sight at something to our front. Bobby then signaled me forward and handed me his weapon so I could take a look. There, against the black screen of the thermal, was a bright white spot made by a heat source, most likely a campfire, but still a few hundred meters away.

We had moved close to 1,000 meters without being detected by the patrols, and now we went back into the swamp and set up the hide inside all the brush and bamboo, out of sight. Across the runway, we could see the light from a campfire with the "enemy" personnel standing around it—unlike the three of us, warm and dry. We set up our cameras, ready to photograph the compound, and waited for the sunrise. The sun came up, and we couldn't see a thing—the campfire had given us a faulty idea of what we would be able to see in daylight.

"Okay, let's make the hide site a 'mini-MSS,'" I told Jeff and Bobby. "Let's leave our rucks here, and we'll crawl up to the runway on our bellies to get those photos."

We low-crawled about 100 yards without being detected and were able to get some pretty good photos of the details of the compound. One of the important features was a railroad tank car, and we got photographs of that, and of the shipping containers and the guards, just as we were supposed to. Carefully, we crawled back to our mini-MSS, then downloaded the photos from the camera and sent them back to Andy at the primary MSS. Andy and Eric looked them over, then sent them to the FOB (forward operating base). *Mission accomplished,* we all thought, being very pleased with ourselves.

Then we got a message back from the FOB: "Pictures no good—wrong angle! We want you to go back and get us angles that show us where the opening in the wire is, the distance from the shipping containers to the tank car," and all sorts of other details that they hadn't told us before.

There was no way we could do this in daylight, so we decided to try again at night, this time with the infrared camera. After hiding out all day, we once again infiltrated the target, crawled up close from a new angle, and even got across the airfield and managed to sneak within 50 meters of the compound. Now we could actually see and hear the guards and other personnel on the site. We turned on the thermal camera and started taking the photos demanded by the FOB.

Once again, we snuck back across the airfield, crawling in the freezing grass and mud, and sent the images back to Eric. Once again, the photos were no good—the thermal camera recorded the fire and the bodies of the enemy personnel, but nothing of the details.

"We need daylight photos," the guys at the FOB said.

"We'll never be able to get those photos during daylight," we replied. We didn't know what the other teams were getting, but we had severely pushed the envelope in the process of making the night shots, and sooner or later we were going to get caught. And getting caught would just confirm the low opinion our company commander seemed to have of us.

As the sun came up on the second day, Bobby, Jeff, and I were readying ourselves to execute our daylight suicide photo mission and trying to meet the FOB's demands for close-ups of the target. Just as we were getting ready to move out, Capt. Wright called me on the radio, using the team internal frequency.

"Frank, the Old Man has put us on admin hold and wants us to pull back to the company area ASAP."

"What the fuck?" I replied in disgust.

"I don't know," Eric answered, "but it must be a big deal because the battalion commander is calling everybody back, including the OPFOR [OPosing FORce]. Pack up your gear and head back to the MSS."

"Roger that," I told Eric.

Bobby and Jeff gave me confused looks and asked, "What's up?"

"I have no clue," I said. "FOB wants us to head back in to the company. Somebody must have stepped on their crank real bad for the BC (Battalion Commander) to put the FTX on hold. Let's ruck up and head out to the road."

After Gerry picked us up, we linked up with the rest of the team at the MSS. As soon as I got out of the GMV, I headed right over to Eric.

"Admin hold, for what? We're in the middle of an FTX!" By this time Eric had more info.

About this time, the Special Forces community had a very public problem: several guys had come back from Afghanistan and had killed their wives, some committing suicide afterward. These killings had made the papers, and all the articles made a strong connection between the murders and Special Forces. The USASOC (US Army Special Operations Command) commanding general directed a mandatory stand-down for everybody in the whole command. Every one of us was required to attend a training session where we would be told to refrain from killing or abusing our wives.

With the exception of two young, single privates left on the objective to guard the OPFOR's heavy weapons, all of us—including the guys who were role-playing the enemy on the compound—climbed into our vehicles and headed back to Bragg.

What happened? we all wondered, thinking that some new crisis had developed and that we'd be launched on our real-world mission early. Instead, we were told that the rash of spouse-abuse cases had prompted this mandatory briefing, much to our disappointment because we would have been happy and ready to deploy overseas. It was late morning by the time we'd made it back to Bragg, and our briefing would not be until 1300, just after lunch.

"Go get chow," we were told, "then be back in the battalion classroom before 1300. The group commander is going to talk to you, then the chaplain is going to conduct a class on stress and family problems; it should be over by 1400. We'll launch back out and restart the FTX by 1600 hours."

Now, one thing you need to know about the way Special Forces soldiers think—we do not accept the notion that there is only one way to solve a problem. We are typically quite creative about the way to accomplish our objectives. When we train with conventional units, they sometimes think we break the rules and cheat. We prefer the idea that we are simply being tactically creative and that we think "outside the box." Along those lines, I had an idea.

This would be a great time, I thought, *to run back out to the compound and get those photographs for the FOB. There is nobody out there except those two kids from the support company pulling guard.* Kenney and I had done a lot of deer hunting together, and deer season was still open.

"Kenney, do you still have all your hunting gear in your truck?" I asked him.

"Sure," he said. "Why?"

"I have an idea. I want you and Bobby to drive back out to the objective in your truck and pretend that you are lost hunters. Take the camera with you and take all the photos you can of the PIR (primary intelligence requirements) and IR (intelligence requirements) that the FOB wants—the layout of the compound, the distances between the buildings, the way the wire is set up, where the machine guns and fighting positions are located. Get all the angles we couldn't get before. Make sure to wear your orange hat and vest, just like you were hunting, and play stupid. Bobby, you get in the back of the camper, out of sight, and use the little windows on the side of the camper to take the photos. While Kenney drives around the compound and is talking to the guards, you take all the photos you can."

"What about the meeting?" they wanted to know.

"Don't worry, I'll sign your names—they'll never know."

I went off to lunch with the rest of the ODA; while we were at lunch, Eric asked me where Bobby and Kenney were. "You don't want to know, but don't worry about it." He rolled his eyes, knowing if something went wrong, he'd be the guy catching hell for it. With a smile I said the words every SF officer dreads: "Trust me sir—I'm working something."

At 1300 we all sat down in the briefing room, signed in on the clipboard, and learned about the evils of spouse abuse. By the time we got out of the class, more than two hours had elapsed. There, in the parking lot, was Kenney's truck. And inside the team room were Bobby and Kenney, both grinning from ear to ear, checking out the photos on the computer. We were busy selecting photos when a couple of captains and team sergeants from Bravo Company walked in the door. They were the leaders of what would be the assault element that was sup-

posed to hit the compound the following night. They were doing a little outside-the-box thinking themselves, and came over to get a little
covert information about the objective.

"Hey, guys," they said, "what can you tell us about the compound?"

"We've got photos," we told them, and we brought them into the
team room, where the images were still being sorted on a computer.
They were really impressed, so we decided to give them the images
now, several hours in advance of when they would normally expect delivery, so they could get started using them to refine their assault plans.
But we attached some conditions.

"These things are TOP SECRET, guys," I told them, "and you can't
tell anybody where you got them. These are only for you and
your team—be sure you don't let your leadership see them or know
where they came from."

"No problem," they said. "We won't tell anybody." So we burned a
CD for them and picked ten of the best photos to send in once we got
back to the mission support site. Then we hopped in our GMVs and
drove back out to the NTA to resume the FTX.

By the time we got back out there, we realized that it was getting
dark and that the light levels of the photos wouldn't correspond to the
current light conditions, so we decided to wait until the morning before we started sending the photos back. In the morning, Andy began
transmitting the photos, two at a time, up to the FOB. He hadn't sent
very many before we got a message from battalion: "These photos are
great. Do you have any more like the third one? Do you have any
closer? These are just what we need—send more." Andy sent a couple
of others, and the guys in the Intel section were going nuts, they were
so happy with the photos. The resolution was good, the angles were
perfect, and despite being made through the camper window, they
were much clearer than the earlier photos.

Although we were pleased with this response, all of us were waiting
for somebody to put two and two together—anybody who looked carefully at the photos and thought about them could figure out that the images were not taken from a concealed position but right out in the
open . . . standing in the middle of the runway.

Even better, we were sitting in our mini–mission support site/hide site, in comparative comfort, instead of low-crawling out in the wet grass at the edge of the runway. But as far as the FOB knew, we were back in the weeds, shivering in the cold, transmitting the photos while we were taking them. Andy kept sending them photos, and the Intel team kept gushing about how wonderful they were. We sat quietly, drinking the hot coffee that Bobby had brought out with him, wondering when somebody would catch on, but they didn't.

As planned, Bravo Company assaulted the target at 0300 next morning, and the takedown was executed perfectly. By the time the exercise was completed, we were all exhausted. We'd been up all night and had been going full throttle for two days previously, and everybody was looking forward to getting cleaned up and going home. That, however, was not going to happen soon; all the teams got the word that we would have our "after-action review" (AAR) debriefing first, at 0800, with all team leaders, team sergeants, and warrant officers in attendance. Eric, Gerry, and I headed up to battalion and bumped into the S-3 Operations sergeant major on the way in the door.

"Nine-One," he said. "Man, you guys did awesome! Those photos were top-notch. The only team sending back useable photos was you guys. The battalion commander was really digging it—your guys did shit hot out there! Your commo guy was the only one out there who was squared away on the photos—none of the other teams could get the photos from the angles we needed, but you guys did it. Good job!" This was before we even got in the front door, and suddenly we didn't feel quite so tired.

Everybody assembled, and the after-action review (AAR) began.

Lt. Col. Binford opened the AAR with an overview and his conclusions, then the Operations officer took over. The first thing the S3 said was, "I've got to give a lot of credit to ODA-391—those guys sent back some of the best surveillance photos we've ever seen. I want to thank Capt. Wright and Nine-One for making our job easier by doing such a great job out there." The guys from Bravo Company were snorting into their sleeves because they knew what we'd done, but the other ODAs didn't have a clue.

It wasn't over. Bravo Company's commander got up and said, "The reason our hit went down so well is thanks to the awesome photos Nine-One sent back and the great Intel people we had to work with. Capt. Wright, you should be proud of your guys—they set us up for success; we did a good job because you did a good job!"

It was hard to keep a straight face during all this, but we did. We tried to sound humble. Even Maj. X came over to compliment us, saying, "Eric, Nine-One did great, and I want you all to know I appreciate the great job."

Eric said, "Sir, we told you we know our stuff; our methods might be a little unusual, but we get the job done."

At last it was time to head back to the company and go home. The three of us laughed all the way back to our team room. When we got there, the other guys were waiting, and we told them about all the praise at the AAR. All of us were punchy from lack of sleep. Even though it was only nine in the morning, we opened the ceremonial "end-of-mission" beers and began our internal team AAR, which was really nothing more than a laugh session.

We had gone from zeros to heroes, from the black sheep of the company to its role models, in just one night. We had gone from the bottom of the unit's political food chain to the top. For a little while, ODA-391 was the success story of the battalion. We knew all this approval couldn't last, and it didn't.

EIGHT

MISSION IMPOSSIBLE

One day after the AAR, Lt. Col. Binford was ordered to fly out to Fort Carson, Colorado, to receive the operations order for his battalion. We were still cleaning weapons and gear from the FTX when somebody came in to report, "The colonel has our 'op order,' and he's going to give each company its 'warning order.' Stay in your team rooms but stand by for the colonel."

We continued to work on the gear, but the mood in the room changed immediately. Once you get an op order, something is going to happen; before you receive that order, it is all more or less a rumor that may easily turn out to be false. The new guys in particular were worried that the whole thing would be cancelled before we were launched if, as was expected, Saddam complied at the last minute with the demands imposed by the United Nations and President Bush.

Lt. Col. Binford's order specified that 2nd and 3rd Battalions of 10th Special Forces Group would be the Joint Special Operations Task Force (JSOTF) North, and that 3rd Battalion, 3rd Special Forces Group (that was us), would be "chopped," or temporarily attached to the 10th, to make sure they had a full group of three battalions and enough muscle to complete their mission. Lt. Col. Binford made the trip that night and was back the next day. Then he visited each company in turn, reading the official battalion op order to the teams. When it was our turn, he went through our missions; these included—no surprise—a lot of targets similar to the ones we had just practiced against up in the NTA, sensitive site explorations. Our job would initially involve checking out the roads, trails, bridges, and other possible routes that could be used by larger forces to capture these sites. "On the way down to these sites, however," Lt. Col. Binford told us, "you will be assigned other targets to recon or hit."

Everybody was assembled in the C Company conference room—a tight fit but with room for us all. It was sort of a John Wayne moment, so Lt. Col. Binford gave a sort of John Wayne speech.

"Okay, men," he began, "for those of you who think we're playing games, now's the time to leave. We're going. I just left the JSOTF [Joint Special Operations Task Force] and the 10th Group guys up at Fort Carson; there is a major planning effort underway. We are going into northern Iraq. We have numerous targets to hit, airfields and WMD sites to investigate, routes and bridges to check out—you name it, we are doing it. So those of you who thought we were playing games up till now, you have a choice: you can walk out of here now, or you can stay here and go with us. If you have family issues or anything else that is going to keep you from doing your job, now is the time to quit. Come up to my office after this meeting and sign a DA Form 4187, and I will have you out of the battalion tomorrow—but if you stay, I expect you to do your job."

Lt. Col. Binford made a point of this because there had been a recent rash of people quitting; some of them were actually team sergeants. The quitting caused big problems for the whole battalion, and he was tired of it. He was counting on each of the teams to deploy with the same people who had trained together for months and had learned to depend on each others skills.

Then it was time for him to read the operation order. First he read the JSOTF's mission: "On order, JSOTF-North conducts unconventional warfare and other special operations in JSOA [Joint Special Operations Area] North to disrupt Iraqi combat power, IOT [in order to] prevent effective military operations against CFLCC [Combined Forces Land Component Command] forces."

Higher headquarters' missions were usually broad and vague. They basically summed up an "end state" and not really the specific missions in between that get you there. That's where Col. Cleveland, the 10th SFG commander, and now commander of JSOTF North, came in. Col. Cleveland and the JSOTF staff had one heck of a job in front of them; slicing the mission pie up for each of the battalions was the easy part.

Next Lt. Col. Binford read our battalion's mission: "On Order, Third Battalion, Third Special Forces Group, will conduct special reconnaissance of specified NAIs [Named Areas of Interest], conduct SSE [sensitive site exploration] operations on suspected WMD facilities, and provide route reconnaissance and screening operations, in support of CFLCC Forces [4th Infantry Division (ID)]."

As we listened, we began to realize that that was one heck of a broad mission statement. That was actually a lot of work for one little Special Forces battalion. The other two battalions would be tied up with the UW (unconventional warfare) effort with the Kurds. That left little Three-Three to handle the conventional work. The reason we were selected for such a task was simply that we had vehicles. In order to keep up with a large mechanized force (4th ID), you just had to have wheels; choosing Three-Three was a no-brainer.

Then it was on to Charlie Company's piece of the pie: "On order, Charlie Company, Third Battalion, Third Special Forces Group, will conduct Special Reconnaissance of the following NAIs. . . ." And he read off the grid coordinates for these places. "Charlie Company will BPT [be prepared to] provide route reconnaissance to include road trafficability and bridge assessments in support of coalition forces [4th ID] operations and provide flank security and screening operations to prevent effective military operations against CFLCC Forces [4th ID]."

At this point Lt. Col. Binford walked over to the map showing all of the Middle East, southeastern Europe, and North Africa.

"Tenth Group will be deploying to Batman, Turkey," Lt. Col. Binford said, pointing to its location on the map. For a second we all thought he was kidding.

"Did you say 'Batman'?" one of the other teams asked.

"Yes, Batman," he responded. "Look at the map of Turkey when I'm done; there really is a town called Batman." He continued, "After the JSOTF is established there, we will deploy a short time later. After we get enough forces in Turkey, we will begin to launch teams out to cover these NAIs that Col. Cleveland wants us to keep an eye on or have guys on them to coordinate strikes by the Air Force on them just before the invasion starts. The basic premise is that once 4th ID gets their forces to the staging area at the Turkey/Iraq border, we will launch the teams. The current plan has us going in D minus seven [seven days prior to the start of fighting, known as D-day]. Once 4th ID starts its advance south toward Baghdad, we will pull off the NAIs and screen their forward right flank to the west of them until they get to Tikrit. We may have to do some quick bridge assessments to ensure that their M1s can cross them and that they're not rigged to blow. Make sure all of your Charlies [MOS 18C/Special Forces engineers] are up to speed on how to evaluate the weight capacity of bridges. From there they will pass beyond us, and we will begin doing the SSEs on the WMD sites. This plan will require you guys to be really flexible because there are a lot of variables, and I'm pretty sure it will be changed as we get closer to D-day."

If Lt. Col. Binford only knew just how accurate that last statement was. The plan would not just change a little, either, but in a major way. "Are there any questions?" he asked.

"Sir, when's D-day?" someone asked.

"Right now, the JSOTF is planning on early February. We won't know until we get the official word from CENTCOM. We've been told to have our forces in Turkey by the end of January. I see us leaving sometime around the first and second weeks of January."

That was good news; it looked like we'd get Christmas with the family. He then answered a few more questions. Then, with no more to answer, he said, "Now go to work; I'll see you in a couple of days for the brief-backs."

He then turned to and handed off the order to Maj. X, whose job it was to assign A-teams to those NAIs and issue us our individual team OpOrders. Maj. X called the company to attention, then waited for Lt. Col. Binford to leave the room. Then he addressed the whole company.

You could see the excitement in his eyes. "Team leaders, team sergeants, and the warrants, stay here—we need to talk; everybody else, go back to what you were doing," Maj. X said.

"The B-team and I will analyze the order. Later today we will give you your team warning order; then later this evening you'll get your team OpOrder. In the meantime, go back and get your team rooms set up to work on your plans."

Special Forces officers wait entire careers to lead men into combat, and soon Maj. X would be leading his entire company into Iraq. We had a mission to get ready for. The team rooms were a mess from all the gear we had been ordering, on top of which were all the guns and gear from the FTX, and the guys did a great job cleaning it out and getting it ready. All the trash disappeared, the map boards were set up, and somebody ordered pizzas; we settled in to the serious business of predeployment preparations. Eric gave Marty and Jason a call and told them to get back to the team room. I made a call to SWC (Strike Warfare Commander) to try to get Mike out of ANCOC (Advanced Non-Commissioned Officers Course), but to no avail.

We got to work on the development of our role about nine the next morning, planning our missions with all the available information, knowing that more would be provided as soon as the Intel sections at battalion and group had more to send. We expected changes, too, and got them early and often.

What I didn't expect was to be called into Sgt. Maj. Ward's office for what would be a difficult choice.

"Frank, I know you're not going to like this, but there's some last-minute shuffling happening before the teams start their final planning. We need to give up two guys from the company to Bravo Company."

"What? Now, after all the training?" I said. "They want to start moving guys around?"

"The CSM [Command Sergeant Major] wants us to give up two guys with experience from Afghanistan. They have a lot of young guys over there that are hot out of the Q course, and they need some senior guys to round out the company." He went on, "You and Nine-Four have eleven guys on your team; the rest only have ten, so I'm going to ask you both to give up either a Bravo [weapons specialist] or a Charlie [engineer]. I'm going to give you first dibs, but you're going to have to give up either Jeff or Kenney."

"This sucks," I snapped. "Jeff and Ken are both good guys. How the heck do I decide which one?"

"I'll let you go back to the team room and talk about it," Joe offered. "Take it up with both of them and with your team leader and warrant. I'll give you an hour before I ask Nine-Four. If they come back with an answer before you do, you won't have a choice."

"Roger that, Sergeant Major," I said with a bummed-out tone as I left his office. I grabbed Eric and Marty and pulled them outside to the back of the company.

"The smadge [as we informally call the sergeant major] says we have to give up a guy to B Company." The look on their faces showed me they were just as miffed as I was.

"Who?" asked Marty.

"He's giving us a choice," I told him. "Jeff or Ken . . . and we have an hour to decide."

Marty looked at me and said, "We're not giving up Kenney; he's our only IMPAC credit card holder. We lose him, and we'll have to go through another team to buy shit. That will royally screw up purchase limits, budgets, card limits, and other admin things when we try to figure out who bought what. I say we give up Jeff."

"I have to agree," added Eric. Both were right. I had never considered Kenney's other job on the team, which was Team S-4 (supply) and IMPAC card holder. Since the IMPAC card is actually assigned to an individual, if he leaves, the card goes with him. Without him, we'd be in a mess.

"Well, I guess it's settled. I'll go give Jeff the bad news and let the smadge know Jeff will be going over to Bravo Company."

Needless to say, Jeff was not happy, but like a trooper he went off to Bravo Company, where they needed his help. The team was also a bit pissed that we were giving up guys just a few weeks before we were going to war. That left us a weapons guy short. I went back to see Joe Ward, to let him know that Jeff would be going and that I needed a weapons guy and a medic. Joe said he'd try his best to get those slots filled.

"Guys are pouring into the battalion from the Q course every day, but they're cherry. You're probably not going to get a senior 18B [weapons specialist]," he told me.

"I'll take the first guy in the door. I need the bodies," I said. "Jason is doing a good job, and Marty's an old weapons guy. We'll get a new guy up to speed."

The sergeant major told me, "I'll go up to battalion and group to see what MOSs (Military Occupational Specialty) we have coming in and what I can get you." I told him thanks, and I went back to the team room to keep the guys focused. We had a bunch of things to get done before the specifics came down from the company.

We were soon tasked with an order to prepare to execute recon missions along the main supply route (MSR) that American units would use to travel from the north into Iraq. At the time, the plan called for us to enter the country through Turkey and follow a power-line road down around the city of Mosul, sneak past three Iraqi divisions, then get around the town of Tal Afar, and then over to the Tal Afar airfield. This meant that, instead of screening the movement of the heavier forces as they moved toward Baghdad, we were to watch for the possible transportation of WMD materials from the Tal Afar military compound to Syria, a scenario then considered likely.

"Nine-One, your PIR [primary intelligence requirement] is to watch this road," we were told by Maj. X as he pointed to a map during the "mission-assessment" briefing.

"We expect the enemy to try to move WMDs by truck from the Tal Afar compound by road to the north and west. There are only a couple of roads in the area, and they can be watched from an intersection to the east of the airfield. We want to make sure nothing moves out of Tal Afar without us knowing about it. For your IR [intelligence requirements], while you're there, do a quick recon of the airfield, the bunkers, and the ASP [ammunition supply point] for the compound—find out if it is full or empty."

This was a classic strategic reconnaissance assignment, but with a variety of twists, one of which was that it was asking a lot. The PIR was reasonable enough, but as usually happens, everybody on the staff wanted to add something else for us to do as long as we were in the neighborhood.

Our package of information from the Intel shop included excellent overhead photographs, which we studied carefully. It soon became obvious that the only way to get to our assigned location was to drive right through an enemy-held military facility. Now, this was supposed to happen even before the invasion began. That meant that the enemy units in the area, who were no dummies, would be expecting trouble but would not be distracted by combat operations. They could devote their entire attention to ODA-391 if we were discovered.

Each SF company has its own "war room," a secure place where maps and photos can be pinned up on the walls. There are large tables where many people can work on different aspects of the planning process, and before the mission is "launched," the war room is a very busy place around the clock. Here, in the days before Christmas, is where we began working toward performing our small role in the big invasion.

Eric, Marty, Gerry Kirk, and I sweated over the mission analysis, the beginning phase of the planning process. How could we get from our insertion location to our objective area without being seen? Where could we hide our GMVs once we were at the target? Where could we watch the roads while remaining hidden?

We started submitting RFIs, the Request-for-Information forms that told the Intel section what we needed to know, and soon thereafter we began to get maps, overlays, aerial photos, and all sorts of reports and written documents. These were provided by the battalion S-2 (Intelligence) Section, where a group of specialists were responsible for producing the maps and photos for us very quickly. Gerry was our Intel specialist, and he was busy writing down all the coordinates for our targets; when we had them all, he wrote up the RFIs and submitted them.

This process started with a computerized mapping program called Falcon View, which allowed us to quickly study maps on our own laptop computers. From those we got high-resolution satellite photos by asking for them through RFIs. Software like Falcon View isn't secret, and anybody can get similar programs, but it is an amazing technology and part of a series of changes that have happened during my career in the Army. Just a few years ago we were entirely dependent on paper maps and handheld compasses to know where we were on the battlefield. One of the first things we did as we began to digest our task was to start looking at the computer screen and its display of the terrain; what we saw was daunting.

All this happened almost immediately on receipt of our warning order and while the guys were still cleaning up the team room. We knew from past experience the value of "leaning forward in the foxhole" at this stage of the game, anticipating the workload, which we knew would overwhelm us if we were not prepared to deal with it. Gerry took his RFIs and walked them up to the S2 shop and turned them in, then stood over the technicians, breathing down their necks to get them to work a little faster and to make sure Nine-One's RFIs were on the top of the stack.

As we studied the problem, it began to look like we'd be discovered long before we got close to our overwatch position near the intersection of the highways. We couldn't drive in from the north because of the location of the town. The countryside surrounding the area was generally flat and treeless except for occasional wadis, none of which were suitable for travel in our GMVs.

We studied the map some more and considered the terrain. There were absolutely no places for cover and concealment—no hills, no trees, no places to hide during the movement to the target, and not much of a place to hide once we arrived.

There was only one place to hide, and that turned out to be on the airfield itself. Only there could any vegetation be found—the rest of the area was wide open. One spot at the corner of the airfield looked good, if there was a way to get to it. This location was inside the perimeter fence, far from the buildings and hangars where everybody thought chemical weapons might be stored and which didn't seem to be patrolled often enough for a path to be visible in the photos. If we could get to this place, we could build a hide and start watching the traffic on the roads nearby.

After studying the target for a while, Eric, Gerry, Marty, and I all reached the same conclusion: there just was no way we were going to get to the site in our GMVs. "We have to be nuts," Marty said, "to think we can drive anywhere close to this location without somebody seeing us."

We could use the same sort of white Toyota pickup trucks that all the locals used, and that would help us blend in, much as it did in Afghanistan. But there was another problem, and that was the size of our team. One or two pickup trucks driving around in this part of the world would not arouse anybody's curiosity, but it would take four vehicles to move us, and that would attract interest right away. Four pickups are a convoy, and a convoy near a military installation is worth checking out.

So we started to get creative. "Okay," Eric said, "we can put two of the pickups in two helicopters each, then put them in over here, to the west of the airfield, and put the other two in another two helicopters and insert them over here, to the south. That way we can link up near the target without attracting a lot of attention."

That wasn't a bad idea, except that the more complexity you introduce in the plan, the more difficult it becomes to pull it off; something always goes wrong—you get inserted in the wrong location, an aircraft breaks down, or the road you planned to use is blocked, or any of a hundred other problems pop up. That is why we spend so much time in the planning process, making sure we understand exactly where we are going and what is on the ground, and keeping everything as simple as possible once we get there.

Suddenly we were looking at using four CH-54 helicopters to insert four pickup trucks into two different locations in enemy territory, and do it at night, and do it near a military installation. Not only that, we could expect the enemy to be on high alert, to expect us to be interested in this particular installation, and to expect us to move through this area once the war kicked off.

Even so, we could probably pull this off if we took some precautions. One precaution was to make sure our guns were out of sight, and that meant that we couldn't mount them on the usual pedestal behind the cab. Instead, we thought we could put one guy in back with an M240 in his lap, covered up with a tarp to look like a common Bedouin tribesman of the area.

The tactical plan, though, kept bumping into complications. As we tried to imagine the insertion, the movement to linkup, and the process

of occupying the objective, the whole idea looked more and more dubious. There were only a few roads available, and off-road travel was not
an option because of the wadis that bisected the area. All the available
roads went through villages and one sizeable town. Even if we got to
the intersection undetected, there was no place to watch it that was not
exposed to view. The only available location was on the airfield itself.

Next question: how could we get onto the airfield? Looking at the
map and the overhead photos, we saw there was only one way—we
would have to stash the vehicles in the nearby wadi and establish
the MSS there. Then one of the guys from the MSS would have to
drive us up to the edge of the perimeter fence surrounding the airfield.
From there we'd have to dismount the R&S (Recon and Surveillance)
team, breach the fence, and walk 3 kilometers across an active military
installation, all the while trying to avoid notice by the Iraqi soldiers
guarding the place. Once in position, the team was supposed to dig a
hide site in what was most likely sun-baked soil without making any
noise. And all of this had to be done in one night.

The dismounted R&S team would be at least 4 kilometers from the
MSS if they got into trouble, and any prospects for a rescue or reinforcement at this position were poor. It got worse.

The S-3 shop provided us with some great high-resolution satellite
photos that were just two weeks old. They showed the Tal Afar complex in great detail; clearly visible were manned antiaircraft sites at
various points around the perimeter, aircraft on the runway, and trucks
and cars moving around the facility. Then they told us that Intel esti-
mates had between two hundred and three hundred enemy soldiers
guarding the place, with a total of five hundred to six hundred people
on the installation.

"We're in trouble," I said.

Despite our doubts, we went through the whole planning process
and developed two alternative schemes for meeting the commander's
primary requirements for the mission. We came up with Plans A, B,
and C, each of which seemed destined to be miserable failures. Late
that night, after working on the problem for many hours, Marty told
Eric, "Frank and I think there's no way we can pull off this mission.

There is no realistic way we are going to get on this airfield without getting shot. Those antiaircraft guns are trailer-mounted, quad-barreled Russian ZSU-23s."

The Russians ensured everything they made was multipurpose. Even though these were antiaircraft guns, they were also designed to be fired in a direct-fire ground mode, specifically at troops and light-skinned vehicles. The 23mm bullets, almost twice the size of our .50cals (12.7mm), would turn any vehicle into Swiss cheese in seconds.

Marty continued, "If we do manage to get in, there is no way we're going to get out alive. We need to ask for another objective, maybe north of the road, but getting into the airfield itself is not possible. We're not going to do it."

Eric gave us a mixed look of both agreement and disappointment.

"You're going to have to tell him no,'" I said, knowing how much he disliked using that word, especially with the battalion commander.

"Frank you remember what happened the last time you tried to get me to say no?" Eric reminded me.

"We've gotta tell him no, Eric! If we don't, we're going to get our guys killed. If we tell him okay, and we go in on those CH-54s, we're going to loose our guys. It is better to take the crap the major and colonel are going to give us for saying no now than to have to explain why the mission was a disaster and half of us got killed."

Eric knew the mission was next to impossible and he was the last guy that wanted to put his men at risk, but he also knew what turning down a mission would mean. Eric remembered a lesson he learned in Afghanistan. One of the commanders from a "special" organization relayed a message to Eric. "Never turn down a mission or you'll never get another one," he told Eric. "We've been sitting around for six weeks waiting for another one."

Eric did not want this to happen to us, but he didn't want to put his men at risk either. Instead, Eric decided to go and ask for another named area of interest (NAI), one nearby that might be a bit more accessible.

Eric walked down the hall to the company commander's office and told Maj. X that we would recommend against doing the mission on that particular NAI.

Local militiamen inspect the aftermath of the ambush of the convoy at Gardez. This is the pickup truck that took the brunt of the enemy's initial fire. A grenade that was dropped in through the driver's open window blew out all the windows and killed one of the occupants. (*US Army, taken by Bruce Fitton*)

The floorboard of same truck with a hole created by the grenade. Note the blood from the only fatality. (*US Army, taken by Bruce Fitton*)

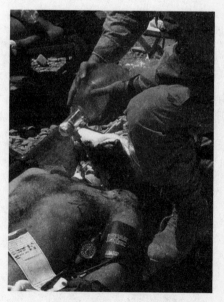

Afghan casualty who suffered a severe head wound. Note the breathing tube that was surgically inserted in the neck. (*US Army, taken by Bruce Fitton*)

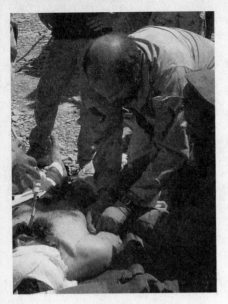

Frank starts an IV on the same Afghan casualty. (*US Army, taken by Bruce Fitton*)

Frank and Capt. Eric Wright clown for the camera in Romania as they prep vehicles for infiltration. (*US Army, taken by Robert Farmer*)

It is a tight fit in an MC-130 once the GMVs are backed in and chained down. Three members of ODA-391, their long wait to get into the fight nearly over, pose for the camera just prior to engine-start. (*US Army, taken by Gerry Kirk*)

US Air Force MC-130 moments before loading ODA-391's vehicles at the Romanian air base used to stage units before Operation Iraqi Freedom. MC-130s are modified versions of the old Hercules airframe that are intended to support Special Operations Forces. (*US Army, taken by Gerry Kirk*)

ODA-391 poses in front of their vehicles and equipment moments after briefing Col. Cleveland on their capabilities. Col. Cleveland and his staff were surprised at the firepower and mobility of the GMVs. (*US Army, taken by Joe Ward*)

Company Charlie, Third Battalion, Third Special Forces Group, sit idle at the 10th Group safe house in Halabja during Operation Iraqi Freedom. These Third-of-the-Third Humvees, heavily modified and far better armed than the 10th Group vehicles, were objects of envy and admiration. (*US Army, taken by Gerry Kirk*)

Monument erected at Ground Zero in Halabja, where Saddam ordered the chemical attack that killed 5,000 Kurdish women, children, and elderly men on March 16, 1988. The young men were working in the fields at the time and survived to deliver some delayed payback with a little help from Special Forces in 2003. (*US Army, taken by Gerry Kirk*)

Photo of a camp that Colin Powell showed to the UN. Note the effects of heavy bombing from cruise missiles, JDAMs, and AC-130s on the structures as depicted in the satellite photo below. (*US Army, taken by Gerry Kirk*)

Actual satellite photo used by Powell in his briefing to the UN. (*US Army, taken by US State Department*)

ODA-391 supports the chemical weapons detection team's inspection of the heavily bombed Ansar al-Islam camp at Surgot. Jason Brown provides security with his M2 .50cal heavy machine gun while the team surveys the shattered remains of the camp, looking for ricin and similar chemical and biological weapons. (*US Army, taken by Gerry Kirk*)

A surface-laid antitank mine, one of many that were randomly placed at the Ansar al-Islam camp near Surgot. (*US Army, taken by Kenney Wilson*)

Master Sgt. Tom Sandoval's split team established ODA-044's temporary base in a hasty, shallow fortification in the middle of a wheat field near the Kurd town of Pir Da Ud. ODA-391 arrived to help ODA-044's assault on enemy positions about 10 kilometers (6 miles) to the south of this location. (*US Army, taken by Gerry Kirk*)

Tenth Group has traditionally emphasized working with indigenous militia and dismounted patrol operations and used lightly armed and locally acquired vehicles like these Land Rovers. Although capable of good rough-terrain movement, they lacked heavy firepower, long-range fuel capacity, and most of the radios of Third Group's GMVs. (*US Army, taken by Michael Ray*)

Jason Brown uses his M2 to cover Kurds advancing on Objective Rock. (*US Army, taken by Mike Ray*)

The beginning of a very long day: Three-Nine-One (foreground), with Three-Nine-Two, and Zero-Four-Four in trail, moving to the Line of Departure early on the morning of 6 April 2003 prior to the assault on the enemy positions on the ridge south of Pir Da Ud. (*US Army, taken by Rich Turner*)

Iraqi prisoners are loaded into one of the Kurd trucks after the taking of Objective Rock. (*US Army, taken by Kenney Wilson*)

Frank (left), with Jake Chandler, Steve Brunk, and unidentified Kurd, on the enemy T-55 tank disabled and abandoned near Objective Rock. This tank was soon mistaken for other enemy armor about a mile away—confusion that would contribute to the friendly fire incident about an hour later. (*US Army, taken by Robert Farmer*)

Photo of the battlefield just prior to the attack, as seen from near Objective Rock. Note the haze that reduced visibility, obscuring the approach of the enemy tanks. (*US Army, taken by Gerry Kirk*)

Jason Brown, after pleading for permission to fire a Javelin, launches the first missile of the battle, while Frank observes the target disappearing into the haze at what he thought was an impossibly great range. This engagement converted Frank and the rest of the teams from skeptics about the weapon into believers in it. (*US Army, taken by Andy Pezzella*)

Immediately after the teams repositioned to their "Alamo," urged along by enemy tank fire, Sgt. 1st Class Mike Ray ran to this high ground and launched his Javelin at an attacking Iraqi APC. (*US Army, taken by Gerry Kirk*)

Moments after a Navy jet mistakenly bombed the Kurds instead of the Iraqis, most of the vehicles nearby were on fire. *(US Army, taken by Gerry Kirk)*

The BBC's video team arrived just in time to get caught in the disaster, the "TV" marking on their SUV provided ineffective protection against a 500-pound bomb. In the foreground are half a dozen Kurds, one is on fire and all are dead. Body parts litter the pavement. *(US Army, taken by Gerry Kirk)*

ODA-391's Mike Ray and ODA-392's Gino Zawojski work on BBC interpreter Kamran, as John Simpson of the BBC and his crew look on; Kamran died a few hours later. Maj. Howard of ODB-044, who was also wounded in the incident, is seen in the middle. For the first twenty minutes after the bomb hit, Sgt. 1st Class Mike Ray was the only fully qualified SF medic at Rock. He quickly set up a CCP (casualty collection point) and began triage of the many dead and wounded. *(US Army, taken by Gerry Kirk)*

Jason Brown and Lihn Nguyen retrieve more Javelin missiles and make their way back to Three-Nine-One's battle position down the hill. *(US Army, taken by Gerry Kirk)*

T-55 tank destroyed by Eric Strigotte (photo taken two weeks after the battle). Ammunition contained inside caused the tank to burn. (*US Army, taken by Gerry Kirk*)

The hole created from the shape-charged warhead of the Javelin missile fired by Strigotte. It is believed that a round inside the breech exploded when the Javelin warhead penetrated the gun tube just forward of the chamber, sending the explosion into the crew compartment and killing the crew instantly. (*US Army, taken by Kenney Wilson*)

Two of ODA-391's GMVs take up defensive positions after the initial battle. (*US Army, taken by Gerry Kirk*)

Frank Antenori fires final Javelin of the engagement at a T-55 trying to flank the teams. The shot was at extreme range and at a target partially obscured by covering terrain, but it succeeded in hitting the target. (*US Army, taken by Steve Brunk*)

Two weeks after the battle, members of ODA-391 were finally able to inspect their targets. Staff Sgt. Jason Brown's first target, an MTLB armored personnel carrier, burned so hot that the aluminum road wheels melted. Staff Sgt. Brown (standing on vehicle) is Special Forces' first "Javelin Ace," hitting two personnel carriers and three troop trucks during the battle. (*US Army, taken by Gerry Kirk*)

The enemy effectively used terrain to prevent us from engaging their T-55s with our Javelins. This tank is in "turret defilade" and could fire on the team's position while staying well protected against all but close air support. (*US Army, taken by Gerry Kirk*)

Bobby Farmer and Steve Brunk inspect Jake's handiwork, one of the 152mm artillery pieces that had fired on the teams and that now lies twisted from the effects of a JDAM, which was one of the few effective bombs dropped during the fight. (*US Army, taken by Frank Antenori*)

The ZSU-57-2 that fired on the teams. Initially, it was thought that the air-burst flak rounds were actually proximity-fused mortar shells. (*US Army, taken by Kenney Wilson*)

Frank Antenori stands in front of the tank he took out of commission. (*US Army, taken by Gerry Kirk*)

The path of the Javelin can be seen from the impact point on the front of the tank. (*US Army, taken by Gerry Kirk*)

Eric Wright and Marty McKenna inspect the hole created by the Paveway bomb dropped on the Iraqi enforcement team that murdered a surrendering squad in full view of the US teams. When the dust cleared, the enforcers and their SUV were gone. (*US Army, taken by Gerry Kirk*)

Nguyen behind the M2 .50cal heavy machine gun outside Kirkuk after the battle. Note the refinery in the distance. (*US Army, taken by Gerry Kirk*)

Joyous young Iraqis cheer and give "V" sign as the SF ODAs enter Mosul. (*US Army, taken by Gerry Kirk*)

Capt. Eric Wright, commander, and Sgt. 1st Class Frank Antenori, team sergeant, of ODA-391, take a break in Mosul. (*US Army, taken by Gerry Kirk*)

ODA-391 poses with some admiring Iraqi men in front of one of the many public portraits of Saddam. This portrait, like many others, has a new bullet-pocked hole between the eyes. (*US Army, taken by unknown Iraqi civilian*)

Jason and Kenney take a minute to eat an MRE at Mosul International Airport. (*US Army, taken by Michael Ray*)

Iraqi kids pose with the team by the
GMVs. (*US Army, taken by Kenney
Wilson and Michael Ray*)

Detachment members of
ODA-391. (*US Army,
taken by Joe Ward*)

Detachment members of ODA 392. (*US Army, taken by Joe Ward*)

Detachment members of ODA 044. (*US Army, unknown photographer*)

The back side of the monument. (*US Army, taken by Gerry Kirk*)

Three-Nine-One poses in front of concrete monument that was located in the center of Highway 2. Note the hole created by Nguyen's Javelin shot. The missile went through the roof and side and into the base. (*US Army, taken by Jimmy Adams*)

"Eric, that's the only NAI in the area and it's one that the battalion commander really wants a set of eyes on." Maj. X told Eric. "Well then, I'll have to tell him that we can't do it." Eric said.

"My guys and I went over it, and we decided it can't be done," Eric said.

By this time, it was late at night. All of us were living in the team room. The same thing was happening in all the other team rooms in C Company, and throughout the whole battalion. Everybody was a little punchy after working on this for the past fourteen or more hours, but we were not done yet.

Maj. X told Eric he wanted to take a look at our mission analysis, he and Eric came back down the hall to our team room to see what we were up to. "Talk to me," the major said. "Tell me what's going on."

We walked him through the whole problem, showed him the maps, the photos, pointed out the terrain features, the roads, the towns, and the complete lack of tactical choices, which meant that the plan did not have a reasonable chance of successful execution. Previously, Maj. X seemed to think Nine-One was a bunch of lunatic cowboys, but now he was seeing our practical, realistic side. We showed him every possible angle of approach, in and out, and showed him that there was no realistic place to hide vehicles, no place to hide personnel, no way to move without being seen. If, for some reason, we made it to the objective, the chances were excellent that we would be discovered and shot while there. And, in the extremely unlikely event we didn't get caught going in or while on the target, they'd nail us going out. The prospects were remarkably ugly, and Maj. X began to see things our way.

Maj. X then made a suggestion. "I see where you guys are coming from and I agree, but I suggest you let the battalion commander make the decision about pulling the NAI. If you guys come straight out and tell him no, he'll never give you another one." Maj. X was right.

Now saying no wasn't the problem, it was how we were going to package it in a way Lt. Col. Binford would see we really did our homework, that we looked at every likely approach to the problem, and that he would come to the same conclusion we did. It was "Mission Impossible."

As I said, our planning sequence is extremely detailed and follows a kind of standardized ritual. It begins with the warning order, to get you started, then comes the operations order, with the complete information about the task your team has been assigned. From that moment, you are supposed to get twenty-four hours to develop your basic concept of the operation, a tentative plan of action; the plan isn't expected to be fully developed, but it is supposed to be fully outlined.

At this point, the battalion commander wants to be briefed on the plan in the mission concept (MICON) meeting; this assures the commander that you and he are on the same proverbial sheet of music and that you haven't gone off track. If your plan doesn't match the commander's intent, there's still time for him to give specific guidance to adjust your planning before you expend too many resources during the final planning process, which takes about three days. At the end of the planning process, the teams give what's called a brief-back. The brief-back is a very detailed briefing to the commander about the specifics of the mission. It's after this briefing that the commander decides if your team has planned adequately, considered all contingencies, and is capable of executing the mission with a relatively high degree of success. Rather than wait until then to break the bad news, we decided to do it now in the MICON, in hopes of moving our NAI to the north, or getting another NAI altogether.

Our MICON was scheduled for the next morning, and sure enough, Lt. Col. Binford and his battle staff were right on time. They came down to the company war room where we had our maps, overlays, and photos on the walls. They each took their seats at the long table that ran down the center of the room, the battalion commander sitting in the center, with his S-3 (Operations officer) to his immediate right. Each had a full cup of coffee and sipped it as he waited for the presentations by each of the teams to begin. These MICONs are very formal presentations, and each team goes in numerical sequence, so Nine-One was first.

Capt. Wright got up and led the briefing. He gave an overview of the mission, then handed it off to Gerry Kirk, our Intel NCO, who continued the briefing by discussing the enemy situation. His analysis was excellent, full of detail that showed he had done a lot of work developing the information. In essence, Gerry told the colonel, *This place is crawling with enemy soldiers.*

Then I got up and briefed the operational part of the mission, explaining our three possible plans by just giving the commander our concept of the operation and how we planned to execute it if so ordered. I gave Lt. Col. Binford our primary, alternate, and contingency plans.

"Based on our analysis," I said, indicating the wadi on the overhead photo, "we think we can put our vehicles in here; although we do not believe the wadi is deep enough to fully conceal them, we will provide additional camouflage with netting if needed." I continued to describe exactly how we planned to move in the area, where the fence and the other critical terrain features were, where we would have to low-crawl on our bellies, and what would be required to execute the plan.

Then it was Capt. Wright's turn; he said, "Sir, based on our mission analysis, based on the intelligence we have on the enemy situation, based on the route required to reach the objective—I have to say that the likelihood of our successfully completing this mission without compromise is low. I ask you to give us an alternate NAI."

The room was silent. Lt. Col. Binford sat back in his chair for a moment; this was not the sort of thing he normally heard during briefbacks. He looked over at Marty and asked, "Chief, do you think this target is too high-risk?"

"There's no doubt in my mind, sir. There is no way we are going to get in and out of this location without getting caught or killed. The mission is way too complicated; too many things could go wrong. We'd just be asking for trouble."

"Sgt. Antenori, what do you think?" Lt. Col. Binford asked me.

"Sir, I have done some crazy, hairy things in my time, but this takes the prize! I have never considered driving on to an Iraqi military base and crawling through fences just to get to a target. Even if we tried coming around the back side, I don't see how we could do it without severely compromising the overall mission. It is possible that we could get in for twenty-four hours, but we would certainly get caught during the exfil, and then we would be fighting our way out. You'll have to mount a rescue effort, the whole thing will fall apart, and it will be a mess."

Gerry Kirk, our intel specialist, had studied the problem at its fundamental level. Lt. Col. Binford turned to him now and asked again, "Sgt. Kirk, what do you think?"

"Sir, we are all in agreement that the risks of this mission are unreasonably high and that the execution of this mission is likely to be an unwanted failure," Gerry said bluntly.

The tension in the room was high. Some commanders would interpret our doubts as a fear of danger. We didn't really know how our commander would respond to our recommendation. Finally, he said, "Capt. Wright, I admire you for being honest about this. I think you've done a good mission analysis . . . and I agree. The target is too risky. I am going to take that target off the list. You guys stand down while I go back to the battalion and try to find another target for you." He dismissed us and called in Nine-Two for their brief-back.

Eric didn't know it at the time, but he had scored major points with the battalion commander. Lt. Col. Binford had a tendency to intimidate his junior officers. Many went through drastic measures just to avoid the guy; surely they never wanted to tell him they couldn't do something. But later Lt. Col. Binford told us that Eric's honest analysis and genuine concern for his men were qualities he looked for in young captains. Simply stated, no one likes a "yes" man, and sometimes it takes a lot more courage to tell your commander "no" than it does to face half the Iraqi army. Eric also gained a lot of points with the team. It was clear to the guys that Eric put the team ahead of his own career, that he wasn't a "yes man," and had the courage to tell his superiors things they might not want to hear. He had also become pretty savvy at finding subtle ways to say no.

MEN WITHOUT JOBS

We had dodged a bullet, but suddenly had nothing to do. While all the rest of the teams had missions and things to do, we had turned down our assignment. Each of the other ODAs confidently briefed Lt. Col. Binford about how they would accomplish their proposed assignment, and each summarized by saying, "We believe there is a high probability that the mission will be successful." We were the only team to say a mission wasn't likely to be successful. All the other teams then began the next phase of an operation, the detailed planning. We, however, had no planning to do. So we continued training for Iraq, hoping we'd eventually get a mission.

After a week or so, the order came down from Maj. X to prepare our vehicles and equipment for air shipment. This involved lashing everything on pallets to be loaded on the aircraft that would carry us from Fort Bragg to a staging base near Iraq. Normally this palletizing is done just before deployment—it doesn't take very long to prep the gear, and once it is palletized you lose the use of your equipment for training and mission rehearsals. But when we were getting ready to launch into Afghanistan, somebody at group decided to pack up the gear without knowing when the aircraft would be available to transport us, and the stuff sat by the runway for a month, during which time we were almost completely idle. To his credit, Maj. X tried to convince Lt. Col. Binford to wait, but lost.

LIHN NGUYEN JOINS THE TEAM

Just before we started to palletize, Joe Ward came to the team room with a new guy, hot out of the Q course. Staff Sergeant Lihn Nguyen. Lihn was a perfect example of the true spirit behind what embodies Special Forces.

Lihn's dad was an American soldier who served six tours in Vietnam. During one of the initial tours he met Lihn's mom, and in 1968 Lihn was born in Siagon. His dad eventually returned to Vietnam on his final tour as a member of the 5th Special Forces Group. It was during this final tour in 1972 that Lihn's dad was able to complete the paperwork to bring Lihn and his mom out of Vietnam and eventually into the United States.

Lihn was eternally grateful that his dad saved him from a life of communism and he was the motivation behind Lihn joining the Army himself in 1987. Lihn completed his initial enlistment and decided to get out of the Army in 1991. Lihn always told himself, if he ever had the chance to go back in and do it again, he'd join the Rangers or Special Forces. In 1999, the urge to join overcame him again. After enlisting a second time, he became a Cargo Specialist (MOS 88H) and learned to drive a fork lift, but Lihn wanted more.

He wanted to fulfill his dream and repay his country for the freedoms and liberty he enjoyed while growing up in the United States. He wanted to bring that freedom to other people who weren't as lucky as he was. Where better to do that than as a member of Special Forces. So he put in the paperwork, and in October of 2000 Lihn went to Fort Bragg for the Special Forces Assessment and Selection course, eventually starting the Q course in June of 2001 to become a weapons sergeant.

After graduating in November of 2002, Lihn took some leave then signed into the 3rd Special Forces Group. Initially, he was assigned to Bravo Company, Third Battalion. But this is where a good company sergeant major comes in.

Joe Ward heard a cherry weapons guy had come into the battalion and he quickly reminded his counterpart in Bravo Company that we gave him Jeff Hull, expecting to get a rookie in return. Joe went next door and picked up Lihn, bringing him back to Charlie Company and eventually handing him over to me, bringing our number back up to eleven.

JASON AND THE JAVELIN SIMULATOR

In the days just before Christmas, we had no mission, no vehicles, no weapons, and nothing to do but wait. While the rest of us complained, Jason came up with a brilliant idea. "Let's go use the Javelin simulator," he suggested.

Fort Bragg has many buildings where, through the use of very elaborate simulators, soldiers can learn to use all kinds of weapons without actually going to the range. Using these facilities, you can become quite proficient in some kinds of shooting, and the Army has invested heavily in making them as realistic as possible, especially for expensive missile systems like the TOW, Dragon, Stinger, and Javelin. Although all these missiles are supposed to be available during war, they were too expensive to shoot in routine training. The Javelin missile, as an example, costs $78,000 without the CLU ("command launch unit," the reuseable sight system), and so the launch of one was such a rare event that none of us except Jason had ever seen one actually fired.

Ordinarily there was a long line of people waiting to get some time on the Javelin simulators, but with Christmas approaching, Fort Bragg was emptier and quieter than usual. That meant that the simulators were available, and we spent many free hours becoming proficient on these systems. In a span of thirty hours, Jason had us all qualify twice on the Javelin Basic Skills Trainer (BST), we all became quite good at killing enemy tanks, but none of us really thought we were likely to put these skills to work in the real world.

THE AIRPLANE SHUFFLE

Christmas came and went. Our pallets sat in the marshaling yard and didn't move. Once every week or so, perhaps to keep us awake, we would be ordered to break down the pallets and repack everything for a different sort of aircraft. First we configured the loads to fit on USAF C-17s, but no aircraft showed up to collect them. Then they had to be rerigged for L-1011s, and nothing happened then, either. After a few days of additional waiting, we were ordered to prep the pallets to go on a KC-135, and then on C-5s and back to C-17s all over again. ODA-391 became very good at palletizing vehicles and equipment for air shipment; we broke them down and rebuilt each pallet eight or ten times, and each time I became more annoyed. My only satisfaction from all this was the chance to say, "I told you, sir," every time Maj. X came within range of my wrath. "We shouldn't be doing this until we get tail numbers from the Air Force," I told him. "Why in the hell are we getting jerked around so much?"

"There is a reason for it," he replied. "Evidently, the Turks were giving the JSOTF staff the runaround. First we were good to go, and then they said no military aircraft. So we switched to civilian L-1011s to make them happy. Now they're saying they want us to hold off until their parliament votes on it in February. Col. Cleveland isn't going to wait that long, so now we're going to Romania."

Finally, in the last week of February, the Air Force gave us aircraft tail numbers—C-17s. Only when that happens do you know for sure that somebody is coming to pick you up in three days. Sure enough, seventy-two hours later, the aircraft showed up. We loaded the pallets, kissed our families good-bye, and climbed in. At last, ODA-391 was off to war.

STAGING IN ROMANIA

The first leg of the trip was to Germany. After twelve hours on the ground, some chow, and some sleep, the flight resumed. After another few hours in the air, we landed in not very sunny Constanta, Romania, on 27 February 2003. Meeting us there was Lt. Col. Binford. After a quick welcome, he handed us off to our battalion AD-VON (Advanced Echelon, a person responsible for setting up support services prior to the arrival of a larger group), Capt. Jorgensen, the former commander of Nine-One, the same guy Eric had replaced in Afghanistan nine months previously. Immediately I could see why everybody had been upset when he left—the guy was very sharp and had done an excellent job of preparing for our arrival. He was the Headquarters Support Company (HSC) commander, and as such was responsible for a lot of things that are taken for granted in civilian life but that can be hard to do during military deployments, things as simple as providing food and shelter for people. While many other arriving soldiers and airmen bunked on the cold concrete of the hangars, Capt. Jorgensen got Nine-One and the other Third Battalion teams into a hotel downtown.

BUILDUP

While we waited during early March 2003, a steady stream of aircraft arrived with more people, ammunition, and all the resources necessary to launch major combat operations.

At last the word came down: "We're going to start putting people in the box." (This is the term we use to describe our area of combat operations, or AO.)

Maj. X read the final warning order: "Since we can't use Turkish airspace, we're going to send the teams with missions to Cyprus, where the British have an airfield. We'll shuttle you into Iraq by C-130 from there."

Immediately Nine-Two, Nine-Four, and Nine-Five started gearing up for the trip to Cyprus and the execution of their primary missions.

"How about us?" I asked Maj. X.

"You aren't going," he said. "You guys don't have a mission, so we are going to hold you here."

Of course, the guys on the other teams were just as competitive as we were, and they could not let this situation go by without reminding us that we had brought it on ourselves by refusing the mission we had been offered. Nobody considered us cowards, but the implication was that they would have accepted the airfield mission and would have executed it successfully, too.

Then one of the guys from ODA-394 came over to rub it in. It seemed to me without any shred of sincerity or sympathy he said, "Don't worry, guys—you're going to get into the fight sooner or later."

Another member of their team reinforced the message by yelling to us from the airplane, "Hey, Nine-One! Have fun guarding those pallets. We'll see you back here at the end of the war."

At last the other three ODAs and their vehicles were loaded on the C-130s, the ramps came up, and off they went while ODA-391 sat on the airfield watching them go, like Cinderella as everybody else left for the big party.

Until this point, we all shared responsibility for guarding the battalion's gear. Now, instead of pulling guard duty every third day, we did it every day. Team morale went down to zero again, and the comfortable hotel was now the last place we wanted to be. All of us were depressed about the role we had been given, so every day we went over to beg for something to do from the 10th Group staff, who, for the time being, owned all the 3rd Group teams. Although they didn't actually throw us out, the attitude was essentially, *Get out and go away. We don't have anything for you. If we do, we'll let you know. Leave!*

COL. CLEVELAND AND THE "DOG AND PONY SHOW"

A few days after the rest of the teams departed, Joe Ward, our company sergeant major, looked us up with a simple little job for us to do. The job didn't involve combat or travel, but was a "dog and pony show," officially called a Modular Demonstration, or Mod Demo. Joe said, "Lt. Col. Binford wants you to take all your vehicles down to one of the hangars and set it all up so Col. Cleveland can take a look at it. He thinks Col. Cleveland doesn't really understand what kind of combat power our teams have because his experience is with 10th Group and their ruck teams. Don't go overboard with the demo, just bring down your vehicles and weapons and lay them out for him."

This was our big chance, and no matter what Joe or the battalion commander said, we were going to make the most of it.

"We need to show him all our stuff," Eric said.

"I agree, sir," Bobby Farmer said. "Let's lay everything out—every toy, every gun, all the ATVs—so he can see what kind of combat power we have."

And that is exactly what we did—all four of our specially modified GMVs, all the Mk19s and M2 machine guns, all the the M240s, and all the Javelin CLUs. We laid out our Barrett .50cal M107 sniper rifles and the smaller M24 .308cal versions, too, along with the SOFLAM (Special Operations Laser Marker) laser rangefinder/designator, the SATCOM radios, our high-power surveillance telescopes, our thermal cameras, and all sorts of gear that the 10th Group teams could only dream of. We set it up to be as impressive as possible, with all our special radios, our GPS navigation receivers, and the rest, and it was a hell of a display. Joe came by to check our progress.

"What the hell are you guys doing?" he said. "I told you not to go overboard! Col. Cleveland knows about most of this stuff. He just wants to see your GMVs, that's all," Joe said.

Maj. X showed up a few minutes later to show us off to a lieutenant colonel, the 10th Group S3 (Operations officer). The S3 was amazed. "One team has all this stuff?" he demanded, incredulous. "You guys have all these weapons and all this firepower in just one ODA?"

"Sure," we told him, knowing that his guys had only what they could carry on their backs.

"All this fits in those Humvees? The ammo too?"

"Yes, sir," Eric said.

"Holy shit! When the Old Man sees this, he's gonna crap," the S3 said.

"Well, we were hoping to make a good impression," Eric told him.

Twenty minutes later Col. Cleveland and his Group CSM arrived with Lt. Col. Binford, and, just as we hoped, his jaw dropped in amazement.

We showed him everything and explained how the vehicles were set up and what they could do. The extra range possible because of the auxiliary tanks and the racks for fuel cans impressed him. The extra firepower from the M240 added to the passenger side, the satellite commo systems that worked even while the vehicle was being driven, and all the other features of each GMV were a tremendous shock. His guys had white commercial pickup trucks, each with a single radio mount and no heavy weapons, with very limited ability to actually do much fighting on their own. You could see the gears turning in his mind as he reconsidered what he could do with us.

At last, Col. Cleveland turned and said to us all, "I have got to get these vehicles in country." Then he looked over at Maj. X, saying, "Your other three teams are in Cyprus, right?"

"Yes, sir," Maj. X replied.

"Bring them back. We're going to get these guys in tonight." He turned back to us and said the words we'd been waiting to hear: "Don't worry, guys, there is plenty of work for you to do. I have lots of ideas about how to use you and your stuff here, but first I have to get you in the box."

We didn't give him a hug or a kiss, but the feelings of us all were approximately the same. Once again we'd gone from unwelcome outcasts and black sheep to star performers, and once again our morale had ridden the roller coaster from the depths of "MWOJ [Men Without Jobs] hell" up into the clouds. The decision to lay out all the gear had paid off.

I thought I'd strike while the iron was still hot, so I asked Col. Cleveland if the JSOTF could find our team a TACP (Tactical Air

Control Party) to go in with. The ODAs that had gone to Cyprus each had a TACP assigned. Since we weren't going initially, we didn't get one.

"Sure," Col. Cleveland responded. "Have your battalion S-3 put in the request; I'll tell my J-3 (JSOTF Operations officer) to expect it."

"Thanks sir. I'll do that," I answered with excitement. With a TACP, that would give me twelve guys—the perfect number to fully man the GMVs. While the guys broke down the display, I ran down to battalion to hand-carry the TACP request up through channels to make sure I got one.

The JSOTF approved the request with no problem and gave me a name, Staff Sgt. Jake Chandler. *Hmmm,* I thought. *That name sounds like it belongs to a movie star and not a TACP.* They then told me where we could find him.

When I showed up at the TACP "hooch" I was told Jake was running around on the airfield somewhere on an ATV, and there was no telling when he would be back. I couldn't wait, so I figured who better to find a guy on an ATV than the team ATV guy.

"Bobby! I have a mission for you," I yelled as I got back to the team staging area. I need you to grab an ATV and try to go out and find our TACP. His buddies say he's running around on the airfield somewhere."

Bobby literally dove for his ATV, Kenney asked me if he could tag along. "Sure, just make sure you find him."

About twenty minutes later an unfamiliar face arrived. "This must be Jake?" I asked.

"In the flesh," Jake responded. I introduced myself as the team sergeant, gave him a quick rundown, and told him to pack his bags, grab his gear, and get back in two hours.

"Jake, glad to have you on the team," I told him, "we're really going to need your TACP skills."

Suddenly the jovial mood soured as Jake gave me a look that practically burned through the back of my head. "I'm not a TACP," he said strongly. "I'm a controller with STS (Special Tactics Squadron). I didn't know it prior to that moment, but evidently there was a big difference between TACPs and STS guys. Jake went on to explain that he was significantly different, and better trained than the average TACP. Evidently Jake was actually more closely related to an actual air traffic controller, with the additional training of having terminal guidance operations involving ordnance as an added skill. For a final clarification I asked, "All I want to know is, can you drop bombs on bad guys?"

"I can drop any bomb, from any plane, on any target you want."

"Great, see you in two hours." And off Jake went to gather his gear.

JASON'S MISSING MISSILES

We had almost everything we needed for combat, with one exception—the Javelin missiles had not yet arrived. We had the command launch units, the CLUs, for the system, but not the missiles themselves. Jason was our missile expert, and I asked him, "Jay, where are these missiles?"

"They still aren't here yet, Frank," he said, just as worried as I was. They were coming on an aircraft that had not yet arrived, and were the only missing part of our basic load. In fact, we had much more ammunition for the other weapons than would normally be carried, because—and this is an old military tradition—we took as much as we could carry.

Just as we were preparing to take the GMVs to be weighed and to have their center of gravity calculated, I looked up to see a forklift zooming down the side of the airfield. Staff Sgt. Kelcher, our battalion ammo NCO, was driving a big forklift, and Jason was hanging on the side, whooping and hollering. On the forklift was a pallet loaded with four big, black Javelin shipping containers. He dropped the containers by our GMVs and said, "We gotta go back—we've got another one coming."

While Jason dashed back for the rest, we broke down the shipment and started distributing them to each GMV.

As soon as the Javelins had been secured in their racks on the Humvees, we drove down to the ADAG guys—the specialists the Air Force calls Arrival/Departure Airfield Control Group—who make sure anything going on a cargo aircraft is safe for flight. Once each GMV had been weighed and its balance calculated and recorded, we were, as we say, good to go. The drivers backed each GMV into its assigned aircraft, and then the Air Force loadmasters chained them down.

INFIL TO IRAQ

For all sorts of reasons, Special Forces operations are conducted in the dark whenever possible, and that especially includes insertion of teams into potentially hostile territory. Once all our gear was stowed and chained down, we had nothing much to do until the sun went down; only then would the Air Force be ready to take off for the long flight into Iraq. The crew explained to us how they would fly the mission—they would go around Turkey, then in over the northern end of Syria, then pick up the Green Line just north of Mosul, Iraq, and fly it down to an airfield on the west side of the city of As-Sulaymaniyah in Kurdish-controlled Iraq. Since no one could pronounce *As-Sulaymaniyah* easily, the airfield was dubbed "Ass West" for short. While the Turks at least were asked about overflight authorization, nobody bothered asking the Syrians; the answer would have been not just no, but, *Hell, no!*

We learned at the same time that this process would be riskier than we hoped; one of the MC-130s carrying a 10th Group team was shot up so badly flying over Iraq that it was forced to make an emergency landing in Turkey, where the aircraft was impounded by the Turks, who weren't happy about the military plane landing without prior permission. Losing the aircraft created a ripple effect in the process of shuttling all the teams in to Ass West; only half of Nine-One went on the first night—Eric's vehicle and his other two guys; Rich and Lihn; and me, my GMV, and my two guys, Bobby and Jake. Marty and the rest were scheduled to go in the following night.

Taking a trip with the Air Force Special Operations Wing folks is not like a flight on a normal airliner. For one thing, passengers and crew are all armed to the teeth. The seating is awful, the noise is incredible, and there is no movie. Your stewardess is likely to be a guy wearing a shoulder holster, and he will not bring you a pillow. If you are extremely lucky, there may be a box lunch and hot coffee. The floor is slippery from hydraulic fluid spills and diesel from the vehicles, and everything reeks of JP-8 fuel exhaust. Once you are airborne, all cabin lighting is extinguished. The plane is relatively slow; one version of eternity is a flight on a C-130 going anywhere at all. The design is now fifty years old, and some of the airframes used by the Air Force go back nearly that far because the design is strong and reliable, so that the plane will haul just about anything you can jam in the cargo compartment, even half a Green Beret A-team off to war. But luxurious comfort was not part of the specifications. As we boarded the plane, the loadmaster pulled Eric aside. "I hope you and your guys took a shit before coming on board. Remember, our max weight is 25,000 pounds and your gear weighed in at 24,846." We found the comment funny, but he was right about one thing, we were pushing the weight envelope.

Once airborne, the crew entertained their passengers by reporting that one of their antiaircraft threat sensors didn't seem to be working and that, considering the recently demonstrated skill of the Iraqi gunners, maybe we should turn around and get it fixed. After a few minutes, however, they reported that the crew chief had whacked it a few times with a hammer, and that the system appeared to be working again. After skirting the Turkish coastline, they dropped down to a very low level to avoid detection by radar and pressed on through the dark.

This low-level flight avoids some dangers and risks others. For one thing, you get slammed around—up, down, left, right—as if you are in a washing machine without the soapy water. The vehicles and everything else are bouncing around, and sometimes things get loose. If the something is a grenade or a 5-ton vehicle, you have a problem. The ground is only a few seconds away, so if anything goes wrong, it goes wrong too quickly to fix. Even if nothing goes wrong, the ride is tremendously uncomfortable, and airsickness is common. In Special Forces, you used to have one big advantage over the guys in the conventional Army: if you got airsick, the beret made a good airsick bag.

The SOW guys got us safely across Syria and then past the air defenses of western Iraq. At last they began the approach to Ass West. The crew chief gave us the ten-minute warning; all but two of the tie-down chains on each GMV were released and cleared out of the way. Each driver climbed into his seat and put his hand on the ignition switch, ready to start the engine. Bobby went to the front of our GMV, ready to break the forward chain, while I went to the back and crawled underneath to release the rear tie-downs. Taking no chances, the pilots flew an evasive landing pattern that banged us all around some more, and then he spanked it on the ground. When the wheels hit the runway, the props were reversed with a roar, and it was time to go.

Our signal to break chains was when the props were brought back to normal pitch and the aircraft was slowing but not stopped. The aircrew began dropping the ramp, and as soon as it was beginning to open, that was the signal to start the Humvees' engines, all while the MC-130 was still taxiing to the end of the runway. With the engine started, the chains broken, and the ramp partly lowered, Bobby and I dove into our seats and were ready to take all our "carry-on baggage" into the night. At the end of the runway, the aircrew turned the plane around, aligned it with the runway, and got ready to take off again. Now the loadmaster dropped the ramp all the way to the ground, and, yelling over the noise of the four big turboprops, he gave us the order to drive off. Within a minute or two from the time the wheels hit the runway, we were driving our GMVs on solid ground, and the MC-130 was blasting back into the air on the return leg to Romania and the rest of our team.

Waiting at the edge of the runway was Erik Anderson, an old friend and now the "first shirt" (or first sergeant) for the 3rd Battalion, 10th Group, Support Company. After a quick reunion, Erik pointed to where he wanted us to park the GMVs until he had the chance to run us over to where we'd be spending the rest of the night. There were more planes coming in behind us and Erik had a lot more work to do.

HUMVEES FOB AT ASS WEST

We waited at the FOB, a sort of headquarters that is officially termed a "forward operating base," but that is, like so many other things in the Army, called by its initials. The FOB is an A-team's secure foundation when it is conducting an operation. This is where the battalion commander hangs his hat and where all the staff guys keep the team in business—the communications guys, the intel shop, the supply sergeants, and the all the people who attend to the little details of running combat operations in a dangerous, desolate place. An FOB is easy to spot—it is the place surrounded by large antennas and generators, where the coffee is hot and fresh, and where senior officers and NCOs arrive and leave at all hours of the day or night. Even when you and your team show up at two in the morning, people will be waiting and ready to chat.

When Capt. Wright and I arrived at the FOB, we walked in, adjusted to the lights, and found Lt. Col. Tovo, our temporary commander, expecting us. "Welcome aboard. Glad you're here," he said. "Have everything you need?"

"Yes, sir—everything except a job for the team," Eric said.

"Let me get the rest of the teams in here, and then I will see what we can do for you," he said. We found a place to unroll our sleeping bags and went to sleep.

Marty and the rest of Nine-One flew in the following night, and we met them as they rolled out of the aircraft. Suddenly our ODA was the first and only team from Charlie company on the ground in Iraq. The tables were turned on all those guys who mocked us as they left for Cyprus while we were left sitting by the runway in Romania. They got stuck far from the action while the battalion's black sheep, ODA Three-Nine-One, were ready to lock and load and move downrange.

While we were waiting at the FOB, the war kicked off in a rather anticlimactic way. Thanks to the battalion's excellent satellite communications systems, we could watch Fox News while camping out in the foothills of northern Iraq. A television set had been set up in one room, and everybody not busy with something more important grabbed a cup of coffee and watched it all unfold. The coverage of the bombing and cruise missile strikes on Baghdad seemed very remote even though we were in the same country and were only a few hundred miles from all the excitement on the news.

We watched for an hour or so, and then went outside to check on the vehicles for the thousandth time. Everything around us seemed quiet and routine considering that a war was underway. Once again we were riding the emotional roller coaster on the way down—why didn't we have a job? Why were we sitting here when there were battles to fight? I started pestering the 10th Group guys about putting us to work, asking the S3, "What's going on? How come we aren't moving?"

VIKING HAMMER

Finally Lt. Col. Tovo walked over to us and said, "I've got a mission for you. I am going to send you down to Charlie Company, Third-of-the-Tenth, and we want you to escort a CBIS team while they check out a site." We knew about CBIS units already; they are the chemical and biological intelligence support teams tasked with evaluating WMD sites. Each team has about eight members, sometimes civilian and military combined, and all are specialists in one aspect or another of these weapons. Typically, a team will have an EOD (explosive ordnance disposal) member, somebody expert in detecting chemical weapons, somebody else for biological weapons, and several other specialists.

Although the people on the team didn't look very impressive, they were another example of how military politics works. The CBIS team wasn't just another little group of folks under the control of the FOB or even of Col. Cleveland; they had been sent to Ass West to go into Iraq and check out sites where people at the "God level" of the Department of Defense believed WMDs were being manufactured. One was a full colonel, another came from the Defense Intelligence Agency, and one of the civilians knew everything there was to know about biological agents. They already had an escort from ODA-382 to serve as bodyguards, and then we were added to the mix along with Three-Ten. The mission for the CBIS team was to investigate an Ansar al-Islam facility deep in the mountains close by the border with Iran. The village was named Surgot and had been a safe refuge for the terrorist organization for quite a while. Secretary of State Colin Powell showed a photo of the installation to the UN General Assembly during a briefing he was giving that showed the presence of WMDs and terrorists in Iraq.

At the same time we were preparing to launch this investigation, and unknown to us at the time, other 10th Group units were preparing an operation against Surgot from the nearby Kurdish village of Halabja, a town where Iraqi units had murdered the entire population of Kurds with chemical weapons in March of 1988.

We were supposed to link up with the 10th Group teams at a "safe house" just outside Halabja, and then from there move north toward

Surgot. Based on what we knew, no other friendly forces were going to be operating in the area, so Capt. Cook the team leader for Three-Eight-Two called a meeting between Three-Eight-Two, Three-Nine-One, and the CBIST. Eric was senior to Capt. Cook, but since Three-Eight-Two would be the main effort, Capt. Cook would be given tactical command for this part of the operation. I knew the team sergeant of Three-Eight-Two, Vic Combs, and a couple of the guys on the team. I knew we'd all get along just fine, and we did. Capt. Cook, using the maps and aerial photos he had brought with him, laid out his plan of attack. It was a simple plan—Three-Eight-Two would be the assault element, and Nine-One would support them with our heavy weapons. Since the camp was in a bowl-like portion of a valley, surrounded by three sides of rugged terrain, there weren't a lot of options. Three-Nine-One, with the CBIST and Three-Eight-Two riding in the back of our GMVs, would move up to the edge of the valley to within about 200 meters of the front gate of the Ansar compound. From there, the CBIST people would dismount and take cover, and Three-Eight-Two would then assault toward the gate, with Nine-One laying down heavy machine gun and Mk19 fire into the compound. As Three-Eight-Two moved through the compound, we would reposition the vehicles to cover their movements, eventually strong-pointing at opposite corners of the perimeter. Once Three-Eight-Two cleared the compound of Ansar fighters, the CBIST guys would go to work to see if there was any WMD production taking place.

Everybody was pumped up at the prospect of a real mission against a real enemy, and for an objective that had tremendous political importance. From what the CBIST guys told us, Condoleezza Rice and others at the cabinet level wanted direct and immediate reports on the WMDs that everybody thought were being manufactured at Surgot by Ansar al-Islam.

Once we arrived at Halabja, though, the excitement began to evaporate. Instead of assaulting the position, we had a job like that of taxi drivers. On arrival at the safe house, we found that the company commander for ODB-090 (C-3-10SFG) had not been told of our participation, and he was annoyed. He stated that he told the FOB he did not need additional forces, just heavier weapons like .50cals and Mk19s. It took him about fifteen seconds to eye the GMVs and tell us that he was taking our trucks. Marty and I immediately jumped to Eric's side.

"The trucks and the team are inseparable. You want the trucks, you get us with them," Marty stated.

He immediately snapped back at Marty, "You'll give up the trucks, Chief. That's all there is to it."

I grabbed Eric and Marty. "Lets go out to the trucks; we have a phone call to make." The major was clearly aware of what that comment meant. We were going to go over his head. Since we knew it was his battalion and group commander who sent us, we felt that the truck issue leaned our way.

When we got outside, I told Eric, "Get on the horn to our FOB and let Lt. Col. Binford know that these guys want to take our trucks. Have him get on the horn to Tovo because I'm sure at this very moment he's on the horn to his FOB making the case to take them away."

Eric quickly picked up the SATCOM and got ahold of the FOB. It only took ten seconds for Eric to explain what was going on and for Lt. Col. Binford to say, "Capt Wright, you are not to surrender those vehicles to anyone. I will handle this; you stand by for my further guidance."

"Roger that, sir," Eric responded. In just a few minutes we got the word that the GMVs were to stay with us and that we were to stay in Halabja.

This obviously didn't sit well with the Zero-Nine-Zero commander. When we asked where they wanted us to bunk, he told us to get with his company Operations sergeant, who showed us the one small room available and said, "If you guys want it, you can sleep in here." The room was small and it would be a tight squeeze to fit almost thirty guys in it, so many of the guys decided to sleep outside on the vehicles.

Since we had been sent to join the 10th Group teams, they had to keep us for a while, but that didn't mean they had to be cheerful hosts. The ODB commander and his guys briefed us on Operation Viking Hammer, and they also made it clear that none of us, including the CBIS team, would be allowed to leave the little compound. Nine-One was not going to be part of the operation, and only when the other teams had secured Surgot would we be called on the radio, and only then would we be allowed to enter the Ansar al-Islam site with our WMD inspectors. The 10th Group teams would assault the site with their M240 and M249 machine guns and would ride into battle in their Toyota pickup trucks, leaving us and our heavier weapons and our much more capable GMVs to sit tight at the safe house.

They began the assault on 28 March, and our only involvement for the next two days of the operation was that of spectators. We could hear shooting and the explosions of bombs for two days and nights, and then at last we got the call we'd been hoping for: "Okay, Nine-One, you can move up to Surgot now." Everybody climbed into the vehicles for the short trip to the camp, all excited to be able to finally investigate the WMD reports. We decided to put our protective suits on, just in case there really were biological agents present. As we neared the camp, we linked up with a Kurdish guide who would escort us in. He cautioned us on the roads saying, "Whatever you do, stay on the road. Don't ever go off the road; the place is covered in land mines." We gladly followed his guidance.

The place was nothing but a smoking ruin. Condoleezza Rice might have wanted a detailed report about the place, but now there wasn't much to investigate. The CBIS guys were irate—they had been ordered to find WMDs, and now, if any WMDs had been present, they were destroyed beyond recognition by a rain of cruise missiles and bombs.

When we arrived, the local villagers were still combing through the rubble and scavenging anything of the smallest value. We began doing the same thing, but the things the CBIS guys were looking for were evidence of what had been going on at the site for the years it had been in operation. While they got out their sophisticated detection systems and started sniffing around for chemical and biological agents, my guys provided perimeter security with the GMVs, and the guys from Three-Eight-Two went looking for documents and objects that might be useful to the Intel analysts.

Right away they discovered all sorts of incriminating evidence—airline tickets to and from the United States, cookbooks for various toxic agents, and Rand McNally maps of American cities, along with address books with names and phone numbers of possible Ansar operatives in America. These discoveries were seriously frightening, especially the cancelled plane tickets to American cities. The Kurd commander told us that the terrorists kept these tickets to prove to their Islamic brothers that they had actually infiltrated their enemy nation—that they had succeeded in visiting the "great Satan" and had performed a mission for Allah.

Somehow an MSNBC (Microsoft National Broadcasting Company) crew showed up just as we were exploring the Surgot site and managed to demonstrate once again why soldiers usually despise most reporters and media people. "Is this the WMD site that Colin Powell described to the United Nations?" Preston Mendenhall asked.

"Yes, this is the place," we said.

"Well, did you find anything?" he asked.

The answer was, of course, no, but the smart thing to do in this sort of situation is to play stupid. "No, we don't know anything about it," we told him. "Our job here is just to provide security; that's all we know." Of course the reporters went after the inspection team and began to pester them, but with the same result. "Ricin," the reporter exclaimed to the WMD team leader. "Did you find any ricin?" They blew the reporters off too.

After the CBIS team let us know they had completed a thorough search, we headed back to Halabja and the safe house. Our CBIS guys wrote up their report that they found no actual WMDs or components at the site, and sent it back over one of the secure radio systems.

The next morning we got the word from Capt. Cook that we had to go back to Surgot. "What? Why?" I asked.

"The MSNBC crew brought their own WMD-detection kit with them," the captain said, "and they are telling the world that they got a positive response for ricin when they did the tests. It was on the news last night."

MSNBC used a kit called the BADD, or BioWarfare Agent Detection Device, sold by Osborne Scientific. The BADD is a single-use kit that comes in a small pouch, and the UN inspectors had used this kit extensively before the war kicked off. Detection kits for poisons like ricin look for protein molecules that can be found anywhere. Simple detectors are used for screening tests to get preliminary response, and they produce many false positives. Experienced investigators like our CBIS team didn't put much faith in the results generated from these kits, but the reporter did.

Based on the BADD kit result, the reporter broke the story that WMDs had been present. We didn't know it at the time, but MSNBC would post a very detailed and confident report on their Web site several days later, on 4 April 2003, explaining how accurate the test was and how confident the test's developer was that the results were correct.*

When this report hit the news, Condoleezza must have hit the roof because some very senior people in the Pentagon were calling up on the SATCOM radio to tell the CBIS guys that they got the wrong answer and that MSNBC found the WMDs that we missed. *Go back and look again, dummies* was the gist of their message, so we loaded everybody back in the GMVs and drove back for another visit to Surgot. Once again the team went through the rubble, and once again they came up with negative results.

TO THE SOUND OF GUNS

As the CBIS guys made another futile sweep of the site, we suddenly heard a sound to gladden the heart of any real Green Beret—gunfire echoing off the mountains and loud enough to be coming from someplace nearby. "Let's go, let's go," I called to the team, and I ran for my GMV.

We told the CBIS guys to get in the GMVs, and we bounced off the rocky path toward the sound of the gunfire.

It wasn't far away, and it wasn't hard to find. We came around the side of a mountain to discover a group of Kurds firing an old Russian

---

*Osborne Scientific remains confident that their kit found traces of ricin at Surgot. A representative of the company recently said that the BADD kit is considerably more accurate than the system used by the CBIS team.

howitzer at the side of another mountain. Their accuracy was awful, partly because of the range, partly because they really didn't know much about artillery.

"What are you shooting at?" I asked them. Their officer handed me his binoculars and pointed at the distant mountain slope. I could see several tiny figures climbing upward through the snow and the rocks toward the border with Iran at the crest, only a few hundred more meters away.

"Ansar al-Islam!" he said. "They are trying to go to Iran. They are escaping!"

Considering the Kurds' gunnery, the terrorists didn't have much to worry about—they were about to escape without a scratch. "You need to get closer," I told him, but he told me that their vehicles wouldn't make it any farther; they got stuck in the snow and mud.

"We'll get them for you," I said. We hopped back in the GMVs, along with the Kurd commander, and we started driving up the goat path, up the side of a steep mountain.

There wasn't a road, and there was hardly a path, but we soon crossed the snow line and were thrashing through mud, water, and ice. There were sheer cliffs and drop-offs to the side at times as we climbed up the side of the mountain. It was short of amazing how the overloaded GMVs easily climbed the steep slopes. After a few minutes of exciting driving, we got to within about 800 meters of the Ansar al-Islam guys. Rich Turner was behind the gun on Eric's GMV, and he opened fire with the .50cal and got the honor of being the first guy on Nine-One to squeeze a trigger on the enemy in this operation.

Standing behind him, I spotted for him with the binocs and adjusted his fire. "Right, Rich," I told him, "come right a couple of clicks on the T&E (Transverse and Elevation. A knob that stabilized the M2 in its vehical mount, allowing for better accuracy at longer ranges)." Then he began laying down some serious five-round bursts, and you could see the tracers smacking into the snow and rocks around the enemy up the hill.

Rich's fire was effective in at least one way—it got the attention of the terrorists. One of them turned around and cut loose a burst with his AK in our general direction, knowing that the range was impossibly long for him to connect with any of us except by luck. We heard a couple of his bullets whiz by, well overhead, and saw the distant muzzle flashes of the rifle. I thought it was somewhat amusing, but what was really hilarious was the reaction from our CBIS experts, especially the civilians. Many of these guys were older and heavier civilians who had not done a lot of physical training or tactical training recently, but they dove out of the Humvee and went looking for cover when those virtually harmless bullets flew past.

Rich was pretty well dialed in on the Ansar al-Islam guys. We could see the API (armor-piercing-incendiary) rounds exploding against the rocks near the enemy soldiers, forcing them to take cover where they could find it. The mountainside was steep, and the border still several hundred meters from the men. As long as they stayed hidden in the rocks, they were safe from the machine gun. But as soon as they got up for another dash up the hill, Rich could "light them up."

Up at the crest of the ridge, we could see other figures waiting for the Ansar al-Islam men. Rich was about to shift his fire to these other targets when the Kurd officer said, "Don't shoot them—they are Iranian border guards." It was hard to evaluate our fire, but at least one of the enemy seemed to have been hit; one of his buddies came back down the hill to help him, but changed his mind when Rich put some additional API rounds nearby.

After half an hour or so, the survivors got so close to the Iranian guards that we suspended firing on them. They joined up with the guards and disappeared from view into Iran. We got back in the Humvees and turned around, headed back to obscurity at Halabja, like Cinderella at midnight.

MEANWHILE, BACK IN HALABJA

Tenth Group just didn't know what to do with the teams from 3rd Group; we didn't fit anywhere in the SOP, and it seemed to be easier for them to just let us cool our heels instead of trying to figure out what to do with us, our strange vehicles, our excessive firepower, and especially our aggressive attitude.

"You've got to have an A-team that needs help—like fire support, or anything at all! Get us in this fight," we told him.

"No. Nothing for you guys yet," their major would say. "I don't need you—I need your vehicles."

Then, four days after we arrived in country, Nine-Two showed up from Cyprus. "The whole company is behind us," they reported, "and they will all be here in the next couple of days." Now we had two full ODAs with GMVs and a ruck team from 3rd Group on the ground with more on the way, and we were not feeling quite so lonesome. The following day Maj. X arrived with the B-team, and we implored him to get us in the fight.

We got up on Day Three of Operation Viking Hammer to find a guy from 10th Group sitting in the front seat of one of our GMVs being interviewed by a crew from the program *Good Morning America*. We heard the reporter ask him about the GMVs, and he started talking about all the great things the vehicles could do as if he and his team owned them. The reporter ignorantly sucked it up. Little did he know that the guy sitting in the seat probably never saw a combat-loaded GMV before that day.

We were steaming mad. "Get us out of here, or get us in the fight," we told Maj. X.

Then Nine-Four and Nine-Five arrived—our whole company was now ready to go. There were two full-up Special Forces companies ready to be launched, one armed to the teeth, mobile, and powerful, the other lightly armed, less mobile, and with limited capabilities. Thanks to politics, the direct-action 3rd Group unit stayed idle while the unconventional warfare 10th Group teams were kept busy herding Kurdish cats in the mountains. We were incredibly frustrated.

At last, two of our ODAs were released to provide fire support for a mission, just to placate us, but without any significant action. We sort of got a hint to the logic applied to come to this conclusion when one of the 10th Group guys made the comment, "You guys had all the fun in Afghanistan; now it's our turn."

It was obvious that the 10th Group personnel felt that this was their war and that they didn't need or want any help from us. We had our "trigger time" in Afghanistan, they seemed to think, and now it was their turn to get operational experience. Maj. X went to meet with a company commander from 10th Group to lobby for a role in an impending operation and was ignored. *This is our war,* they seemed to be saying, *and you guys can stay out of it.*

Finally, Maj. X got permission from Lt. Col. Binford for us to pull out of Halabja, and we drove in convoy up to the forward operating base (FOB) of Three-Ten at Sulaymaniyah.

Just as we pulled in, a CIA officer named "Sergi" ran up. "I need your help," he said in a heavy Russian accent. "There is an Iraqi tank battalion over there, and I would like you to have some bombs dropped on their position. I have been discussing surrender terms with them, and they refuse to surrender because they do not believe there are Americans in the area. I wish to bloody their nose to convince them that Americans are in the area and that it is in their best interests to surrender. But I cannot do that unless we bomb them. Will you go with me and have your TACP call an air strike on them?"

This seemed to be a wonderful idea to all of us, but we didn't intend to get the Air Force involved. "Great," Jason said. "We can sneak up there, move to within a kilometer or so of the tanks, and get some kills with the Javelins."

Of course, we could not just take off on our own and start engaging enemy tank battalions without getting some sort of authorization, so we found the 10th Group S3 Operations officer, a major, and reported in, with Sergi coming along to help explain the mission. After telling the S3 that Nine-One had arrived, Marty told him, "We've got a mission. We're going to go help out this CIA guy."

"What are you talking about?" demanded the S3 major.

"Sergi, one of the CIA guys, just told us that there is an Iraqi tank battalion right over that hill. He says they are in defensive positions blocking the road. He wants us to call in an air strike on the tanks, and we're going to get a couple Javelin shots in as well."

"No, you are not!" he said.

"Why not?" Marty wanted to know.

"Just because you come riding in here on your sexy trucks, don't think for a minute that you can just go over the hill and pick a fight with the Iraqi army. You guys are nuts if you think you and your little Humvees can mix it up with armor. It ain't gonna happen. The reason there are guys like me here is to keep guys like *you* from getting your whole team killed while doing stupid stuff!"

I was amazed. "You guys have had us sitting here for a week," I told him, "and we haven't done a damn thing. Now there is enemy armor right over that hill, and we have our Air Force TACPs, who can call in a ton of bombs on them, plus we have our own Javelin missiles, and we can smoke them. We're telling you that we can engage them without putting ourselves at risk; we can do it from the crest of the hill. We aren't going to drive down into their effective engagement range; we're going to spank them from a click or more away. We just want to go to the top of that hill!"

"No," the S3 said, "you aren't doing it!"

"Okay," Marty told him, "I want to talk to Col. Tovo. This is bullshit. We aren't here to sit on our butts while you guys play games the way you did in Bosnia." Once again, we were bumping into 10th Group's entirely different way of conducting operations. We were all members of the US Army, all members of Special Forces, all products of the same training programs, all subject to the same fundamental doctrine, but we had entirely different attitudes about what missions we should do and how we should do them. They had spent a lot of time in Bosnia, where the physical and political terrain was different than where we had spent our time, Afghanistan. They wanted to fight little skirmishes against little units, and to stand back and call for close air support at the first opportunity.

Right now, 10th Group was in control and could tell us what to do—or, all too often, not to do. "No," the major said, "you are not going to talk to Col. Tovo about it." And that was the end of the discussion.

Marty and I walked out of the "three shop" (as the S3 Operations office is called) fuming mad. I walked over to the guys in the GMVs, who were all checking weapons and gear, getting ready to take off on this mission. "We're not going," I told them. "Tenth Group won't let us play."

JAKE LOOKS FOR A NEW JOB

Jake Chandler was our USAF controller, and he'd signed up to work with us back in Romania. Back then, he was sure that we'd be in the middle of the fight and that he would be calling in air strikes and dropping hundreds of bombs. He could hear all the other controllers on the radio, calling for air strikes and playing their role in the big event. For a whole week, Jake had been out of the action as a result of teaming up with us, and he was disgusted. "Frank," he told me, "I am going to put in a request to be assigned to another team. I came over here to drop bombs, not ride around in Humvees."

"Look, Jake, I understand how you feel, but we're just as frustrated. We would really like to have you stay with us."

"No, I am going to call my captain up in Romania and tell him that I am not being utilized and ask if there's someplace else where I can make a contribution."

So Jake got on the radio and made his request, but it was denied. He had to stay with us, and he was naturally frustrated. We were all frustrated. None of us were happy at the inactivity; we wanted to get in the fight, immediately, and didn't care too much who or what we had to take on.

While we were feeling sorry for ourselves, Lt. Col. Binford had managed to get our own FOB on the ground up north in the vicinity of Irbil. Those FOBs were complicated headquarters, and it took a few days to get them completely up and running, but Binford was establishing his presence and authority as the third Special Forces battalion commander in the area. Until now, because our FOB hadn't arrived, we were "chopped," or attached to 10th Group, but now Lt. Col. Binford called Col. Cleveland and asked to have his teams back. He pointed out that he was now in Iraq, had the FOB in operation, and was ready to resume operational control of 3rd Battalion's teams.

We got a call on the radio from the FOB that said, in essence, *Say good-bye to the 10th Group and get yourselves up here to the FOB at Irbil*. It was the first time I could remember being glad to be recalled to battalion headquarters, but we were all thrilled at the prospect of being back with our own people.

Lt. Col. Binford wasn't always the easiest guy to work with, but he was fundamentally a *warrior*. He wanted to kill the bad guys, he wanted to take the battle to the enemy in an aggressive way, and even though he wasn't the most charming guy in the battalion, we respected him highly.

He constantly told us, "I want you to kill the enemy forces where you find them. If you can't kill them yourselves, I want you to lure them out into the desert, where you can call CAS in on them and kill them that way."

He was another old member of the 5th "Legion," and he had shared the same attitude most of us had who had come from there—we were all warriors, and we all wanted to punish the enemy with everything we had until he quit or was killed in place.

ODA-391 waved good-bye to Sulaymaniyah and the S3 shop in our rearview mirrors, and made haste to Irbil and our FOB. The advance party had done well when they set the place up; we had an area of our own where we could park the vehicles and store our gear and sleep. We refitted, refueled, and got some more ammo to replace what we'd already used.

NINE

NORTHERN SAFARI

L t. Col. Binford's plan was typical of his style—blunt, direct, powerful. He intended to attack at several places along the Green Line,
and when one of the attacks was able to punch through the enemy defenses, Lt. Col. Binford planned to exploit that breakthrough by sending the whole battalion into the valley beyond, then turn the whole
force left (east) and downward to capture Kirkuk. Each team would be
provided with a force of Kurds as backup to help clear urban areas of
enemy infantry, and together Lt. Col. Binford thought that we could
capture Kirkuk and its essential oil-distribution facilities.

While we had our FOB set up on one side of Irbil, 2nd Battalion,
10th SFG, had their forward operating base on the other. Col. Cleveland,
who commanded all the SF units in northern Iraq—about forty-five
ODAs—assigned operational control of this sector to Second-of-the-
Tenth. This meant that, although Lt. Col. Binford had control of his battalion again, he and all his teams were still under the operational control
("OPCON") of good old 10th Group, and the same old conflicts about
what sorts of missions to execute and how those missions should be executed remained. It was SF politics again, as ugly as ever.

Lt. Col. Binford was ready to rock and roll. He called the teams in and briefed us on the concept of the operation, then brought in Col. Cleveland and briefed him on the plan, too, indicating on the map exactly where each of the 3rd Group teams were to attack. Maj. X and the other company commanders then went into their planning cycle, produced their plan, and called Col. Cleveland back to listen to it all in a brief-back and, hopefully, approve.

The plan looked like this: The Green Line followed a prominent ridgeline that formed the border between territory controlled by the Kurds in the north and Saddam's government in the central and southern parts of the country. The Iraqis had defensive positions all along the line—infantry, armor, and artillery units dug in and oriented toward Kurdish territory. Behind them, in the open terrain to the south of the Green Line, was the 34th Iraqi Infantry Division, with its thousands of men and its extensive combat power.

Col. Cleveland was a bit stunned at the audacity of the plan. He turned to Lt. Col. Binford and said, "So you are telling me that you're going to go over that hill, and you are going to pick a fight with an entire enemy infantry division? You do realize, don't you, that you're dealing with the complete 34th Infantry Division?"

"Yes, sir," Binford answered.

I had to butt in and said, "Sir, as you know we spent a lot of time in Africa, and you know there's an old African saying that goes: 'How do you eat an elephant'?"

Before I could complete the phrase, Cleveland interrupted me. "You're going to tell me, 'One bite at a time,' aren't you?" Col. Cleveland said, unconvinced.

"You're damn right, sir. We're going to go over that hill and start eating them up, one bite at a time, sir! We will bomb them, move, shoot them, move again, and keep doing that until we pile them up, sir, one bite at a time."

Col. Cleveland put his head down and started to laugh, shaking his head in disbelief. Then he turned around and said to Lt. Col. Binford, "Okay, I have your plan. I am going to think about it and will let you know."

We all liked the plan and thought the briefing went very well. Col.

Cleveland went back to his headquarters and then talked it over with Lt. Col. Waltemeyer, commander of Two-Ten, who then objected to the plan. Yet again, political differences between our two organizations complicated our ability to fight the enemy.

Col. Cleveland came up with a compromise. He combined Waltemeyer's ODAs, their lightly armed pickup trucks, and their Kurds with us and our GMVs as a kind of task force. He came back to Lt. Col. Binford and said, essentially, *I approve your plan and you can go with it, but with some modifications. I want you to go over to see Lt. Col. Waltemeyer's FOB and you guys coordinate with each other.*

Maj. X was sent over to Two-Ten to do the coordination. When he arrived, Waltemeyer's staff essentially tossed him out on his ear. From what we heard when Maj. X returned, Waltemeyer himself said, "Who the hell are you, and what the hell are you doing in my FOB? Get out!" Maj. X got out.

Binford called Waltemeyer, reminding him that the two battalions were directed to work together. After a very heated discussion on the radio, Maj. X headed back to Waltemeyer's FOB, this time with Lt. Col. Binford to back him up. As they were leaving, Lt. Col. Binford said to us, "Your major took a couple of fast ones high and inside to the head for the teams today. We're going back over there to straighten this out." He didn't ask us, but it seemed that the major had been taking quite a lot of hard hits high and inside lately, and we were all glad he thought it was time to hit back.

After a couple of hours, they came back, and we all huddled. "Okay, here's what we decided," Maj. X said. "You guys are going to be the supporting effort for 2nd Battalion while they conduct the assault across the Green Line. The other teams are going to provide fire support for them with the .50cals and Mk19s. I'm going to use you as a quick reaction force [QRF]. You're going to link up with Four-Four at Pir Da Ud. Get your stuff and get down there after the briefing."

"You're going to use *who* as the QRF?" I asked, incredulous.

"I've got to have somebody available in case we have trouble," he answered.

"What about using the B-team? They have GMVs and guns and all the stuff we do; use them." It made sense for some to stay back, but we didn't think it should be us.

"No," he said, "I want an A-team. You're going to go here." And he pointed to the place on the map. "Tenth Group's got a position here where they are watching the ridge and dropping bombs on it. You guys set up here. You'll be able to move to any place on the battlefield from there."

The team's morale roller coaster zoomed down to the bottom again. Once again, we had to tell the guys we would be sitting on our butts while somebody else did all the fighting. We were all disgusted. As long as they asked us to help fight somebody—at this point, anybody—we were good to go. Nine-One was in a killing mood, and at this point we were mad at everybody. Early the next morning we drove south to hook up with Four-Four at Pir Da Ud.

TEN

OBJECTIVE ROCK

Early on the morning of 4 April, Nine-One's GMVs lined up and moved out of the FOB compound located in the northern Iraqi city of Irbil and headed south to the designated mission support site (MSS) and assembly area. The team was in a bad mood once again because of our second-string status within the company. The distance from Irbil to Pir Da Ud was only about 15 miles. The road was in good repair in Irbil, but traffic was relatively heavy as we drove through what was the largest city and the provisional capital of Kurdish-controlled Iraq. Jubilant Kurdish civilians, particularly children, constantly ran toward us to cheer as we passed, tossing flowers into our vehicles as they attempted to get a handshake from one of the Americans. They forced us to slow down, but we were still able to make it down to the spot on the map within an hour.

ODA-044 was part of Alpha Company, 2nd Battalion, 10th Special Forces Group. While their battalion was full-strength, their assets were spread over hundreds of kilometers along the Green Line. In order to prevent gaps in coverage, some teams were required to exercise the "split team" option and divide the team in half in order to adequately cover their sectors of responsibility. Such was the case for

Four-Four, with the team sergeant, Tom Sandoval, running one part of the show in Four-Four's sector while his team commander was miles away to the northwest with the other half of the detachment.

We found Four-Four easily enough—their position stuck out like a sore thumb and was easy to find because they had dug themselves a huge hole in the center of a wheat field about 150 meters from the pavement. As we pulled into the position, all of us on Nine-One marveled at the way these guys were operating. Two immaculate Land Rovers, both painted bright white and visible from long distances, were neatly parked just outside the berm, providing sure evidence of a 10th SFG presence. Next to them was a huge truck of the type commonly used throughout the area for transporting large numbers of people or animals, cargo, or any combination thereof. A pair of camouflage-painted Toyota pickups completed this little motor pool, and we combat-parked our vehicles alongside the rest.

From their positions high up on the ridge, the Iraqis must have been able to see Four-Four and their Peshmerga (literally, "those who face death") Kurds, but Tom had wisely placed his position just outside the range of their heavy artillery, keeping the Iraqis from firing on them. This fresh dirt was in stark contrast to the bright green wheat, and that made it highly visible from a great distance. Even though this made the location of the team pretty obvious, Tom had decided it was necessary to protect the force from suicide car bombers—a serious threat. The berm also protected them against possible artillery fire, although the enemy guns appeared to be out of range.

As we arrived, Master Sgt. Tom Sandoval emerged from this hole in the dirt to greet us. Eric, Marty, Gerry, and I went over for the introductions. Although we weren't personally acquainted, I knew that Tom was technically the commander of this sector and that by default we were under his OPCON. Since Tom had operational control, he would be the man who would give Nine-One its orders, meaning he would have the ability to make our lives either pleasurable or miserable. We introduced ourselves, and he said, "Come on in here and let me show you what's happening."

For a hole in the ground, it was a pretty comfortable place. Tom and

his guys had been there for several days, and like all good soldiers manning a fighting position, Four-Four had spent the time developing and
improving theirs. Off to one side was a cooking area; off to another was
a spot for doing observation, with the laser designator, binoculars, radios, and a big spotting scope. They'd rigged ponchos to provide some
overhead protection from the rain and sun.

They, like the rest of the teams, had a USAF tactical air controller.
Theirs was Staff Sgt. Saleem Ali, and he had been annoying the enemy
soldiers up on the ridge by dropping bombs on them from time to time.

We had a look around the position and were impressed with how
well Tom and his guys had set up housekeeping. It was early, and we
had missed chow at the FOB, and Tom noticed our interest in the
breakfast his radio operator was preparing on their little stove—he had
eggs boiling, and there was coffee and a big pile of local pita bread
nearly ready for consumption. I had quickly learned to love pita
bread—you buy it at the local market in big stacks, and then reheat it
for fifteen seconds on each side before serving it with cream cheese
and jelly. In the Middle East, that is the breakfast of champions.

The delicious smell of all this cooking was irresistible, and Tom gra-
ciously offered, "Would you guys like some chow?" He didn't have to
ask the question twice. The mood for Nine-One began to change. Suddenly, we weren't being treated like dirt. Even though Tom and his
team were from 10th Group, the source of so many of our recent problems, his attitude was friendly, hospitable, and cooperative. When our
guys got out of the GMVs and met Tom's team, some of the newer
guys on the teams discovered they had been through the Q course
together, while others had served together on previous assignments
and were on friendly terms. Previously, with the exception of Nine-
Two, we'd been at odds with a lot of other teams. Now we seemed to
have an ally just when we needed one.

While we were digging into the eggs, pita bread, and coffee, Tom
said, "We've been eating like this for a week. The Kurds have been
bringing us food, and we're getting fat. Get the rest of the team, bring
them in here, get some chow, and I will tell you what's going on."

While the rest of the guys got acquainted with the men from

Four-Four, Tom began to bring Eric, Marty, Gerry, and me up to speed. He told us that the enemy soldiers could be seen clearly up on the ridge. Somewhat as an experiment, he tried bombing the position to see how they would react and discovered that they appeared to evacuate their bunkers then came back when the dust settled. Tom told us that they watched after each bombing as the Iraqis brought fresh timbers and building material in by truck to repair the damage.

Tom had the maps and overhead photos from Falcon View laid out where we could study them. From our present position near Pir Da Ud, all that was visible was the northern face of a low ridge. The maps and photos showed that a second ridge was beyond the first, with a small depression or saddle between the two. On the far side of the ridge was a major highway, and beyond was an open valley. Enemy units were believed to be scattered throughout the region, but exactly where was mostly a mystery.

Tom also told us he'd been able to obtain some critical information in a way that is typical of SF, which meant it was from the kind of source that conventional forces would seldom rely on, or even bother with at all. Tom had noticed a shepherd bringing sheep down off the ridge and took an interpreter to talk to the man. He discovered that the Iraqis were letting the shepherds move back and forth through the area unhindered. "Were you on the other side of the mountain?" Tom asked through the interpreter.

"Yes, I was there yesterday," the shepherd told him. "The grass over there is better grazing for the sheep."

"What did you see over there?" Tom wanted to know.

"Lots of Iraqis," he said. "Lots of tanks, jeeps, and trucks."

"Show me on the map," Tom told the shepherd. The man was the only fresh source of information about the enemy's composition and location because, at this time, we didn't have any recon photos or other intel. While other units had UAVs (Unmanned Aerial Vehicle) and all sorts of other support, we were dependent on a Kurdish shepherd.

The man was very helpful and knew enough about maps to be able to point out places where he had seen tanks and other enemy units. From what Tom learned, he concluded that the enemy had established a classic blocking position along the crest, anticipating an assault up the very route we intended to use. The infantry were dug in along the military crest, with the tanks farther back.

"Here's what we're going to do," Tom told us. "We are going to call in two strikes, the first along the military crest, on the infantry positions, then another farther back, where we think the tanks are dug in. That should kick them off the ridge temporarily, giving us enough time to get up there before the Iraqis come back."

"That's great for you guys, Tom," I told him. "We've been sent down here to sit on our butts—we are your QRF."

"The QRF?" he said. "The QRF for what?"

"Our commander's plan is for the other ODAs and you to make this big assault on the Green Line, and if any of you get into trouble, we are supposed to be sitting here, ready to be used as reinforcements."

Tom looked around at us. "Twelve guys? Twelve guys are going to be reinforcements?" He laughed at the idea, but it wasn't funny to us anymore.

"Well, that is not what we have in mind for you," Tom told us. He then laid out the plan as it had been briefed to him by his leadership, and it was entirely different from what we had been told by ours. Binford and Maj. X had briefed us on their intentions for Nine-One and had carried the plan over to Waltemeyer, but now we learned that he had changed the plan a bit. Since Col. Cleveland had approved the general plan for the assault on the Green Line, Waltemeyer had to accept that general plan, but he also had the authority to adjust anything within his area of operations (AO) to suit himself.

Tom Sandoval laid out the plan as it had come down from Waltemeyer and his AOB (Advanced Operational Base) commander, and some of what he said was unexpected good news: "I don't think you're being used as the QRF," Tom said, "but as part of the assault." That news was just what we needed to hear. Tom promised to check with his company commander to find out what was really going on, and suddenly there was hope for the black sheep of Nine-One once again. Sandoval and his guys might have been part of our nemesis, Two-Ten, but our introduction to him and Four-Four, over pita bread and coffee in a hole in the ground, was making us reconsider the whole relationship.

We spent the first of what was to be two long days waiting at this assembly area, getting ready, and enjoying the excellent chow provided by Four-Four and the Kurds. Tom's company commander, Maj. Howard of AOB-040, drove down to meet with all of us later that afternoon. We explained to him the guidance we'd been given, and when it didn't jibe with what he had been told by his leadership, he went back to FOB-20 (Forward Operating Base) to get clarification.

Upon his return the following day, Maj. Howard gathered Tom, Marty, Eric, and me up, and we walked back to his Land Rover. Even though there was only one 10th Group team involved in our little piece of the fight, it was owned by Maj. Howard, and he was in command of them, the stretch of Green Line in front of us, and what was now our little task force.

"I'm in command of this part of the operation," he said, "and here's what I want to do. I am going to bring in all the teams, and we're going to have a meeting of all the team leaders, team sergeants, and warrants to sort this out. Two-Ten thinks we're doing one thing, and Third-of-the-Third thinks they're doing another. I don't want any confusion or any screwups, and the only way to prevent them is to bring in everybody that's playing for a face-to-face. One way or another, we're going to get this part of the operation unscrewed."

He looked at Eric and said, "Get ahold of Maj. X and have him and all his teams report in here tomorrow to Tom's position at 1500 hours for an OpOrder and 'chalk-talk' so we can iron out one cohesive plan. Just because our FOBs have difficulty working together doesn't mean the AOBs and our associated teams can't work things out amongst ourselves." After a few more minutes the meeting broke up, and Capt. Wright immediately went back to our GMVs and got on the radio to call Maj. X to give him and the other ODAs—Nine-Two, Nine-Four, and Nine-Five—the word.

The following afternoon, all ODAs pulled out of their battle positions and began to assemble as directed. One by one, each team pulled into Tom's position and took up positions around the perimeter, with Tom's hole located in the center. Maj. X and Sgt. Maj. Joe Ward had linked up with Maj. Howard, and both arrived in a small convoy. The team leaders, warrants, and team sergeants left their team areas and gathered around the AOB commanders. Maj. Howard began to spread his collection of maps on the hood of one of Nine-Five's GMVs. Pointing to his map, Maj. Howard indicated his sector of responsibility along the ridgeline and the current disposition of friendly forces. Nine-Four and Nine-Five, along with the other half of ODA-044, were already in position facing the same ridge about 6 miles to our right, near the village of Mastiwah, while Nine-Two was set up a couple miles or so over to our left.

Drawing a small circle on the map with his finger, he showed us the section of the ridgeline where he thought we should make our attack. Nine-Four and Nine-Five had studied the area to their front earlier and suggested a better way to get up the ridge. After a quick explanation by Captains Spivy and Staton, Maj. Howard agreed. For once we were involved in a planning session with guys from 10th Group where our opinions seemed to be valued and incorporated.

Then, in true Special Forces fashion, Maj. Howard pushed the maps aside, and he and Nine-Five's commander, Capt. Staton, used a pencil to draw the new plan directly on the flat tan paint of the GMV's hood, sketching the ridge and outlining the whole attack just like John Madden diagramming a football play. The pencil was handed off to each of the team leaders in turn, and each sketched out his attack while the others scrutinized it and made suggestions. It seemed almost everybody had something to say. Everybody except Maj. X, who stood to the side to listen and watch as his team leaders and team sergeants took their cues and orders from another AOB commander.

When they were done, we had a chalk-talk drawing that summarized the entire operation. It distilled all the grand ideas from Cleveland, Binford, Waltemeyer, and their staffs, as well as fresh ideas from the ODAs that would actually be doing the fighting. We had finally found an AOB commander from 10th who was willing to use us as we wanted to be used. All the personality conflicts—the differences of opinion about who should do what, where, and when—had been re-solved by this meeting.

Col. Cleveland needed a breakthrough on the ridge a few miles to our front. Now we had a simple, practical plan to do our part in it, and all the players were happy with it. Cleveland wanted us to get on the other side of that hill, and now we had a time and place to make the attempt.

When the meeting was over, Nine-One had been transformed from understudy to one of the leading actors. The quick-reaction-force mission was exchanged for an attack with the other ODAs. Now we were paired up with Nine-Two in support of Tom and his Kurds. We were go-ing to be out on the flanks with our heavy weapons while the Peshmerga attacked on foot.

The entire situation would seem odd to anybody in the conventional Army. First, the command structure was all out of adjustment—Tom had just six guys and a motley crew of indigenous irregular fighters, very few heavy weapons, and only several Toyota pickups for trans-portation, while we had our eight GMVs, four .50cal machine guns, and four Mk19s. We had him severely outgunned. Tom was a master sergeant, and our two teams were both commanded by captains, so he was also badly outranked.

But they don't call us Special Forces without reason, and the reason here was our ability to adapt to the unique situation of a 10th Group area of operations. Tom's attached Peshmerga were expected to do most of the killing during this attack, so it made sense for Tom to be in charge. While officers from the conventional Army might not have made the adjustment and taken their cues from an enlisted man, Capt. Wright and Capt. Saunders had both been in such situations before and understood their roles perfectly.

A large part of this plan was based on the participation of the Kur-dish fighters, an interesting group of patriotic men. In many ways, they reminded us of our own Revolutionary War Minutemen. Each was a volunteer, and each had a civilian business or profession—some were farmers, others shopkeepers or merchants—and they combined sol-diering with civilian employment. They each had an AK-47, a Russian-style load-bearing vest, and five magazines of thirty rounds for their rifle. These men were expected to show up with their unit only on specific days of the week, rather than soldiering full-time, so the faces in the unit changed from one day to the next.

In addition to these irregulars, there were a few better-trained-and-equipped full-time Kurd soldiers sent to serve as bodyguards for Tom and the other Americans. The Kurdish high command was very concerned that the deaths of a few Americans would quickly result in the withdrawal of the American Special Forces and the support they brought. The Kurds needed the overwhelming force of the American airpower that could be brought to bear and that kept the Kurds in their enclaves safe from Saddam.

The "Peshies" came from two competing groups, the KDP (Kurdistan Democratic Party) and the PUK (Patriotic Union of Kurdistan), and that created occasional conflicts. But they were generally brave, tough, and anxious to fight the Iraqis. Unlike some indigenous soldiers that Special Forces units work with around the world, these Kurds were strong and motivated American allies. You never knew for sure who would show up on any given day, or what time they would arrive, but each would have a weapon, ammunition, and a willingness to find Iraqis and kill them. Tom had been told to expect two hundred Kurds for the big attack, but he had been working with them long enough to be skeptical of that number.

After a few hours, by early afternoon of the day before the big attack, all the key players from all five teams and both AOBs expressed approval of the plan and its details. Tom and his Kurds would use the road over the ridge as their axis of advance, while Nine-Two would cover the left flank and Nine-One would cover the right. We planned to stay close enough to each other for visual contact and to be able to provide supporting fire all across the whole front of the advance, as well as against any threats that appeared on our flanks.

The majority of Kurds were to be dismounted but would have their two Toyota pickups, each with a Soviet .50 cal DShK mounted in the bed, and a single, Korean War–era jeep equipped with an antique 106mm recoilless rifle (the noisiest weapon on the battlefield). Nobody had any objections. The plan had the virtues of being simple and using us in appropriate ways. Best of all, everybody seemed to approve. ODAs Nine-Four and Nine-Five would follow a similar line of attack, with the rest of ODA-044 and their Kurds as well attacking up their portion of the ridge along the same lines.

Now it was time for the teams to get back to their battle positions, complete their precombat checks, and implement a sleep plan. There was still a lot of work to do.

THE KURDS TRY IT ON THEIR OWN

Marty, Eric, and I were busy with all the details of preparation when one of the KDP vehicles drove up. The commander of the Kurds got out and started walking over to Tom's position. Thinking something was up, Capt. Wright and I headed over to hear what he had to say and heard the Kurdish officer telling Tom, "I am going to be attacking today. I am going now!"

"No, no, the attack is tomorrow," Tom told him, thinking he had just misunderstood.

The Kurdish officer had understood the plan perfectly, but in the complex world of Kurdish politics, he had hastily implemented a plan of his own and was ready to operate independently. As I have said, the Kurds were from two competing groups, the KDP and the PUK. The PUK Kurds were assigned to attack with the other group of ODAs from the Third-of-the-Tenth about 100 kilometers to our southeast. The Kurdish colonel was the KDP commander of the irregulars assigned to us, and he wanted to attack before the PUK irregulars in order to demonstrate superior courage and have the honor of taking first blood and so gain a political advantage. Tom Sandoval's great plan of bombing the ridge first, with its need for excellent timing and coordination, was of no consequence to this commander.

"We're going now, with or without you!" the Kurd colonel said.

Tom, like us, looked a little shocked, even though all of us were used to the sometimes-bizarre politics in these Third World environments. "We're not ready," Tom said, "and we are not going today." The colonel, obviously angry, turned and left, stalking off back toward his Toyota.

We all watched in amazement as he went back to his men and issued his orders and all mounted their big trucks.

"Holy shit, Tom," I said, "this guy's going to go through with it—he's going to assault the ridge without us."

Tom, with the rest of us, looked on in disbelief as they drove past us, down the road and directly toward the ridge in the distance. All the Kurds were smiling and waving, pumped up with the honor of being the first into battle. This brave little armada sailed off to confront the entire Iraqi army single-handedly, driving confidently toward their rendezvous with what we were sure would be disaster.

We started talking about what to do if the Kurds started taking heavy casualties. "We'll just have to wait to see what happens next. If they start getting hammered, we'll have Ali get on the radio for some CAS, and we'll go down there and extract them if we have to," Tom stated. He then told his commo man to get on the SATCOM and alert their FOB to what was about to go down in a few minutes.

We did not have long to wait. The enemy observers must have seen them immediately and called in their fire missions to the artillery batteries over the ridge.

One of the first things an artillery battery does when it occupies its firing position, is to calculate the adjustments needed to hit likely targets within the range of its cannon. This data, called "preplanned fires," is then quickly available when an enemy force moves into these positions. The fire-direction center for the battery doesn't have to figure out the solution to the problem of putting "steel on target." As we watched, the Iraqi army gave a good demonstration of the wisdom of preplanned fires.

Luckily, their timing wasn't good, and that saved the Kurds. As the Kurdish trucks rolled down the road, the observer made his call. The enemy 152mm guns fired a barrage at the road near where it passed a pumping station, an obvious "target reference point," or TRP. The artillery began impacting just a couple of hundred meters in front of the Kurds' lead truck, forming a literal curtain of steel and sending clouds of smoke, dirt, and steel in all directions.

This was quite a show, and we expected the Kurds to be chopped up as the Iraqis adjusted fire and walked their artillery right over the Kurds. But before the Iraqis could adjust, the Kurds quickly turned around and raced back up the road to their original position and us. The Kurdish commander drove over to where we were still standing, right where he had left us a few minutes before.

He walked up to Tom and said, "Tomorrow! We will go tomorrow!" Then he drove off. None of his men had been killed or wounded, and perhaps he had learned his lesson. We waited for him to leave before we began laughing hysterically.

STEVE BRUNK VOLUNTEERS

Up to this time, we had one small problem in my GMV. ODA-391 had a vacancy for a "junior medic." We also had our Air Force controller, Staff Sgt. Jake Chandler, along for the ride.

After we first infilled a few weeks earlier, Bobby and I had to trade off between driving and manning the gun while Jake sat in back with his radios, normally without much to do. After a few days I said, "Jake, you get to do the driving. Bobby needs to be on the gun, and I need to be on the radios. Since you aren't very busy back there, you can be our chauffeur." Poor Jake wasn't happy about the lack of work, but he really didn't want to get demoted to driving us around. His talents were being entirely wasted, but he didn't have a choice.

"I'm here to drop bombs," he said.

"Well, until we get someplace where you can do that, you're doing the driving," I told him.

Jake drove us all over northern Iraq, doing a great job but complaining all the time. So when Nine-One hooked up with Tom in the mission support site, Jake came to me and said, "Frank, now that the assault has begun and you are going to need close air support, I am going to need to have my hands free for my radios, and I need to get back to my mission. Find another driver." He was right, too—you don't want your TACP driving when you need to have help from the Air Force in an emergency.

That night I got on the radio, using the company internal battle frequency that ODAs used to talk to each other. Since the B-team was constantly monitoring the frequency, I knew I would have no trouble getting hold of Keith Nann, the Operations sergeant for our B-team. Once I got Keith on the horn, I begged, "Keith, buddy, I need a favor. I need one of your guys down here to drive for me. Can you spare Jimmy Adams?" Jimmy was a weapons guy by trade, very sharp and reliable. He was an experienced senior sergeant who had trigger time in Panama and Afghanistan; he was familiar with our SOPs and would be a great member of our team.

"Not just *no,* but *fuck no,*" Keith said. "I am not giving you one of my best guys to drive you around." Keith knew that even though I told him the need was just for a few days, he was unlikely to have Jimmy back on his team anytime soon, if ever.

While I was talking to Keith on the radio, Ken Thompson, whose team, Nine-Two, was also one guy short and who had the same problem with his TACP, had been listening in as well. As Keith finished telling me all the reasons he couldn't spare anybody, Ken chimed in on the channel and said, "Hey, Keith, get me another guy, too."

"Two guys!" he yelled. "A minute ago you only needed one man, and now it is two? What's going on with you guys?"

"Keith, you know we have to have three guys on every vehicle, and without our TACPs, we're screwed. Ken and I just need guys that can drive—anybody!"

Keith relented a bit and reluctantly said, "Frank, let me go talk to the sergeant major and see if the FOB can give up a couple of guys."

A couple of hours later, the sergeant major drove up and pulled in beside my GMV. "What the hell is this about needing two more guys, Frank?" he wanted to know. Ken Thompson and I had been talking, and the two of us ganged up on him and explained the situation to him—how we had to let the Air Force guys get back to dropping bombs. Without making any promises, the sergeant major drove off, back to the FOB at Irbil to see what he could do for us.

Later that evening, after all the final planning and preparations had been complete, the entire B-team, along with fully loaded-down, giant resupply trucks "Mother" and "Mad Max," stopped by our position on their way to the staging area. The silhouettes of the modified FMTVs (Family of Medium Tactical Vehicles) looked *huge* in the dark as they lumbered along the dirt road toward us. Sgt. Major Joe Ward jumped from one of them in the darkness, followed by two shadowy figures. "Sgt. Antenori," he yelled, "I got your two guys for you." One of the men came over to my GMV; the other headed for Ken Thompson's.

"Hey," I said. "What's your name?"

"Staff Sgt. Brunk," he said.

"No, your first name."

"Steve."

"You can call me Frank. Welcome to Three-Nine-One. Do you know what you're getting into?" I asked, laughing.

Steve Brunk was not a Green Beret; he was a military intelligence specialist attached to our FOB on a temporary basis from the Group MI (Military Intelligence) detachment. These MI guys normally monitor radio transmissions, interrogate prisoners, and stay far, far from the battle. Steve was bored out of his mind, and when the sergeant major asked for volunteers to drive for the teams, he had jumped on the chance to get out of the confines of FOB life and into the fight.

"Okay, Steve, here's what you're going to do, and it is very simple— you just do exactly what Bobby or I tell you. Bobby can see better from behind the gun, so he will occasionally tell you to go left or right in order to go around obstacles. When things start to get busy during the assault, I am going to start yelling at you, too. When I start yelling, forget Bobby and listen to me!"

"Got it," Steve said.

STAFF SGT. ALI AND THE USAF FIREWORKS DISPLAY

After nightfall, a small group of operators left the assembly area and moved forward toward the Iraqi front lines. Marty led the mission, which consisted of elements from all three ODAs. Jason and Andy joined Marty in his GMV; they were met by a vehicle from Nine-Two, with its three-man crew, and a vehicle from Four-Four, with their STS (Special Tactics Squadron) controller, Staff Sgt. Saleem Ali, and the team's radio operator. Under cover of darkness, they all headed down the road toward the Green Line. All of them pulled off the road near a pumping station and set up the night vision viewers and laser rangefinder/designator. Ali spent the rest of the night preparing his "fire plan," calculating targets, entering the data for the bombs, and preparing to put the whole plan into action beginning about 0300Z (0600 local) the next morning.

We were now going to war with a lot of new weapons and systems that weren't available when I got out of the Q course back in 1989. Today they are making a real difference in the way we fight, as well as in the effectiveness of our operations. In the past, Saleem would have called for the bombers to deliver "sheaf fire," meaning, to deliver their bombs into a box on the map using grid coordinates, hoping that they would be effective against the enemy's combat power. In the past, the tactic was referred to as "carpet bombing." Usually, many of the bombs would only make a lot of smoke, dust, and noise as they missed their intended targets. Now, however, he could give each bomb an exact, individual point target. The laser rangefinder each team was issued, attached to a night vision device and GPS receiver, could see through darkness to the enemy positions and mark their locations with relative accuracy.

When the bombers arrived in a few hours, loaded with their 2,000-pound JDAMs (Joint Direct Attack Munition), they would direct each bomb to fly itself to the place Staff Sgt. Ali defined. He had been given two B-1Bs, each with twenty-four 2,000-pound JDAMs, each JDAM needing its own individual target data. It took him all night. He got no sleep at all before the attack. But he got the targeting data uploaded over the secure radios and passed it to the navigators in the bombers, who then programmed the data into the bombers' targeting computers, which then transferred the data to the individual computers in each JDAM—your tax dollars at work.

Marty, Andy, and Jason stayed up with Staff Sgt. Ali at the pump house, both to provide security and to mark the "release point" and line of departure for the attack in the morning. The rest of us stayed back at the MSS, trying to make sure nothing remained undone, pulling guard, and trying to get a little sleep. Most of us, however, were too excited to sleep, especially the new guys. They expected the next day to be a big one, and they were right. It turned out to be bigger than anybody expected.

That night I had a chance to consider our mission. We knew the enemy had at least a full battalion, and possibly a brigade, in the area of the assault. Our force consisted of only five A-teams, plus some brave, but sometimes unreliable, irregulars. We had been told to plan on four hundred Kurds (two hundred per assault element) but would probably have fewer. This was a tremendous imbalance of forces, and a conventional unit would never attempt an attack against a dug-in enemy with such odds, but we were not a conventional unit. Earlier, Eric, Marty, and I had another opportunity to ponder what we were about to get into. "Well Frank, it finally looks like you're going to get that fight you've been looking for," Eric stated. Marty was also happy we would finally have the opportunity to evaluate his training plan and all the training the team had done. I looked at Eric and said, "Well, Eric, this is where the responsibility thing comes in. Tomorrow we'll be taking a bunch of good guys up that hill; I hope we can bring them all back down in one piece." Eric looked at me with a serious look. "I'm with you Frank. My number-one job tomorrow will be to make sure of that." Marty was a bit more optimistic. "We're going to be fine. The guys are ready, we've trained our asses off, and we've got the best gear money can buy."

Despite all the criticism ODA-391 had received during the past months from inside and outside of 3rd Battalion, we didn't think we were biting off more than we could chew. I thought we could do what we had promised—take the problem on one bite at a time, even if it was a big enemy "elephant" on the hill to our front. All of us were fired up. We were impatient to get into the fight at last, after all the training, the promises, the conflicts with our chain of command, and the differences with the other groups. We had promised to pile up the enemy, but so far the war had been fought without us piling up anybody. After the emotional roller coaster of frustration we'd been riding, ODA-391 would have gone up that hill against an enemy division with butter knives for weapons, if that was what we had to do.

Early the next morning, 6 April, Tom and I watched the big "laser light show" as the first air strike was delivered right on schedule. It was beautiful, the flashes and clouds of smoke and dust erupting into the air as the impacts rolled down the ridge. Although still dark, the southeastern sky was getting light as the bombs detonated with brilliant flashes. Naturally, we tried to photograph the fireworks.

The first strike's twenty-four bombs impacted before first light; the second strike, against estimated enemy tank positions behind the ridge, came about twenty minutes later. Steve Brunk watched the distant blasts, knowing that he was about to drive up onto that target. He was a long way from the FOB and must have been having second thoughts about the business in which he had now become a full-fledged partner. Steve, however, was a warrior, and like the rest of us was eager to fight for his country.

The conclusion of the second strike was planned to be our signal to mount the GMVs and get into position for the attack. All of us were ready, but the Kurds were nowhere to be seen. They were told to be at Four-Four's position at 0300Z (0600 local), and had assured us they would be prompt. Time, however, is a variable thing in this part of the world. The guys on our team decided that the Kurds were in the "-ish" time zone—if they said they'd be someplace at six, they would show up sixish, within fifteen minutes before or after.

Sure enough, they were about fifteen minutes late. They rolled up their pickups and big cargo truck to the edge of Four-Four's fighting position. And when we started looking at the Kurd troops, there were only around eighty instead of the two hundred promised. The little adventure of the previous day might have encouraged some of them to sleep late, but we were already prepared for this by previous experience with irregulars—they tend to be irregular about everything.

I noticed that this cultural habit drove members of the conventional Army nuts when we worked with irregulars in Afghanistan, but I was not surprised at the late arrival. A few more Kurds trickled in as we finished getting a few last-minute details sorted out. It was starting to get light as the sun began making its way over the horizon.

Tom began to get nervous. His plan required that we take over the positions from the Iraqis before they had a chance to return following the bombing. They had been a bit tardy about the process before, but the longer we delayed, the more likely the enemy was to get back into their bunkers. "We're going," Tom yelled. "We're out of here." And off we went.

Our first stop was just a mile or so down the road, to pick up Marty and the guys at the pump house after their long night helping Saleem. "What's going on?" he asked. "We're forty-five minutes late." But Marty had worked in the Arab world long enough to know how the locals operated.

While Marty got settled in his seat, all four of our GMVs drove into position along our line of departure and into the staggered-wedge formation we would use for the attack. Tom and his Kurds were a few hundred meters to our left, with Nine-Two a few hundred meters farther down, also in staggered-wedge formation, waiting for the word to move.

The Kurds, as I have said, reminded me of our own Minutemen of 1776; they wore a mixed bag of uniforms: some were in camouflage, others in solid green, and others wore civilian clothes. Besides their rifles and ammunition, they had none of the "battle rattle" Americans require—no CamelBaks, no kneepads, no gloves, no body armor or eye protection. Some wore sandals instead of boots. They had left their homes early that morning, after breakfast with their families. They had probably kissed their wives good-bye, picked up their weapons, and gone off to spend the day at war, not sure they would come home at night. They were true militia, the kind that Special Forces soldiers have trained and led for well over fifty years.

When modern military units engage in planned ground combat, there is a complicated ritual to the business. It begins with the planning process. All our maps had a line drawn at the base of the ridge. This line formed what we call a "line of departure," and when we cross such a line in a battle, we report by radio to our commander, "ROUGH-NECK NINE-ONE, LIMA DELTA, OUT." The call sign lets him know who's calling, and the simple initials "LD" (always spoken in their International Phonetic Alphabet form for clarity) let him know where we are and what we're doing—crossing the line of departure (LD) in our sector, beginning the attack.

A road, abandoned and blocked at this time, led up and over the ridge. In happier days, it had connected Irbil with Makhmur and towns farther south and west. The plan put our four GMVs on the right side of the road and Nine-Two's GMVs on the left side, with Four-Four's Range Rovers on the road itself. With the exception of the few manning the DShKs and 106mm, all the Kurds were on foot. The whole formation spread out on line, about 500 meters from the left flank to the right.

All of us had completed our precombat checks. We had a round in the chamber of every M4 carbine, M2 .50cal heavy machine gun, and Mk19 grenade launcher. The engines were running, SINCGARS (Single-Channel Ground and Airborne Radio System, a secure digital communications technology) radios were set to the designated company battle frequency for the assault, and our individual IMBTR radios were set to our "team internal."

Bobby got comfortable behind the Mk19 on our vehicle, while Steve Brunk, our brave volunteer, sat in the driver's seat, and I waited for Eric's command to move out. We got the word that the Kurds were ready and in position.

"Okay, let's go," Eric said.

The dash up the hill began with our vehicles in two staggered-wedge formations, two pairs operating as a unit, the left GMV of each pair a bit forward of the right. Marty's GMV was closest to the road, Gerry Kirk to his right rear, then Eric, and then me on the extreme right of the formation. Moving this way offered good fields of fire to the front and flank while reducing the risk of friendly-fire incidents.

Ordinarily, using a road like this would have been a bad tactical idea. It would be a simple matter for an enemy to come roaring down this road with any kind of force, especially a few Russian-made MTLB or BMP armored fighting vehicles, and split our formation in two. Our plan used the road anyway because the Kurds were so difficult to control. We knew that even they could follow the road, and this prevented the Kurds from wandering out of their lane. This also allowed Four-Four's Range Rovers to follow along behind, pushing them forward.

The slope of the hill was gentle enough, but the terrain was full of shallow gullies caused by flash floods during the rainy seasons. The gullies were about a foot-and-a-half deep and obscured by grass and brush. This made it hard for Steve and me to see these small ditches until we were right on top of them. Bobby had a better view, and as we worked our way up the hill, he suddenly yelled, "Stop!" but not fast enough. Neither Steve nor I saw the gully until the front end of the GMV pitched and dropped into it.

We slammed to a halt. My head hit the windshield, and then I bounced into the M240 machine gun, injuring my hand and shoulder. Steve slammed into the steering wheel but was unhurt. Bobby, however, had been thrown violently into the machine gun mount and was groaning in agony. His chest struck the butterfly trigger grips on the back of the gun, but since he was wearing body armor, that impact was diffused.

However, a latch handle located just to the right of the gunner's seat and used to secure the rotating turret ring of the GMV hit him on the left hip hard enough that we thought the bone might have been broken. Luckily Bobby had only an ugly and enormous bruise. It was painful and distracting, but not bad enough to take him out of the fight—luckily for us all. Bobby was furious and was swearing constantly—every profanity in the book, pretty much in random order, but Steve's name was mixed in with all the swearing.

"Bobby, I'm sorry," Steve yelled. He felt awful, which was fine with Bobby just then.

Bobby stayed at the gun, Steve kept driving, and I tried to reassure them both. "He'll be okay, Steve," I said. "Keep driving."

"God-damn-son-of-a-bitch . . ." Bobby was fuming. I finally had to tell him to calm down. We had things to do and places to go. Steve calmed down, Bobby recovered, and we maintained position out on the flank. Bobby needed to get his head around his responsibility as the Mk19 gunner and forget about the hip, and that's what he did . . . for a while.

THE TWO-WAY RIFLE RANGE

Tom had done a great job planning the attack. His preplanned strikes came in on time and target; as we looked up the hill, we could all see it was empty of enemy forces. The bombing may not have killed any-body, but it certainly cleared them off the objective. Although every-body was anxious to do some shooting, there was nothing to shoot. As we moved slowly and deliberately up the slope, Marty called me on the radio.

"Frank, the Kurds don't want us to go any farther cross-country; they found a big minefield on both sides of the road."

We were making good time and were about halfway to the objective.

"Their commander wants us to come over to the road. The Kurds are going to clear the mines from the pavement, and then we'll use the roadway to get past the mines."

I called Eric on my IMBTR radio. "What do you want to do?"

"Let's all collapse in on the road just to get through the minefield," Eric responded. A "Roger that" came from each of our other three vehicles.

We drove over to the road and continued uphill. Ahead, three Kurds were busy picking up the antitank mines. They apparently knew how to disarm them because each mine was simply tossed onto the dirt at the edge of the pavement. These were big weapons, each weighing about 10 pounds, with more than half of that being explosive. They were designed to blow the tracks and road wheels off of armor, and would easily shred our Humvees if we happened to drive over one of them. But the mines were simply laid at the edge of the pavement along a stretch of the road only about 50 meters long. Once the mines were removed, we could safely proceed.

But the Iraqi engineers had added something besides the mines. The road was an obvious route for any enemy force, and the enemy had done what they could to slow us down. This kind of situation is common. We call it a "countermobility mission," and both the mines and the huge pile of dirt, at least 12 feet high, that had been pushed onto the road were designed to hamper movement, not prevent it. You can't keep a mobile force from attacking, but you can push them into your kill zones, and you can delay them while you beat them up with your artillery, tanks, mortars, and rocket-propelled grenades.

Right now we were in the kill zone. The Iraqis had definitely de-layed us. Luckily they were not covering this obstacle, thanks to the air strikes, but we were momentarily stuck on the wrong side of the dirt berm. Kenney, one of our engineers, hopped out of his GMV, studied the huge roadblock for a minute, then said, "I can blow this thing."

While he went back for his stash of explosives, the Kurds decided to push on. They climbed over the berm on foot. Immediately they began taking fire from enemy infantry who hadn't abandoned their positions.

"The Kurds are getting fired up," I yelled. "Let's go, let's go, let's go!"

"Hey, it's going to take me ten or fifteen minutes," Kenney yelled back.

Eric rolled up. "What's going on?" he wanted to know.

"We've got to get over there. The Kurds are taking fire from the objective!"

Our whole purpose on this mission was to provide fire support for the Kurds. Even though they took off without us and got themselves into this little scuffle, we had the responsibility to rejoin them immediately and put our M2s and Mk19s to work.

"What do you want to do, Frank, drive through the minefield?" Marty asked. Marty is normally very mild mannered, but even he was getting a little excited by this situation.

"Yes," I said, "we have no choice. We can get around them—the mines aren't really very close together. We have to get out of here and go up there to support those Kurds—that's what we're here to do."

There were really two important reasons to proceed. One was to continue to move, and the other was to ensure our own safety. The Iraqi engineers had done exactly what they intended and stopped us cold, right where their buddies could chop us up when they got their act together. Although there was a risk in driving through the minefield, there was a bigger risk in staying put. We had two full ODAs driving eight GMVs, each filled with over 4,500 pounds of fuel and ammunition.

We were literally sitting ducks and had no idea what type of Iraqi force might be making its way toward our position. Waiting for Kenney wasn't really an option. We had been telling everybody we wanted to fight and had the means to do so. Now we had a fighting mission, and we didn't have the luxury of taking time to blow the berm.

"We're going around," I said.

"Five minutes!" Kenney implored. "Give me five minutes."

"Fuck it," Eric said, "we've got to go now—we're going around the berm!"

We jumped in our GMVs and turned around, back from the berm but still on the road. If any enemy artillery observers had seen us, we would have made an easy target. Tom Sandoval's air strikes may not have cleaned off the entire ridge, but at least the enemy observers had cleared out because we escaped from their trap before it could be sprung.

I led Nine-One off the pavement and out into the dirt, across country, on the right side of the road. Nine-Two's four GMVs did the same on the left side. We found an open area where we could move with comparative safety, searching for the edge of the obstacle blocking our advance.

"Bobby," I yelled, "get up on the hood and watch for mines!" He climbed out from behind the gun and sat on the roof with his legs in front of the windshield. With this elevated viewpoint, he could see the ground a bit more clearly. I stood up and leaned out of the front passenger seat where the door had been removed. I was holding on as well as I could, while Steve Brunk was driving carefully, ready to stomp on the brake if we spotted a mine. Luckily we did not see any in this area. After a few minutes we were able to get around the steepest part of the berm.

As we made it to the top of the hill, we encountered another obstacle, the Iraqi positions. Trenches and bunkers crisscrossed the ridge, forming what looked like an endless chain of connected Ws. While tanks would have had no trouble simply crossing the trenches, our GMVs could not. Thinking quickly, Bobby jumped from behind the Mk19 and ran for a bunker, grabbing sandbags from its walls and tossing them into the trench. Without saying a word, several of us quickly followed Bobby's lead and joined him in tossing sandbags. Meanwhile, we could hear the exchange of fire between our Kurds and the Iraqi defenders, the sounds adding urgency to our little construction project. In no time we had constructed a bridge of sandbags, over which we drove the GMVs without a problem.

After making our way over the top of the ridge, we drove over to the pavement and hustled up to the fight.

Nine-Two's four vehicles succeeded in getting around the berm over on the left side, a little ahead of us. As they crested the rise, the Iraqi defenders were immediately visible in a series of trenches 100 meters beyond the Kurds who were engaging them.

Sgt. 1st Class Van Hines, Nine-Two's weapons sergeant, fired two long bursts from his .50cal machine gun over the Kurds, into the trenches, and the fight was instantly over. The Iraqis quickly dropped their weapons, put their hands up, and surrendered. By the time we arrived, the Kurds had ceased fire, and the Iraqis were walking out to the road without their weapons, hands in the air.

Although Nine-Two had broken their will to fight, what the Iraqis saw was Nine-One's vehicles and the American flag flying from the vehicle antennas. They ended up walking down the road toward our vehicles and the Kurds. Bobby Farmer jumped out of our GMV and started walking over to take the surrender of the forty or so enemy soldiers.

"Bobby, stop!" I yelled at him. "If you get to them before the Kurds do, we are in big trouble!"

We'd been directed by our group JAG (Judge Advocate General, the Army's lawyers) to make sure the Iraqi's surrendered only to the Kurds. According to the Geneva Convention, if you accept the surrender of an enemy, you also assume responsibility for safeguarding, housing, and feeding them. A-teams did not have the spare resources to deal with prisoners, but the Kurds did.

The Kurd colonel ran over to the Iraqis and took the surrender from their officer, a major. I got on the radio to Nine-Two, who had remained in an overwatch position, guns trained on the Iraqis.

"We've got them; they surrendered; come on down."

Bobby broke out his special Mossberg shotgun in case there were problems with the prisoners. Eric rolled up about the same time.

This was a moment filled with tension for everybody—for the Iraqis, who were not sure what would happen to them, and for us and the Kurds, who were not sure what other enemy forces were waiting for us and where they were. Our objective was close, just down the road, but none of us knew when the rest of the enemy battalion would come back to their positions.

We had rushed through a minefield, found a way around one of the enemy's obstacles, and now were watching the Kurds taking the surrender of the first enemy soldiers we met on the battlefield. Bobby and the other new guys wondered what a real combat operation would be like. Now they were finding out that actual combat is far from what is in textbooks or portrayed by Hollywood.

Every SF soldier is expected to speak at least one foreign language from the area of the world where his unit is normally deployed. For those of us in 3rd Group, that means we study French, Arabic, and many of the common languages of Africa and the Middle East. Those language skills can be lifesavers at moments like these, so I hustled over to the senior officer among the prisoners. Trying to remember all that training in Arabic, I said to him, *"Ana raqib Frank, fel kawat el hassa Amriki, feen debbaba?"* ("I am Sgt. Frank of the American Special Forces. Where are the tanks?")

The enemy major listened intently to me, and then he said, "I speak English much better than you speak Arabic. Let's speak English."

"Okay, okay—so where are the tanks?" I barked back at him.

"They're gone," he said. "They left us when the bombs started falling. The bombs were everywhere. The tanks left me and my men to fend for ourselves. They have gone to Makhmur, where they have a headquarters." Makhmur was about 20 kilometers farther southwest on the road we had just used to get up on the ridge. For tanks, that is not really very far away. *The tanks could come back at any moment,* I thought.

Then the Iraqi major said, "We are surrendering to you."

"Oh, no you're not," I told him emphatically. "You already surrendered to the Kurds, not to us, and they will take care of you from here."

The major was dismayed at this news, and with some cause. The Kurds, for good reason, had a reputation for being a little rough on Iraqi soldiers, but the major had no choice. The Kurds collected him and his men, loaded them on the big truck, and sent them to a prisoner-of-war compound back at Irbil, about 40 miles to the north.

What now? At this point, we were almost to the intersection that was our destination for this mission, the place called Objective Rock on our maps. I could see it, just a few hundred meters down the hill from where we had crested the ridge and where Nine-Two had defeated the enemy infantry in their trenches. If the major's report was accurate, the enemy's armor was not too far away. If they kept to their pattern of previous days, they would return sometime within the next hour or two.

Those tanks were a real concern. We could see that they had been positioned in well-constructed revetments. Tom Sandoval's shepherd had been right. These positions were just where he had indicated. The pavement was torn up from the enemy tanks' steel tracks, and the road had been badly damaged because so many of the enemy had used it to escape the air strike.

The tank drivers must have been panicked when the bombs began to fall because one of them ran his T-55 off the road and got it stuck by "high-centering" it. Several rocks were jammed under the hull, lifting it slightly and preventing the tank treads from getting a bite. This didn't damage the tank, but simply rendered it immobile. Instead of having one of the other tanks pull the vehicle out of this fix, the crew apparently bailed out of the tank and ran off, leaving an otherwise perfect, fully loaded T-55 main battle tank parked beside the road. Nobody could have guessed it at the time, but that tank—without anybody inside—would be responsible in only a few hours for the deaths of seventeen Kurds and the wounding of dozens of Kurds and Americans and even a British reporter.

I grabbed a can of black spray paint from out of the GMV and told Steve Brunk to follow me over to the tank. "Come on, we've got to tag it," I told Steve. "Tag it?" Steve answered. "Yeah, we need to put our call sign on it to let the 173rd guys know who got here first." Steve laughed as we both jumped up on the tank. I quickly sprayed "Roughneck 91" on the side of the turret. Little did I know that a spray-painted word on the tank would create a stir all the way back at Fort Bragg.

Jake was watching and saw the tag as Three-Nine-One taking credit for the tank kill and yelled out to me, "You better paint 'STS' on there, too. After all, it was the Air Force that knocked out that tank." I complied and told Jake to jump up on the tank for a picture, which Bobby happily snapped.

Until now, Bobby had more important things to worry about besides his injury, but this lull in the action allowed him a chance to check his damage. Before jumping back into the GMV turret to reman his gun, Bobby dropped his pants enough to get a look at his hip. The skin was not broken, but he had an immense bruise that covered the whole side of his hip and butt.

"Hey, Steve," he yelled. "Look at this! Look at what you did to me, buddy." With the exception of Steve Brunk, we all thought the bruise was funny. Bobby pulled his pants back up, everybody got back in their vehicles, and we prepared to move. It was just a short distance to the goal for the attack, the road intersection down the hill identified as Objective Rock.

With the prisoners in the custody of the Kurds, we moved down the slope to the intersection. Within an hour, we had completed our mission, seizing Objective Rock. Three-Nine-One had fired no shots, and had neither taken nor inflicted any casualties. Other than Bobby, nobody had been hurt. Not a bad start. But it was still early in the morning. The day was far from over.

ELEVEN

ACROSS THE GREEN LINE

Tom Sandoval was delighted. He and the rest of us quickly moved the remaining few hundred meters to the intersection, and the day's mission was accomplished. Our ODAs and the Kurds had seized Rock at the cost of one badly bruised butt. Tom's radio operator was reporting back the glad tidings through the FOBs, where Lt. Cols. Binford and Waltemeyer were monitoring the assaults by all the ODAs up and down the ridge. Tom had accomplished the breakthrough Col. Cleveland wanted. As long as we controlled this ground and its approaches, the way was clear for the 173rd to make its assault into the heart of the enemy.

At the same time, though, a few miles up the ridge, ODAs Nine-Four and Nine-Five were not so lucky. There the bombing was less successful, and the enemy soldiers stayed in their bunkers. When those teams moved up to the ridge, they had to fight their way over the top, and they were heavily engaged for much of the day. Nine-Four and Nine-Five displayed great heroism that day. They were caught in the impact zone of the Iraqi artillery for over forty-five minutes and still continued their attack on the ridge. When the artillery became too heavy or got too close, they would displace a few hundred meters then attack again.

Artillery from howitzers and mortars pounded the two teams with fire skillfully directed by enemy forward observers. Eventually the enemy fire from the D20s and D30s was too much, forcing them to rethink their approach. They decided to pull back and find some cover in a nearby village to figure out another line of attack. Bobby Davis from Nine-Four told me later that his GMV zigzagged across the battlefield as rounds burst nearby. They sought shelter behind a building, and Bobby said they all felt tremendously relieved when their GMV escaped behind the house. That relief didn't last, he said, because the house was promptly blown apart by another accurate round from the enemy's 152mm howitzers. The intensity of the enemy fire was so great that one of the guys from the B-team, located almost five miles from their position later commented, "It sounded like a herd of dinosaurs were playing football."

The Nine-Four and Nine-Five attack was further hampered by the complete failure of the Kurds to make the assault. The other half of Four-Four stayed with their Peshmerga, trying to get them up the hill and into the fight. When Nine-Four and Nine-Five withdrew, the B-team came forward to resupply them. They fired up a lot of their ammunition and were running low. After getting their ammo restocked, Nine-Four and Nine-Five once again assaulted the ridge. Seven Bronze Stars for Valor and over a dozen Commendations for Valor were awarded to both teams for their heroism that day.

We could hear the distant artillery and the radio traffic. Although we had possession of Rock, the Iraqis could try to take it back any minute. If they did, we were in a very poor position to fight them off because—as we saw once we were on the ground—the intersection was actually in a shallow depression in the terrain. Standing on Rock, as Tom and the rest of us were, we were virtually blind beyond 200 meters. Enemy tanks or infantry could be rolling up on us at that moment, and we would never know until they were right on top of us. That was a problem.

There was a larger problem, too—a conflict of orders. Tom Sandoval's orders for his detachment were to seize and hold this intersection until relieved by heavier follow-on forces such as the 173rd Airborne Brigade and all its tanks and infantry. Eric Wright's and Matt Saunders's orders for their detachments were to support Tom while he executed his mission, but after that, to go off on their own. Our *support* mission ended with the successful seizure of Rock.

All the team leaders, warrants, and team sergeants gathered in the middle of the road for a conference of war. The distant boom of enemy artillery added its note of urgency to the discussion. "This is a dangerous spot," I said. "We can't see over that little ridge to the south."

"Well, we are at the objective," Tom replied. "We have to hang out here until we get the word from the FOB about what they want us to do."

"We can't hang out here," Eric said. "We're in a hole. There are tanks out there, and if they come back, we are going to get run over."

"We're going to go forward, Tom," Matt Saunders told him, "just to the top of the hill so we can see better."

"Nope," Tom said firmly, "we aren't supposed to go farther than right here. This is our 'limit of advance.'"

"Tom," I said, "we have got to go forward. The tanks went down that road toward Makhmur. If those tanks come back, we won't see them till they crest that hill over there, and it is only 200 meters from here. If they catch us at that range, we're dead."

In a conventional Army unit, this sort of discussion would never happen. The senior officer present would almost certainly be the commander of the operation. He might ask for the opinions of his subordinate officers about the tactical situation, but he would make the decision and issue his orders, and everybody would execute the mission. The battalion sergeant major might be present for the discussion, but neither he nor any of the other sergeants in the unit would have much of a role in the process of battle command.

Once again, our command relationships in Special Forces are different. Tom Sandoval, a master sergeant, had been in full tactical command right up until we rolled onto the objective. He had two captains and their teams subordinate to him during the entire attack.

In the regular Army, captains tell master sergeants where to go and what to do. But during our attack and for the previous few days, the roles had been reversed, and Tom was the boss. That relationship ended when we radioed back to the FOB that we were on Rock.

Instead of pulling rank on Tom, the entire group—Eric and Matt, the warrant officers and team sergeants—all gathered to thrash out the issues and try to reach a consensus on what we ought to do next. We all recognized that Tom's guidance from 10th Group and our guidance from 3rd Group conflicted, and now we had to resolve the conflict.

Marty McKenna spoke up. "Remember, Tom, now that we've gotten to the objective and across the Green Line, our two ODAs are no longer OPCON [under operational control] of 10th Group. We all heard our colonel tell us that once we crossed the Green Line and got you to your objective, that's ENDEX [end of exercise] for us. We're done. We are cut loose from you at this point, Tom, and we're supposed to 'exploit the initiative.' Lt. Col. Binford wants to bring up the whole battalion through here and go on to take Kirkuk. We're back under the control of 3rd Group," Marty said, "and we are moving up."

Tom was getting frustrated with us. Until now we were a useful resource for him and for his battalion. Although Tom did not say so, we had heard that he had been told, "These 3rd Group guys are out of control—reel them in and don't let them get into any more trouble than they've already created." He was badly outnumbered at this point and did not have a lot of options. We were living up to our reputation as black sheep again after a few days of good behavior.

Kenney Wilson, standing nearby, offered some words of "engineer wisdom" to the group. "We need to take care of that obstacle behind us. If those tanks do come back, they're going to drive us right into that minefield. If it's later tonight, driving through there in the dark with tanks chasing us is going to be a bit more hairy than what we did this morning."

"Kenney's right," Eric said. "Before you guys head over that hill and get into trouble, we need to do something about that berm blocking the road behind us. I am going to take half the team back there and let Kenney blow the obstacle before you guys start stirring things up." Eric took two of the GMVs, Kenney and his demolition materials, plus four other guys, Gerry, Mike, Rich, and Nguyen, back up the road. They would clear the way for the 173rd when they finally arrived, or possibly clear it for us if the enemy pushed us back from our position.

Marty looked at Matt Saunders and said, "Let's just creep up to the top of that rise and see what's on the other side."

Saunders agreed, turning to his team and telling them to saddle up.

Marty looked to me and simply said, "Let's go."

"You coming, Tom?" I asked as I turned and walked toward my GMV.

"I'm staying here!" he said.

"Fine, we're moving up to the ridge. See you later, buddy," we told him. Then we climbed back into our GMVs and drove off down the road, leaving Tom and his split team and their Kurds at the intersection. Steve, Jake, and Bobby were waiting in the GMV with the engine running. Bobby was ready to use the Mk19 if any of the enemy surprised our little force in this hazardous spot. All eight of our vehicles resumed their positions. Nine-Two's vehicles spread across the left side of the road; our remaining two were on the right. At Matt's command, we moved out, and in a few minutes we pulled up to the crest of the second ridge, which had been blocking our view.

With the GMVs safely out of sight behind the military crest (the shoulder rather than the absolute top of the terrain) of the hill, Matt Saunders, Marty, Ken Thompson, and I dismounted and walked up the rise and peeked over the top. Unlike the previous few days, the sky was overcast and very hazy, restricting visibility. Even so, we could see the ground slope gently away from our position. In the distance were wide fields of what seemed to be fresh wheat on a vast, level plain. We knew from the map that the town of Makhmur was directly ahead of us, invisible in the fog, about 15 kilometers farther on the same road we had just used to get over the ridge. Off to our left we could see the little village of Debecka, not much more than a collection of simple houses built from mud bricks. In the center of town there were a few large buildings made from concrete, none more than two stories high. There was a flagpole on a building in the center, with an Iraqi flag flying defiantly at the top of it. Green grass and multicolored wildflowers gave the view a momentary quality of peace. Then we saw the trucks.

At the base of the ridge, about a mile from our position, was a road. We knew from the map that this was Highway 2, and we had been briefed that it carried a lot of traffic. The volume of that traffic, however, and its composition surprised us all. Trucks of all sizes, cars, buses, and motorcycles zoomed back and forth on this highway. While some of the traffic was civilian, much of it was clearly enemy vehicles. We saw troop transports, resupply trucks, command vehicles, and lots of pickups and SUVs with large triangles, the insignia of the Iraqi Land Forces, painted on the doors.

Matt, Ken, Marty, and I were amazed at the traffic, especially at all the targets. "Look, there goes a troop transport," Matt said as a truck full of soldiers rolled up the road toward Mosul.

Our orders and our instincts were to take the fight to the enemy. And, at last, here was the enemy. Each of us had the same idea at the same moment. This was a shooting gallery just like at the state fair, except that the targets were real. The prize was to help make a difference for American forces on the battlefield.

"We've got to shoot these guys," I said. "We've been bitching the whole time we've been here that we want to pick a fight with the Iraqis, and now here is the whole Iraqi army driving back and forth in front of us. Now's the time to light them up. We're too far away to hit anything from here. Let's move forward." The .50cal and Mk19 would reach out to the highway, but at a range of 2,000 meters, neither would be effective. We could occasionally score hits on a truck at that distance, but in this case the result would probably be only to scare the driver and to invite reinforcements. We all knew from our shooting on the tank ranges at Fort Pickett that engaging vehicle targets from distances of over 1,400 meters was a waste of ammunition.

Tom and the guys from Four-Four must have been a bit upset about being left back at Rock because suddenly they appeared just behind us on the ridge. Being only five Americans all alone and on the wrong side of the Green Line must have influenced their decision to move forward with us. But just as Tom pulled up, Capt. Saunders and his guys hopped into their GMVs, and Marty and I climbed in ours. Then we all moved forward again, over the rise and down toward the valley, leaving Tom and his guys behind a second time. We did not have time for a second discussion with Tom on the merits of moving forward. We were about to do what we were trained to do. Now was our big chance.

After driving slowly down the ridge for another ten minutes, we were closer to Highway 2 by another 600 meters. It was about a mile from the highway and was at the edge of what we knew to be the effective range for the heavy machine gun. An enemy truck appeared out of the haze, far off in the distance, moving down the highway. This was a perfectly legitimate target, it would soon be in range, and there was nobody around to tell us to leave it alone. Jason Brown was our senior weapons sergeant, and he was behind the M2 on Marty's vehicle. Jason was carefully evaluating the truck while tracking it with his gun. Once we stopped, I radioed, "Okay, Jay, shoot them up."

Jason lined up on the truck and depressed the spade triggers on the gun with his thumb. We all watched the red tracers streak downrange toward the truck, half expecting it to blow up or run off the road under Jay's merciless hail of fire. Jason operated the gun just as he had so successfully done on the ranges, firing short bursts of six to nine rounds, then evaluating the shots, then firing again. He fired about thirty or forty rounds, kicking up dust beside the road, but without any other visible effect.

The truck drove off up the road, apparently untouched and apparently without the driver even knowing he had been fired upon. After all the tension of the past hours, days, and weeks, there was something comical about all this. Everybody laughed at Jason just as we had when targets were missed during training at Pickett.

We moved down the hill again, this time to just about 900 meters, around half a mile from the highway, and tried again.

"Let me shoot," Marty said as he traded places behind the machine gun with Jason. While he was getting set, another enemy vehicle appeared, this one a tan SUV of the type used by Iraqi officers. The vehicle drove into range, and Marty fired it up, scoring several hits. The SUV veered off the highway in a cloud of dust, going out of sight into a deep ditch over the far side of the road.

Instantly, before we could react, two truckloads of Kurds roared past us down the road toward the SUV. We could see them race to the spot where the enemy vehicle ran off the road. Several jumped out with their AKs and began shooting. We could not see what was going on, but it was easy enough to guess—the Kurds had taken all the prisoners they needed up on the hill and seem to have no intention of taking more. There was no return fire.

Then we watched as the Kurds scurried around on the road, oblivious to passing civilian vehicles. They climbed back in their trucks, turned around, and started back toward our position, but with the

SUV in tow. They had hooked a chain to the wreck of this vehicle and began dragging it back up the road to where all of us watched in amazement.

Whooping and hollering, the Kurds roared past us with the wreck of the enemy SUV dragging behind them. The vehicle was full of holes, and one of the tires was flat. Oil and transmission fluid were leaking from every pore, the windows were shattered, and sparks flew from the wheel rim scraping along the pavement. The chances of the SUV ever driving again appeared to us as impossibly remote. The Kurds did not care. They were thrilled with their trophy. Maybe they planned to mount it on the wall, like a deer head. All of us thought this was a great way to greet the Iraqi army.

"Look! A truck!" one of the guys yelled, pointing off to the left. Sure enough, a large troop truck was just leaving Debecka on a dirt road, headed toward Makhmur. The road headed across our front at an angle. Despite the distance and the haze, we could see the truck was heavily loaded with soldiers. When first sighted, the truck must have been at least 1,500 meters from our position, well out of effective range of both the machine guns and Mk19 for such a target, and it was expanding the range with every second.

"Shoot it! Fire it up!" somebody yelled.

"No—too far out of range," Bobby said.

JASON'S "KODAK MOMENT"

As far as I was concerned, we could not touch this truck, as tempting as it was. We learned our lesson with the .50cal machine gun and moving targets—800 meters was about as far away as a target could be for an effective engagement. But for Jason Brown, this was a kind of "Eureka!" moment.

"I can get it with the Javelin," Jason said. "Frank, Frank, let's get out the Javelins and get it with a missile." The Javelin was then rated at about 2,000–2,500 meters, and the target was already close to, if not beyond, that distance.

"No, Jason, it's too far away." I really thought it was well out of range: it was moving away from us at a good speed, and Jason would need some time to prepare the Javelin. "By the time you get the missile prepped, the truck will be long gone—just don't worry about it. Let it go."

"No, come on, Frank! I can get it!" Jason was like a little kid pleading for a new toy. "I hauled that damn thing around in the 82nd Airborne for three damn years and never got a chance to shoot it. This war is going to be over in three damn days, and once again I will never get a chance to shoot a damn Javelin."

Marty came over to our vehicle. He does a good imitation of Dean Martin, the old-time movie star with a studied, casual personal style. He gave me his funny, deadpan look and said, "Aw, Frank, let him shoot it."

"Oh, hell, okay," I said. "You are never going to hit it, but go ahead and try, Jason."

"Jason's going to shoot a Javelin! Jason's going to shoot a Javelin!" somebody yelled. Then the scurry for the cameras began. Everybody dove into their rucksacks to get their cameras. Every guy seemed to have one—disposables, pocket cameras, digital cameras, film cameras. At least twelve of the guys from both Nine-One and Nine-Two forgot their weapons for a moment to watch Jason fire the first Javelin any of us had seen actually launched, a genuine "Kodak moment."

Jason sat on the road, preparing the weapon. The rest of us alternated between watching the disappearing truck and watching Jason trying to remember all his training on the missile. He quickly extracted the command launch unit (CLU, pronounced *clue*) from its container, attached it to a missile he had already prepared for use and had stowed in one of the ready racks, uncovered the CLU optics, and lifted the missile to his shoulder.

Quickly taking a seated position on the highway, Jason energized the CLU, looked through the sight's green and black video viewfinder, and selected WIDE to acquire the distant truck in the sight. The CLU provides a thermal, not visual, spectrum view of the world, and its sensor needs thirty seconds to chill down before the sight will work. The sensor makes hot things like engine blocks and exhaust pipes show up bright green against a darker background. After the missile is activated, this bright green view is actually transmitted from the "seeker" (a cameralike sensor in the nose of the missile). Once Jason found the truck, he zoomed in on it with the narrow-field-of-view function. The heat from the engine provided a small bright green spot in the finder.

With his left index finger he squeezed the trigger in the left grip handle to activate the "seek mode" and bring up the "track box"; then he used his right thumb to bring the two brackets of the track box in on the target to help the missile-guidance system understand where the target was. Then, using his left trigger finger, he squeezed the left trigger again to lock the crosshairs onto the target. Now the Javelin's guidance unit locked onto the truck, and Jason could see the crosshairs go from blinking to solid and begin to follow the truck as it moved in his CLU's viewer. All that was left was Jason's decision to fire on the truck, now only a cloud of dust off in the fog and haze.

I grabbed my binoculars for another look at the truck. "Jason, that truck has to be at least 2 miles away now. You are never going to hit that thing."

"No, Frank. I got it. Can I shoot?"

"Okay, shoot!"

Jason squeezed the right trigger.

The Javelin squirted out of its launch tube with a little whoosh as the small ejection motor fired, popping it up and into the air. The missile hung there in space for a split second. Then, just as it appeared that it was about to fall out of the sky and land a few feet in front of us, the main rocket motor ignited, and the missile soared up and out of sight into the clouds and disappeared.

While all the other guys were recording Jason's big adventure on film, I kept my eyes on the truck. Five seconds passed, then ten, then fifteen. "Jay, where's your missile?" I teased him.

"I don't know, Frank," Jason said.

We were all pretty much holding our breath. The seconds slowly passed as the distant cloud of dust gradually became nearly invisible. All twenty guys were standing around, watching the target and wondering about the Javelin.

"Hey, has anybody seen Jason's missile?" I asked.

"It went up in the clouds," somebody said, "and I haven't seen it since."

After what seemed like an eternity, we all concluded the missile failed. "So much for your 'high-speed' missile," I yelled at Jason. I stood up and turned away, sure that it had gone astray or self-destructed.

Just then, all the other guys cheered. I spun around to see a fireball where the Javelin had made its attack on the truck, flying down out of the clouds and homing in with unbelievable accuracy, firing its warhead into the cab and engine of the vehicle. The infantry in the back were ejected onto the ground, and the cab was now destroyed and afire. I could see the truck slowly coast to a stop, wrecked.

All the guys were cheering Jason, patting him on the back and giving him high fives. It was a bit like scoring a bull's-eye on an impossibly distant target.

"Okay, Jason," I said with a sense of happy sarcasm, "you got your Javelin shot—are you happy now?"

"Hell yes, I'm happy. I waited three years to make that shot," he said.

"Good. Now let's get back to shutting down this highway."

Jason turned off the CLU power switch, removed the sight from the spent tube, and then tossed the empty container away. He put the CLU back in its storage bag, not expecting to ever need it again. This was later realized as a very significant mistake.

But Jason's missile shot taught us something that would be critical later. Although we had trained on the simulator for the Javelin, none of us—especially us old soldiers—really believed in it. We were skeptics. The shot at the truck was not tactically important, but it converted us all. The old Dragon missile had conditioned us to expect misses even at much closer ranges. We thought we could not count on our ability to defeat tanks and APCs in a close fight. The Javelin spanked that enemy target at over 3,000 meters, almost 2 miles away, automatically and as advertised. It did not have the huge flash and bang of the Dragon or TOW (Tube-Launched, Optically-Tracked, Wire-Guided) missiles, either—the launch signature that told the enemy exactly where you were hiding and where they should concentrate their return fire. Both those old missiles would blow your eardrums out if you did not have hearing protection, but the Javelin was almost silent as it launched. We had not given the missile much thought before, but now we were believers.

SHUTTING DOWN THE HIGHWAY

There was a lull for a few minutes. Bobby again took the opportunity to drop his pants to check the damage to his hip, while Steve, still sitting in the driver's seat about 2 feet away, could not avoid seeing the large, dark bruise that had now spread even farther and was adding brilliant colors to the deep purple of the impact area. "Hey, Steve, take a look what you did to my hip, buddy. Isn't this wonderful? Look at those colors. I think my hip is broken!"

"Jeeze, Bobby, I am really sorry about that," Steve said, probably wishing he was back at the FOB, as boring as that might have been.

But then another truck appeared in the distance. Marty fired on it, too, but it was at a greater range this time, and he missed. The driver realized something was wrong, executed a rapid U-turn, and escaped back up Highway 2, apparently untouched.

Marty looked over at me and said, "Do you want to go down on the intersection? Let's shut this highway down."

"Hell, yes." I said. "Let's go check with Matt."

We ambled over to Capt. Saunders, and Marty told him, "Sir, Frank and I think we should drive down to the intersection and shut the damn highway down completely. What do you think?"

Matt thought a moment and liked the idea. Then he said, "Let's do it."

Tom Sandoval rolled up in his pickup; he had heard the shooting and wondered what kind of trouble we were creating this time. "What are you guys doing?" he demanded.

"We're shooting up these enemy vehicles, Tom," I said. "We can't just let them drive up and down the road." Tom started shaking his head. He knew this was coming, he knew what we were like, and he knew what his commanders had told him. We were getting out of their control again. "We're going down on the intersection, and we are going to shut down Highway 2. You're invited to come along." Tom didn't seem happy about it, but he came along anyway.

This was getting serious, and nobody was laughing about shutting down the traffic on this road. Once again we all climbed into our vehicles, spread out in tactical formation, and moved forward. Steve, with Bobby's attentive direction, avoided putting our GMV into any more ditches as we drove cross-country, through the high grass and flowers.

Down on the intersection we found a crossroads with a traffic circle about 100 meters across, situated on a perfectly flat plain without any cover or concealment in sight. There was not a single tree to provide shade. There was not a house or store or building of any kind visible within a mile, just some small mud huts on the side, used by vendors. In another time and place, this landscape would have been beautiful, with its fresh wheat and pretty flowers and quiet solitude, but not now. With the six guys back clearing the berm, we were now just twenty-five Americans and eighty KDP Kurdish Peshmerga, and we were sitting on top of the second-busiest highway in Iraq. Somewhere out in the haze there were enemy tanks, artillery, and thousands of infantry, all with excellent weapons, training, and knowledge of the ground. We had six GMVs (two were back at the berm), two pickup trucks, and two local cargo trucks. Each unit was extremely vulnerable to anything bigger than rifle fire that the Iraqis decided to throw at us. If we got in a serious fight, there was not a place to hide within half a mile.

Everybody's pucker-factor was high and getting higher as weapons were checked again. We all knew that another target would roll down the road again momentarily, and this time there would be no misses. Matt had the good sense to place two of Nine-Two's vehicles on a low hill about 100 meters from the intersection, where they could provide overwatch protection for the rest of us. This was important because there was no way of knowing just what would come driving down the road, or from which direction it would come.

Since the idea was to shut the highway down completely, we had to deal with every single vehicle that showed up. We expected that the Iraqi drivers would behave in a somewhat predictable way—that they would slow down, for example, when they saw us blocking the road with our vehicles. The civilian vehicles would be turned around and the military vehicles either captured or destroyed. The Iraqis, however, seemed to obey an entirely irrational set of driving laws, and this began making our work at the crossroads more complicated than expected.

Soon after arriving, we saw a motorcycle head up the road in our direction. A soldier in uniform drove it. When he failed to stop, he was shot. The motorcycle skidded across the ground in one direction; the driver skidded in another. Once again, the Kurds roared past to collect their plunder. The cycle was tossed in the back of one of the trucks, somewhat worse for a few bullet holes, and the Kurds returned in triumph.

Almost immediately, we saw a white Toyota pickup truck bearing down on us. It did not have army markings and might very well have been driven by a civilian. We had the binos on the truck, trying to discover if it was military or civilian. We tried to stop the truck by standing in the road and waving. Innocent or not, the truck driver could not have missed seeing the four big GMVs with machine guns on each, and a dozen men on the ground, all with weapons pointed at him, as well as one or two waving madly, signaling him to stop.

A reasonable or prudent driver would have carefully and promptly braked to a halt under these circumstances. I was standing on the right side of my GMV with the M240 pointed at the truck. Steve Brunk was out of his driver's seat and on the left, with his M4 aimed at the driver. Bobby was up in the turret with the Mk19. We'd gotten daily reports about suicide car bombs (called VBIEDs—Vehicle-Borne Improvised Explosive Devices) giving the Marines and the guys from the 3rd ID problems. As the range closed, Bobby grabbed for his Mossberg shotgun, bringing it to bear on the cab.

"Frank, he's still coming!" Bobby yelled. "What do you want me to do?"

"Fire a warning shot," I told him. Well, this was a lesson to me—in combat, there is no such thing as a warning shot. Everybody assumed that the shot was a signal for the fight to begin, and every weapon opened fire on the truck. From where I was, I saw Bobby's buckshot hit the pavement in front of the vehicle, which then seemed to explode. The windshield dissolved. The whole vehicle was shredded by automatic-weapons fire from several angles.

When the shooting started, this truck was only about 50 meters from us and still traveling at what seemed to be about 50mph. Within a few seconds, though, the pickup was an unrecognizable wreck, and so was the driver. The whole thing lasted only a few seconds and ended with an explosion. I thought some sort of munitions on the vehicle detonated, but it turned out to be Jeff Adamec's Mk19 fire. Jeff put four high explosive rounds through the windshield, and the blast from those warheads appeared to be one big explosion.

By the time Jeff's 40mm rounds detonated, the truck was so close that we were in the warhead's effective radius. Bobby and Jake were standing in the back of our GMV and were hit by shrapnel in their chest.

"Cease fire! Cease fire!" several people yelled as the pickup careened off the road and into a ditch.

"Bobby, get up there and clear the truck," I told him. He jumped down with his little shotgun, just in case, and ran forward with Andy to inspect the damage. The driver was shredded and already dead. We wanted to make sure he was a soldier and not just a foolish civilian, so I asked Bob to take a close look. He couldn't tell, so the Kurd colonel came forward.

"He's Iraqi," the Kurdish colonel spat in disgust. He didn't care if he was civilian or military, but we did. He was Iraqi, and he had been about to run us all down, but it was time to remind everybody about our rules of engagement. We did not want to hurt any innocent civilians.

We were standing in the road, discussing the problem of identification, when another vehicle approached, an Iraqi army bus. None of us had any trouble deciding if this one was a legitimate target because soldiers began firing on us from the open windows. They were still too far away for the AK fire to be accurate or very effective, but the gesture got our attention. It quickly ended the discussion we were having about how to deal with questionable targets.

Immediately, all of the .50cal machine guns opened up on the bus. We could see the rounds pounding the vehicle, tracers flying right into its center of mass. The bus did not run off the road like the previous three targets; instead, the driver braked hard, executed a perfect three-point turn in the middle of the highway, and roared back in the direction he had just come from. As he made his escape down Highway 2 and drove out of range, we all sat astounded at the driver's audacity and skill, as well as his amazing luck.

One .50cal bullet will easily destroy an engine or a wheel or break a driveshaft, and we must have scored a dozen hits or more on this bus. At the ranges at Fort Pickett, this target would have been down and scored as destroyed; here on the battlefield, it drove off to fight another day. Of course, the shooting from the windows stopped, and we could only imagine the carnage inside. But that driver was still alive and still driving—he was one lucky guy.

As the bus disappeared into the haze, I had a few minutes to take stock of just where we were and just what we were doing. The day had already been long and exciting, and it was getting longer and more exciting by the minute.

We had left the MSS-assembly area at 0600, arrived at the pump house at 0700. After waiting for the Kurds for half an hour, the assault kicked off at 0730. We were on top of the ridge forty-five minutes later at 0815, and were on the objective at around 0900. We began moving forward about 0915 and had been engaging road targets since about 0930.

Now the time was about 1000 hours, and we were finally doing what we came to Iraq to do. We were a mile or so past the Green Line, stirring things up for Col. Cleveland and Lt. Col. Binford. We had Highway 2 shut down in both directions. Our position on the intersection was very exposed, but we had a couple of routes for withdrawal if necessary, and so far we had seen no serious threats.

FIRE IN THE HOLE

Meanwhile, Eric and the other half of the team had made it to the huge berm that had blocked our path earlier in the morning. Having a little more time, Kenney did the math to determine how much explosive he would need in order to move enough dirt to create an opening big enough to drive a truck through. He quickly came to the conclusion that he did not have enough in the back of the GMVs to do the job, and then he realized he had more than enough explosives after all.

The mines! he thought. *We could recover all those antitank* [AT] *mines the Iraqis laid all over the place just on the other side.* He quickly yelled to Mike and Rich, who were standing just outside their vehicles.

"Hey you guys, go grab me a bunch of those Iraqi AT mines while I get the demo gear out of the truck."

"What?" Mike responded. "You want us to go pick up mines?" All Mike knew about mines was that they blow up when something triggers them. He thought to himself, *I'm a medic; I didn't learn shit about handling mines, just handling the result of what happens when they go off.*

Kenney knew that the Kurds had removed the triggering mechanisms. Once the triggering mechanism screwed into the top of a mine was removed, it was harmless. Besides, antitank mines needed several hundred pounds of weight to set them off.

Kenney yelled back to Mike, "Listen, all you need to do is scarf up all the mines the Kurds threw on the side of the road. They're not armed; there's nothing to worry about." Mike and Rich reluctantly started picking up the mines, which weighed about 10 pounds apiece.

Kenney dove into the back of his GMV, grabbing his demo kit, a case of C-4 explosives, a roll of "det cord" (detonation cord), some fuses, some blasting caps, and his M-60 fuse igniters. Mike and Rich grabbed about four to six mines each, carrying them stacked like poker chips against their chests, taking them back to Kenney. Kenney used his entrenching tool, a small folding shovel, to dig a hole into the side of the berm at its base. They began stuffing all the mines into the hole. Ken placed a couple blocks of C-4 on top of each mine as a "kicker" to ensure each mine went off. There's a rule in demolition circles that you never bury a blasting cap, so Kenny primed the C-4 with what's called a Uli (pronounced *yu-li*) knot. The knot is made by wrapping detonation cord around itself several times, forming a cylindrically shaped knot that is then imbedded into the plastic explosive C-4 blocks. He then ran the ends of the det cord sticking out the back of the Uli knots together, joining them with blasting caps crimped to a time fuse that he cut for about a minute delay.

Kenney sent everyone back to their vehicles and had them start their engines and turn the vehicles away from the berm so they would be ready to drive off to a safe distance. Kenney then attached his fuse igniters to the end of the time fuse, removed the safety pins, and yelled, "FIRE IN THE HOLE! FIRE IN THE HOLE! FIRE IN THE HOLE!" at the top of his lungs to warn everyone within the sound of his voice that an explosion was about to occur. He then pushed in on the pins to set his fuse igniters, gave them a quarter turn, and pulled.

Hearing the audible pop of the primers contained inside and seeing the outer plastic covering of the time fuse start to bubble, Kenney knew that his fuses were burning and that it was time to go. He jumped into the passenger seat of his GMV, Mike punched the gas, and they quickly drove off, with Eric and his guys following right behind them in their GMV. Within a minute, a large explosion threw a big cloud of dirt into the sky.

They returned to the berm and were disappointed to see that only about half of the obstruction had been cleared—not quite enough to allow a large vehicle to pass.

"Go back and get me some more of those mines," Kenney told Mike and Rich.

"We used all the mines the Kurds cleared," Mike noted. "The only ones left are the ones out in the minefield."

"Well, go get them," Ken yelled back. "Just unscrew the triggers and toss them down the hill before you start carrying the mines back."

Mike and Rick started collecting more mines, worried that the Iraqi engineers might have added antitampering devices to prevent the very activity Mike and Rich were engaged in.

When Mike and Rich returned with the second pile of mines, they found Kenney wildly swinging his entrenching tool, digging a second hole.

Once again, Kenney placed a block of C-4 on each of the mines and stuffed them into the hole he dug at the base of the berm. When he was ready, he again repeated the magic words, "FIRE IN THE HOLE! FIRE IN THE HOLE! FIRE IN THE HOLE!"

When the dust cleared this time, there was a gap in the pile of dirt large enough for a truck, and the road was now clear for follow-on forces or, if needed, our hasty withdrawal.

The gap would be used in minutes, but not by anybody we expected. There was a BBC News crew only a few miles away, and they would be the first from outside our little task force to use our freshly created passage.

MEANWHILE, BACK AT THE RANCH

Back at the intersection on Highway 2, we all knew that the enemy had realized by now that they had a problem and where that problem was located. Although they probably did not know much about the size of our force, the burning vehicles and the heavy machine gun fire definitely let them know where to find us. By now, the local Iraqi commander had surely been getting excited reports from survivors of our effort to shut down the highway, and he would be deciding how to respond.

I had been in the First Gulf War and remembered how the Iraqi units surrendered at the first chance. The infantry we had encountered two hours previously had surrendered at almost their first chance, although it had required two bursts of .50cal fire into their positions to make them do so. We knew that a whole battalion or possibly a brigade of mechanized infantry was supposed to be in the vicinity, and could come out either looking for us to fight or to surrender to us. They could also run off, as Iraqi units had done before. This wondering is part of the puzzle of battle—what will the enemy do next?

We found out right away. Marty saw what looked like three large troop trucks slowly driving down the highway, out of the fog, toward us. Visibility was limited to only about 2 kilometers, so they were already pretty close when Marty noticed them. The lead vehicle was flashing its lights to get our attention, and it worked. Iraqi forces had been told to flash their lights as a signal to us that the approaching vehicle was surrendering.

"Marty," Andy Pezzella said as he watched the lights slowly flashing in the distance, "what do you want to do?"

"Let's watch them," Marty said. The trucks were too far away for us to know if they were military or civilian. Maybe they were civilians who had heard about the roadblock and just wanted to avoid being shot.

All of us had our full attention fixed on this little parade for a few moments before something exploded in the wheat field about 200 meters to our left flank. Mortar rounds make an odd sound when they impact, a percussive note that is quite different from the sharp crack of an artillery ground burst or airburst. The sound is partly the result of the explosion, partly the result of large chunks of steel flying through the air.

"WHOA!" somebody yelled. "What the hell was that?" A large cloud of black smoke mixed with a lot of dirt attracted the attention of all of us. The second round was almost in the same spot, and now we knew.

"Mortars!" I yelled.

Four rounds exploded nearby, but they were all in roughly the same place and not "walking" in toward our position. That meant that the tube that fired them was either shooting blind, without an observer to correct their fire, or that the gunners were inexperienced. They were putting rounds on a spot on a map without knowing what effect those rounds were having—luckily for us.

"If they bracket us, we've got to move," Marty yelled. That was fine with me.

Todd Gannon, Nine-Two's TACP, was in one of the overwatch vehicles. Like a good TACP he had his binos up, trying to spot the enemy mortar team. "I see them. I see them," Todd called. "I see them dropping a round. There are two Iraqis with a 60mm mortar at the edge of the village."

Small mortars like the one the Iraqi team was using are highly portable, easily carried by two men, and provide a potent source of indirect artillery that can do a lot of damage when properly used. Being engaged by a mortar team so quickly, even if it had not yet inflicted casualties on our group, was troubling. It suggested that the enemy infantry was nearby, and that they were not yet in a mood to throw down their weapons and surrender.

"You guys hold this intersection," Capt. Matt Saunders yelled at us. "I am going to take my team, and we're going to kill those guys!" They roared off in their GMVs, moving in bounds along the road toward the village of Debecka, a mile or so to the south.

Matt and Nine-Two had not gone very far when somebody else began firing on us. This time it seemed to be mortar fire from our front, and this time it was potentially more lethal. Instead of detonating when they hit the ground, these enemy rounds were going off in the air overhead, spreading their splinters in a wide radius. Airbursts were a very serious threat to us, but fortunately, it seemed we were out of range since the rounds exploded over 300 meters away.

Once again, the enemy gunners were not adjusting their fire. We did not know it at the time, but discovered later that we were being fired on by a ZSU-57-2 mobile gun system, a very versatile and lethal cannon system mounted on a tank chassis. This cannon fires projectiles about the size of a beer can at a rapid rate and at long range. Happily for us, the gunners apparently ran out of proximity ammunition before they were able to adjust their fire. The system's primary role is to shoot down aircraft, but those projectiles would have torn up our GMVs just as easily.

Our day was getting still more interesting. A mortar team was firing at us from our left, a mystery gun was firing at us from somewhere else, and three big trucks were moving slowly toward us, trying to get our attention. We were standing out in the middle of a road, with no place to hide. A large part of our little force had run off to deal with the mortars. We had knocked out a few enemy vehicles, we had shut down the highway, and we had verified that the Javelin missile system actually worked. It was twenty minutes before eleven in the morning, and I was long overdue for a cup of coffee.

A SURPRISING SURRENDER

While this situation was interesting, and even somewhat serious, those of us who had been in combat before were not too worried. So far, the enemy fire had been inaccurate and ineffective. Our position was being probed, obviously, but in a weak sort of way. A few distant mortar rounds were not much of a threat. Even if the trucks proved to be full of enemy infantry preparing to assault, we had the means to pile them up long before they could get in range with their AKs.

Matt Saunders and his team were about halfway to the mortar position when Andy Pezzela called out, "Hey, those guys are shooting at us!"

I pulled up my binos, looked toward the approaching vehicles, and saw the dismounts walking in and around the approaching trucks. Through the haze I could not see any weapons, let alone muzzle flashes. I also could not make out if the trucks were military or civilian. All I could see was the constant flashing of the headlights on the lead vehicle.

"No, they're not shooting, Andy," I said. "They're just flashing their lights at us." Marty was looking through his binos as well. Like me, he saw nothing.

Andy was adamant, "I'm telling you, I saw muzzle flashes! Those guys are shooting at us!"

"They're a mile away, Andy, and even if they were shooting, they couldn't hit us from there. Just keep an eye on them," I told him, but Andy continued to insist, and we continued to tell him he was seeing things.

Andy was right, and I was wrong. What Andy had seen actually turned out to be the muzzle flashes of many AKs, but from such long range that the sound of the weapons could not be heard over the rumble of our own engines. Ordinarily, you hear a bullet passing nearby as a sharp crack; because a bullet's velocity is greater than the speed of sound, it makes a small sonic boom. These bullets had lost much of their initial velocity and were passing by nearly silently and must have been impacting quietly all around us.

We turned our attention back to Nine-Two, who were just about in range to engage the mortar team with their .50cals. Unlike the rest of us, Andy Pezzella had not been distracted from his task of watching the approaching vehicles.

He saw the advancing enemy momentarily disappear behind a large cloud of smoke, and before Andy could advise us, he noticed a dark shadow. It was emerging from the smoke and haze, and gradually he realized that what he was looking at was no truck. Then we heard the words that would forever be engraved in all of our minds.

"TANKS! TANKS! TANKS!" Andy yelled at the top of his lungs.

Bobby suddenly began pounding on the roof of our GMV, right over my head, trying to get my attention. "TANKS!" he yelled. "TANKS! TANKS!"

Tanks? I thought. *What do you mean, "Tanks"?* I stepped out of my

GMV and looked where Bobby was pointing—in the direction of the trucks.

Out from behind the big cargo trucks, just visible above the lush green wheat plants, I could see the tops of MTLB armored personnel carriers (APCs) maneuvering to the left and right of the road. Only the very tops of these vehicles were visible, along with their heavy black exhaust plumes, but that was enough to give every one of us a serious jolt of adrenaline. We all stood there in amazement as, one after another, the APCs deployed into line-abreast formation. The MTLB isn't a true tank, but it can kill you just as well—it presents a low profile, is highly maneuverable, and mounts an excellent machine gun inside a fully enclosed turret. Also, its half-inch armor provides very good protection against our .50cal and Mk19 rounds.

Whoever was in command of the local enemy forces had thrown together a very professional response to our invasion of Highway 2. We had only been on the intersection for a half hour, and already we had been engaged by mortars, the ZSU-57-2, infantry in the bus, infantry in the trucks, and this horde of MTLBs roaring toward us at high speed across the wheat fields. It was one of those proverbial *Oh, shit!* moments for every one of us.

The Iraqis were doing everything right. We stood there like idiots, mesmerized by their surprise attack—I did not know what to do for a few moments. Nobody else did, either. *We're being attacked?* I thought. *The Iraqis don't attack; they surrender or run. This can't be.* We simply had not expected this development, or the ones that soon followed.

The MTLBs started putting out smoke, either through their on-board generator or with grenade-projectors, adding to our difficulty in evaluating their threat. The MTLB is one of the world's great cross-country combat vehicles and can easily do about 20mph across open ground.

To this day, I don't know who broke the spell, but somebody yelled, "SHOOT! Start shooting!" All the heavy weapons opened up, first Andy's .50cal machine gun and then Bobby's Mk19. We knew we could not kill the enemy vehicles, but at least we could make them button up (close their hatches and so reduce their visibility), and this would maybe buy us a little time.

Marty ran for the radio and called Nine-Two. Ken Thompson answered. "Ken, get back here! We're being attacked by tanks!"

Ken Thompson glanced across the field and could see only one MTLB in the haze, an apparently minor threat. Marty's voice on the radio, however, told a different story. Ken relayed the report and turned the team around, and all four GMVs raced back up the road toward the intersection.

While Nine-Two was breaking whatever speed limit applied to Highway 2, our guys were pouring everything they had at the line of APCs. Then two things happened, one good, the other bad. First, the APCs braked to a stop. *Great,* I thought. *We've stopped their advance!*

Have you ever had one of those days when things go from bad to worse and the process never seems to stop? This was shaping up to be one of those days because the MTLBs were only getting out of the way for the big boys in this fight, four T-55 main battle tanks. The Iraqi tanks came out of the smoke screen, past the MTLBs, and began closing on our position at the intersection.

The T-55 is the most popular tank on the world market, with a simple, reliable, almost idiotproof design. This tank has been the foundation of many armies around the world for over thirty years. It has a 100mm high-velocity main gun that is so powerful that even a near-miss could destroy a GMV. At that moment, I think we all thought we had been caught in a very well-designed and well-executed trap.

Ever since Nine-One had been reconstituted nine months previously, we had been pushing the proverbial envelope of what an ODA could do. Time and again, Nine-One and I had been challenged about our aggressive tactics, our abrasive style, and our big talk about taking the fight to the enemy. When Col. Cleveland challenged us on our ability to take on a bigger force, we said we could do it. When that S3 major from 10th Group called us a bunch of out-of-control gunslingers, we pushed him to let us fight. When our own company commander, Maj. X, had a choice, he selected other ODAs instead of Nine-One because we wanted to pick fights. Even Tom Sandoval, who at the time seemed to be our one and only friend from 10th Group, had just tried to rein us in and prevent exactly this kind of situation.

For about three seconds, I remembered all the people in our food chain who had been warning us that we were biting off more than we could chew, and that we would get ourselves in a spot just like this. They all predicted that someday we would be looking down the main gun tubes of some enemy tanks, and they were right—we had put ourselves in the sights of all those tank guns, and so had confirmed the worst fears of our detractors.

Jason Brown feverishly dug his CLU out of the back of the GMV . . . and realized with dismay that he had turned it off. He turned it back on but knew the sensor would need about thirty seconds to cool down again. It was thirty seconds we did not have right then. Even so, Jason quickly grabbed a fresh missile, locked it onto the CLU, and jumped off the vehicle. He sat on the pavement, the missile on his shoulder, holding his breath while the seeker chilled. Caught up in the excitement of the moment, Jason forgot that he could just simply go to "Seeker Mode" and use the missle's thermal vision, which only took a few seconds to cool.

Awestruck, I watched one of the tanks pull to within 900 meters of us, then turn its main gun tube directly at the vehicle that Bobby, Steve, Jake, and I were manning. I saw the huge muzzle flash from the main gun, and then almost instantly heard the sonic signature of the projectile, sounding like a cross between a speeding locomotive and a space shuttle launch, as it passed a few feet away, right over the hood of my GMV, exploding on the rising ground just 50 meters to our rear.

"Let's go, let's go!" I started yelling at Marty, who had reached the same conclusion and was yelling the same thing. All of us knew that we had to move, and fast. Steve Brunk had wanted some excitement after the boredom of the FOB; now he had all the excitement a young soldier could ask for.

Matt Saunders and Nine-Two rolled in just as the first tank round struck. Jeff Adamec and Ken Thompson immediately jumped from their vehicle, Jeff with a CLU, Ken with a missile tube. They chose their position at the edge of the road, and Ken mounted the missile to Jeff's CLU as Jeff searched for a target. They ran into the same problem as Jason. They had to wait for the CLU to cool. Unlike Jason, Jeff was not a school-trained Javelin gunner and simply didn't know about the seeker option.

Tom Sandoval and his guys were still with us, although the Kurds had decided that it was time for them to get back up the hill. The Iraqis quickly fired several more main gun rounds at us, but they all went high, over our vehicles, impacting 50 meters or so behind us on the hillside.

While the enemy tank gunners were not particularly accurate, they were at least disciplined. Each one fired in turn, down the line, as if their commander was telling them each when to shoot, and possibly where to aim. If any of them would hold their crosshairs just a little lower on our GMVs, they would blow us apart. We could not figure out why they missed at such close ranges, and with so many rounds fired. Were they trying to scare us? Did they think we were Kurds? Were they trying to just push us back across the Green Line? Were they just inept? We could not tell, and, at the time, we were too busy trying to survive to worry very much about these details.

I looked over to Marty's vehicle and saw Jason sitting in the middle of the road with the Javelin on his shoulder.

"Come on! LET'S GO!" I yelled to Marty.

Marty was way ahead of me. He was yelling at Jason, "Take the shot. Take the shot!" Marty wanted to get at least one Javelin off to send a message to the Iraqis that we could kill their tanks. He was hoping it would slow them down long enough to buy us time to get back up to the ridge. He continued to yell at Jason, "Take the shot!"

Jason seemed to be consumed by the desire to kill the tank. Looking through the CLU viewfinder literally gave him tunnel vision. He casually answered Marty, "Just give me a couple seconds, I almost got it."

Jason may not have realized the gravity of the situation, but Marty did. He ran forward and grabbed Jason, pulling him up off the asphalt, yelling, "Let's GO, Jay!" at the same time.

Now Jason was able to see how close the tanks actually were. He realized he did not even have time to get inside the GMV. Cradling the entire missile tube and CLU under his right arm, he dove onto the front hood of the GMV. With Andy behind the .50cal, Marty made a dive for the driver's seat, popped the vehicle in gear, and stomped on the gas. As Marty spun his GMV around, Jason grabbed hold of the sling lift guide in the center of the hood with his free hand. With a bear hug around his precious Javelin and a white-knuckle grip on the GMV, Jason rode the hood of the GMV for the 900-meter drive back up the hill.

Meanwhile, Jeff Adamec was desperately trying to get *his* CLU ready, but with four tanks firing at us from such short range, we had no more time to spare. Ken Thompson did not need to see Marty pulling away to realize the big trouble we would be in if we did not get out of that intersection. He stood up, then reached down and grabbed Jeff by the lifting strap of his body armor, hauling him off the pavement, yelling, "GET UP! Let's go!"

Ken practically dragged Jeff back to their vehicle, pushing him into the rear of his GMV. Unable to climb into the back with the heavy missile, Jeff hung on to the spare tire mount, literally for his life, leaning over the top of the fuel cans strapped to the rear bumper. He, too, rode the distance back up the ridgeline holding on with one hand.

Steve, Marty, and the other drivers pushed their gas pedals to the floorboards as they made those GMVs race for the exit as fast as they could go, back up the hill in the direction we had come from. Our motto might have been "Nine-One Don't Run," but we decided to make a "tactical withdrawal" as fast as those Humvees would take us, cheered on by the enemy 100mm tank rounds flying past and exploding nearby.

The Iraqis must have thought we looked pretty comical racing away from the intersection. Bobby was lobbing 40mm rounds at the tanks the whole time, and I was shouting, "Keep shooting, Bobby, keep shooting!" in the hope of keeping the tanks buttoned up. There was no cover at all, and the Iraqis kept banging away at us, always shooting high.

We had at least a kilometer to go before there was any chance of finding cover, and the only route was the little road back to Objective Rock. The terrain beside the road was too rough for rapid travel, and all of us needed to get away as fast as possible. But we had another problem—the Kurds.

The Kurds made their break for the exit first, while we were still re-acting to the tanks and trying to get the missiles ready to shoot. That meant that the Kurds and their large, old, and very slow trucks were ahead of us, and the little road suddenly looked like a Los Angeles freeway at rush hour. Those old trucks crawled up the hill at about 10mph, completely blocking the road. Steve and the other drivers leaned on the horns while the rest of us just yelled at the Kurds, urging them to go faster or get out of the way.

Finally, as Marty crested the first hill, he saw some defendable ter-rain. He decided to pull his GMV off to the side of the road and get out of the line of fire.

This would be the spot, he thought. *We'll circle the wagons and "Alamo" here. Alamo* was actually an operational term to describe a place to consolidate your forces and mount a defense until reinforce-ments arrived. In the Special Operations community, the term *Alamo* was only used in dire situations; it certainly applied now.

Jake Chandler, Saleem Ali, and Todd Gannon were all on their UHF radios sending out their emergency close air support requests.

"Flash! Flash! Troops in contact, troops in contact! Clear the net," Jake yelled into his radio. "This is ROUGHNECK NINE-ONE with an immediate CAS request, over." The sound of machine gun fire and exploding tank shells could be heard in the background.

A voice in the sky answered, "Go ahead, ROUGHNECK—send it." Jake began sending enough information to get us some air cover, giving simple coordinates to vector a fighter to us in order to provide some much-needed fire support. When the voice asked him for a description of the situation, Jake's answer turned all ears to our situation.

"We're taking fire from a bunch of tanks just a couple hundred meters to our front." Jake answered. "We were almost overrun but have managed to Alamo up on some high ground. What's the ETA for the fighters?"

"Roger, we copy all—ETA thirty minutes," was the response.

Jake couldn't believe it. "Thirty minutes! We won't be here in thirty minutes—we need fighters now!"

I was on the radio too, frantically trying to reach Eric and the other half of my team, without success. The downside of the IMBTR radio was that it was "line of sight"—Eric was on the other side of the hill. I continued trying to reach him.

Nine-Two pulled off the road to the left of Marty's GMV. Their .50cal and Mk19 gunners were hosing down the advancing armor, trying to keep their heads inside at least. We pulled off to the right, up alongside Marty and Jason, who had both jumped from the vehicle. Jason was hauling his Javelin, still attached to the CLU, up to the top of a small rise in order to get in position and engage the approaching armor.

Marty was running directly toward our vehicle. "Give me your Javelins!" he yelled to Jake, who was still sitting in the back of the GMV monitoring his Air Force radio. Jake quickly complied, popping the straps on our two Javelins and handing them over the side to Marty without saying a word. Marty grabbed the lifting handles on top of the tubes and took off running toward Jason's position.

I looked over and saw Andy Pezzella, now all alone in the GMV, firing his .50cal. Soon his gun would be empty, and he would need some help lifting the heavy 60mm mortar cans from the back of the GMV up to his gun. Instead of mortar rounds, each can was now filled with three hundred rounds each of .50cal ammo, enabling the gunners to maintain a heavy rate of fire without having to reload so frequently. Standard .50cal cans come with only one hundred rounds in them, and one hundred rounds go a lot faster than you would think.

"Steve! You stay here and help Bobby—just keep feeding him ammo. I'm going to go help Andy." Steve jumped from the driver's seat of our GMV and climbed up top alongside Bobby, who was now starting to dial in the rounds from his Mk19 on the Iraqis below us.

As I got to Andy's vehicle, I climbed into the back and started lifting ammo cans up on top of the GMV's roof. Andy had already gone through two cans and was almost done with the last can, which we kept in a special rack that we had modified on the turret. The timing was beautiful; his gun went dry just as I pulled the lid off one of the cans.

"Pop the feed tray! I'll drop the new belt in," I yelled to him. Andy quickly complied, and within seconds he was firing again. I looked

over his shoulder and saw that the T-55s and MTLBs were still coming. They would naturally pursue us up the road and chase us all the
way to Irbil if they could, before reoccupying the positions they had
abandoned earlier in the day.

Ordinarily, we would have been forced to agree with them. Their
plan would have been an excellent idea, but now . . . we had the missiles! The rules of the game had just changed for all of us, although the
enemy did not know that yet.

IF IT GLOWS, IT GOES

The CLU thermal sensors were now all fully chilled and ready to acquire targets. Jason put his eye to the CLU and could not believe
what he saw. With enemy armor spread all across our front and moving toward us, Jason did not bother to worry about which one would
be first. He locked onto the first vehicle that appeared in his CLU, an
MTLB armored personnel carrier, activated the BCU to cool the missile's seeker, brought the track gates in his sight in on the target, got a
lock, and squeezed the firing trigger. The missile left the tube and
popped into the air with its characteristic "soft launch," then roared
off downrange.

Jason wasted no time watching to see if the missile hit. He quickly
dipped his right shoulder and hit the release lever to drop the expended tube from the CLU. Marty had a reload ready at Jason's side.
Jason latched the CLU to the fresh missile, brought it to his shoulder,
and found another MTLB in his sight. Almost instantly, he locked the
seeker onto the new target and sent the Javelin on its way. Jason had
two missiles in the air before anybody else had launched.

Jeff was right behind him, and his first Javelin fired just after Jason's
second launch. Suddenly, at this critical moment, Bobby's Mk19
jammed. I could see him pounding on the weapon with a cleaning
rod, trying to eject a jammed casing, and I ran over to help. Bobby applied the immediate action drills we had practiced at Fort Pickett so
many times, and he cleared the stoppage in seconds.

"Way to go, Bob," I yelled up to him. Bobby, like the others, was truly performing superbly. Even with enemy tank rounds and machine gun fire flying past his vehicle, he maintained his composure like an experienced combat veteran. Not the least bit frazzled, Bobby once again began raining 40mm projectiles down on the enemy. We expected the enemy to deploy their infantry against us, and the Mk19s were the best argument we had at the moment to keep them inside their APCs.

At that time I saw Andy throw another empty ammo can off to the side of the GMV. Andy was going through ammunition rapidly, so I hopped in the back of the vehicle and started feeding him more fresh boxes of .50cal rounds. While the other guys were getting ready to launch their missiles, Steve and I made sure the gunners had plenty of ammunition.

Jason's first missile crashed into its target with the same precision as his earlier shot at the truck, but at an even greater range, 2,700 meters, again beyond the rated maximum engagement distance. The MTLB was struck from above, the warhead blasting through the thin overhead armor and into the engine compartment with disastrous consequences for the crew and passengers. Although the vehicle was destroyed, the rest of the enemy force appeared not to notice. Since that target was on the extreme left flank and to the rear of their formation, the Iraqis may not have seen the vehicle blow up. Certainly, the crew was in no condition to make any radio calls, so the rest of the tanks and APCs continued their attack.

Jason's next missile found a second MTLB, and then Jeff's first Javelin destroyed a third. Within just a few seconds, three of the eight MTLBs were in flames, their crews dead, their infantry passengers blown out the back doors and lying wounded and dying in the fresh green wheat.

Now we had the enemy's attention. If they had thought our escape from the intersection was funny, none of them were laughing anymore. Instead of pressing their attack in the disciplined manner of a few minutes before, their MTLBs began executing antitank missile-defensive drills while the tanks continued straight ahead. Now it was our turn to laugh, although nobody did.

Those MTLBs started driving around in unpredictable circles, a maneuver that might have been effective against a TOW or Dragon but that was futile against the Javelin. Those first three missiles, fired by Jeff and Jason, essentially shut down the enemy attack. We had been caught out in the open, surprised by an enemy who could not be effectively engaged with the weapons we had immediately available. Suddenly, it was the enemy's turn to be caught in the open with no place to hide and without an effective weapon.

Down on the intersection, we had nothing to protect us from the direct fire of those 100mm main-gun rounds. Up here, we had the crest of a small hill, all the protection we needed from anything the tanks or APCs could throw at us.

Until now, the enemy had fought well. Now their whole command structure began to come unglued. First, the enemy infantry dismounted from their MTLBs, perhaps because they thought the vehicles were death traps—which suddenly they were. But out in the open wheat field, within the effective ranges of both the .50cal and the Mk19, they were just as vulnerable, and the gunners began to cut them down.

Our second volley of missiles engaged their trucks. The MTLBs probably carried the best infantry available to the enemy commander, but the bulk of his men were in these big trucks to the rear of the armor. Why they kept coming forward was a mystery to us all, but that did not prevent Jason and Jeff from spanking them as they drove up the road toward us. Jeff and Jason managed to shoot a missile at the same truck at the same time.

Now the enemy pressure was too great for much coordination between us. Jason said later his attitude at that moment was, *If it glows, it goes,* meaning that the first heat signature that showed up in his viewfinder produced an immediate lock and launch.

Gino Zawojski, Nine-Two's senior medic, took out his team's second CLU, mated it to a missile, and prepared to fire from the right side of the road. He quickly scored a hit on another MTLB. Then he reloaded and killed another.

Eric Strigotte, the junior weapons sergeant from Four-Four, got into the Javelin act too, and destroyed a truck. Within five or six minutes of our arrival behind this small rise, we had destroyed five MTLBs and two troop transport trucks. Out of eight Javelins fired, seven hit their targets and killed them, while one of Jason's missiles seemed to have disappeared. Three of the four MTLBs on the left of the road were on fire, their passengers and crews killed. Two of the four on the right were already knocked out, and two of the three trucks on the road along with their troops had been reduced to burning wreckage.

The four T-55s wisely sheltered themselves behind the berm on which Highway 2 had been built. Elevating the road this way allowed drainage during storms, and now it provided defilade protection for the tanks. The surviving infantry also ran to take cover behind this berm. Some made it; others were cut down by the machine guns and 40mm grenades.

Two smaller military pickup trucks had been trailing the assault. Now that the attack had stalled, both rushed forward. The commander of the force might have been in one, and if so, he made a mistake by moving up toward the lead elements.

Andy was still behind his .50cal, and he was tearing up the dismounted infantry as they tried to run behind the tanks. I watched him fire a burst, then stop to evaluate the fall of the shot and make small corrections, and then fire again.

"Andy," I told him, "don't stop, you're dead-on. Keep shooting!" Hitting a moving vehicle at this distance, about 1,000 meters, was a challenge, but Andy was knocking the enemy soldiers down like bowling pins. As the pickups now drove up, I could see the tracer rounds from all three .50cals concentrate their fire to the leader. I could see glass, plastic, and steel flying through the air as Andy's, Van's, and Scott's rounds hammered the truck.

As the pickup rolled off the road to a stop, they engaged the second truck, stopping it as well. The occupants dashed from the disabled vehicle, trying to make it to cover. With a quick twist of a knob on his T&E (Traverse and Elevation) mechanism, Andy traversed his gun to the right and let off a long burst. I saw the armor-piercing rounds exploding as they ricocheted off the asphalt and cut into the enemy soldiers. Large pieces of flesh flew from their bodies moments before they fell dead in the intersection. Andy and the other .50cal gunners from Nine-Two worked their weapons back and forth through the exposed enemy infantry, chopping them up. They were literally running them through a human meat grinder.

I tried to call Eric again on the team internal radio frequency, and this time I was in luck. They had been making their way back to our position after blowing the berm and were now in radio range. "Eric! Where the hell are you? We're being attacked by tanks. I need you down here ASAP."

His voice was calm and ironic. "I leave you guys alone for twenty minutes and look what happens. We'll be there right away," he said.

Then he asked if I had called the FOB to let them know I was in contact.

"Negative," I answered. "Can you give them the heads-up?"

"Roger," Eric replied.

"Also, see if you can get ahold of the B-team," I told him. "We're running out of Javelins, and we're close to 50 percent on ammo. We're going to need a resupply here soon."

Eric then asked, "Do you need me to bring you guys some ammo?"

"Negative! Negative; get someone from the B-team to do it." I quickly said. "I need you to kill those damn tanks."

STANDOFF

Now the fight entered its third phase—a standoff. The tanks succeeded in getting behind the berm without loss, but they must have understood that the tide of battle had turned against them. They used the ground effectively, each of them in what we call "turret defilade," a position where only the gun tube and the top of the turret are exposed to direct fire. The four tanks continued to fire, one at a time, each taking its shot in turn, as if they were at a gunnery exercise.

The enemy gunners knew exactly where we were and had finally adjusted their fire a bit, but they were still not accurate enough to score hits. Many of their rounds struck the front of our position, throwing huge clouds of dust and rocks in the air. This material rained down on us—we called it a "dirt bath."

For the time being, all four T-55s were safe, because the CLUs could not see enough of the hull to get a good heat signature for the missile. As long as the tanks stayed put, we could not touch them. It was time for Saleem, Jake, and Todd to try calling for CAS (close air support), and so they did.

The emergency calls for CAS were finally answered as two Navy F-14 Tomcats roared overhead. It had been just over thirty-five minutes since the TACPs called, "TROOPS IN CONTACT." Jason, Jeff, Eric, and Gino's volley of missiles had shut down the enemy attack and bought us thirty minutes of precious time while we waited for the fighters to arrive. The lead F-14 checked in on Todd's radio frequency, not Jake's, so Todd started painting our situational-awareness picture for them.

I also got back on the radio with Eric, telling him we could not get a shot on the tanks with the Javelins from our position. "Eric, I need you to go off to our left flank as far as you can. See if you can get an oblique shot on those tanks from farther down the ridge."

"Roger that," Eric answered, and he began to maneuver his split team around to our right.

Todd quickly explained the problem to the pilots of the F-14s. "We have enemy T-55 tanks near a road intersection, 900 meters from our position, many dismounted infantry near the tanks, and a few trucks also in the vicinity."

Until now, the Navy aircraft had stayed above in the clouds. This shielded them from enemy ground fire, but it also prevented them from seeing the battlefield. Once they had the target description, they descended under the cloud deck to where both the pilots and weapons systems officers could actually see the ground. The F-14s were literally only a few hundred feet off the ground. They flew directly over our position, positively identifying our six GMVs and the two white Range Rovers. The pilot then turned north, did a hard bank to the right, and zipped back up into the clouds.

The pilots reported back to the TACPs that they could see the intersection, a tank, the pickup trucks, and the dismounts milling around. While we were keeping the enemy pinned down and waiting for a resupply of missiles, the Navy Tomcat crews were preparing to deliver

500-pound bombs on the enemy tanks. Those Iraqi T-55s could hide from us, but not from CAS.

We watched the jets overhead, expecting to see them make their runs on the tanks any moment. All of my split team's Javelin missiles had been used up. Nine-Two still had some and were trying to engage the tanks, and Eric Strigotte from Four-Four had one or two missiles left, but no good targets.

Capt. Wright and the rest of our team raced out to our left flank until they ran into a small ravine that blocked the Humvees from further travel. "We're on foot from here," Eric yelled. "Grab the Javelins, and let's go!"

As Mike Ray jumped from his vehicle, he saw our position at the Alamo off to his right. He also saw all the armor maneuvering below him on the valley floor. He yelled to Lihn Nguyen to grab their CLU, Rich and Kenney each grabbed a Javelin from their vehicle, and Gerry, who is responsible for documenting events like these, got his camera. As an F-14 passed overhead, they all began running down the hill with the missiles, looking for a good vantage point for a shot on the tanks. The enemy spotted the vehicles and opened fire on both GMVs. Mike and Rich, running across the open ridge, could clearly see the muzzle flashes of the tanks' main guns, but thought they were firing at the guys in the Alamo. That assessment was shattered when a tank round impacted with a loud crack into the dirt about 50 meters in front of them. Rather than keep moving, Mike told the rest of the guys, "This looks like a good spot; let's shoot from here." He sat on the ground as Rich helped him load a Javelin onto his CLU. Mike looked through the viewfinder and began searching for a target.

Back at the Alamo, Todd started yelling the standard warning that close air support will be arriving in seconds: "First aircraft inbound. Bomb in. Bomb in."

UNFRIENDLY FIRE

All of us looked down at the intersection, waiting for the bombs to start taking out the tanks in front of us. Instead, there was a tremendous explosion behind us, up the hill. There was a collective feeling of, *Oh, no!* We looked back and saw a huge black plume rising from the ridge behind us. We all knew that the Kurds, as well as the rest of our team, were up there. We wondered how close the bomb had come.

Across the net came the cry of "CEASE FIRE! CEASE FIRE! Friendlies hit!" Everyone's heart sank. The TACPs immediately got on their radio nets and started yelling, "ABORT! ABORT! ABORT! Blue on blue, blue on blue." They then told the F-14s to return to the IP (Initial Point, a location from which an attack begins) and await further instructions while we tried to sort out what happened.

Capt. Wright had been on the hill behind us and turned his attention from the tanks to see disaster just a few hundred meters away: several of the Kurd vehicles were in flames, and there were bodies strewn all over the intersection. Eric's heart sank. Moments earlier he had spoken to Major Howard and two other member of ODB-040 at that very intersection before maneuvering to help us at the Alamo. "The major is up there!" Eric yelled to his split team. "Back to the vehicles."

"Frank," he called on the radio, "we have friendlies hit. We got lots of casualties. I need your help up here!"

"Eric," I called back, "I have tanks to my front, and they are still shooting at us. Sorry, I can't help. You're on your own for now. We have to stay here and fight these guys." If the enemy tanks saw us pull back, they would surely renew their assault on us, and we would all be exposed and vulnerable.

"There are at least forty wounded up here," he said.

"Do the best you can," I said, "and we'll send people to you as soon as we can."

Until now, the fates and fortunes of war had been entirely on our side. We had had every possible lucky break. We had been shot at by dozens of enemy infantry in the bus, from the back of their big trucks, and from their MTLBs. We had taken dozens of 100mm high-explosive, main-gun tank rounds. Our withdrawal from the intersection under fire had been well executed. Despite facing an enemy that outnumbered us five to one and that held nearly every advantage, including surprise, we had been unscathed until now. None of us had been scratched. No vehicles were hit, and the whole operation had been too perfect to be believed.

The Navy pilot had been told to look for an intersection with T-55 tanks just off the road, troops, and pickup trucks. The Navy pilot looked out of his cockpit down at the ground and saw an intersection, a T-55 tank just off a road, troops, and pickup trucks. His first bomb was delivered with great precision into a crowd of troops, killing many instantly. Unfortunately, they were not the Iraqi infantry. The Navy bomb landed among Tom Sandoval's Kurds waiting back at Objective Rock.*

---

*According to Sean D. Naylor in a September 22, 2003, article in *Army Times*, a briefing on the battle said, "that after correctly identifying the six GMVs at the Alamo, the pilot lost his sense of cardinal direction. Instead of targeting the Iraqi T-55s that were firing on the SF troops from about 1,000 meters to their southwest, he focused on one abandoned T-55 located a similar distance to the northeast at the intersection the Americans had named Objective Rock." This friendly fire episode was investigated by all three services and there was no consensus on where the blame, if any, should be placed.

Eric yelled to his split team, "Let's go! We're going to help the Kurds!"

Just seconds before the Navy bomb hit, Mike had initiated the BCU in his Javelin. Now he needed to fire it. With Eric yelling for him to pull back and help the Kurds, Mike searched for a target, any target. He saw a heat signature from one of the APCs, closed the track gates on it, and fired. He released the spent tube, stood up, and started running back toward his GMV. The missile went over the top of the APC and crashed harmlessly into the ground behind it, detonating with a thump.

Within seconds, they made it back to their vehicles. Eric Wright and the other half of our team rushed back up to Rock. While we were busy trying to kill people, the other half of Nine-One was busy trying to save people. Gerry Kirk, Kenney Wilson, Lihn Nguyen, Rich Turner, and Mike Ray were with Eric, and the six of them reached the site of the disaster within a very few minutes.

They brought their vehicles to a stop about 70 meters from the burning Kurd vehicles. What they saw in front of them was a kind of hell on earth. Many of the Kurds' trucks and SUVs were mangled and destroyed. Most of the vehicles were afire. Of the eighty Kurds in the group, most had been within a few feet of the bomb's impact.

They could see and hear the cries of the wounded and dying Kurd soldiers. Mike yelled, "Grab the aid bags," and the guys immediately scrambled for them. Once again our predeployment training was put to the test. Every man was trained as a combat lifesaver. Mike had spent hours teaching the basics of hemorrhage control—putting on tourniquets and pressure dressings and packing large wounds. In a few seconds, all that training would be put to use.

Mike and Kenney started running toward the first group of casualties, with Rich following close behind. They could clearly hear small arms "cooking off," but ignored the explosions as they ran toward the carnage. With a loud crack, one of the Kurds' RPGs (Rocket-Propelled Grenades) that was in one of the burning vehicles "cooked off" and flew toward Mike and Kenney. The RPG passed between them at knee level, missing both by less than a foot. It continued on an upward trajectory, flying by Rich's head, forcing him into a reflexive duck. It zipped by so close that Rich could actually feel the whoosh of air on his face that the weapon displaced as it traveled at several hundred feet per second.

Eric and Nguyen were in the back of one of the GMVs, still digging for aid bags, when the RPG flew just a few feet above them. Eric quickly realized that this would be only the first round to cook off and yelled for the guys to quickly move the vehicles back another hundred meters. A single RPG hitting a GMV heavily loaded with fuel and ammo would inflict just as severe a blow as the Navy bomb.

While running to the scene, they passed a group of men lying in a ditch. The men called out to them in English, catching them by surprise.

"Did you call off the planes?"

They were a BBC reporter, a cameraman, and their producer. The reporter was John Simpson. He had been staying in a hotel in Irbil, trying to be close to the evolving action as Kurdish and American forces prepared to cross the Green Line. Simpson had somehow overheard a radio report from Tom's Kurds back to their headquarters in Irbil that the town of Debecka had been captured.

This report, of course, was not true. We never set foot in Debecka before or after the fight, although the path had been cleared to make it possible. Simpson, believing that the Kurds had taken this key ground, jumped in his SUV with his crew and dashed off down the same road we had used earlier that day.

We did not know this at the time, but Simpson was just the beginning of a media onslaught that would soon arrive and begin causing us tremendous problems. Within a few minutes after his arrival, he watched the Tomcats circle overhead and line up for their attack. He watched the fatal bomb as it fell to within a few feet from where he and his colleagues were standing.

Bombs and artillery rounds are interesting devices, carefully engineered to slaughter people and mangle vehicles with great efficiency and effectiveness. The shell of these weapons is designed to fragment into sharp-edged shards that often look like knife blades. These fragments are scattered at very high velocity across a wide area, and the kind of bomb that dropped on the Kurds is dangerous to over a quarter of a mile.

Strange things can happen when bombs and artillery rounds detonate. Simpson was close to the impact but was only slightly wounded, while the fragments sliced down dozens of others in the area. His translator, Kamaran Abdurazaq Muhamed, who had been standing next to him, had his foot partially amputated and sustained numerous shrapnel wounds. Like Simpson, the cameraman was only lightly injured, and they all took cover in a nearby ditch, thinking the F-14s were coming back for another run.

With the chaos all around him, Simpson quickly switched into his reporter mode and began to report on the incident by telephone back to the BBC, describing the carnage live to millions of British viewers watching the war on the BBC back in the UK.

When Mike first got to the scene, he began operating automatically. His training during the mass casualty exercise conducted during the medic phase of the Q course now kicked in. He quickly found a depression off to the side that provided protection from the bullets cooking off nearby and from the exploding fuel from the vehicles. He grabbed a wounded Kurd and dragged him into the depression.

"This is the CCP [Casualty Collection Point]," he yelled to the rest of the guys. "Start grabbing casualties who are still breathing and bring them over here."

Kenney ran into the mass of burning vehicles, where several Kurds were still trapped inside. He quickly pulled a seriously wounded Kurd from a mangled truck and dragged him over to the CCP. Mike took one look at him, saw gaping chest wounds, clearly mortal injuries, and made a decision. "Throw him over there," Mike yelled to Kenney. "That will be the dead pile!"

"What?" Kenney yelled. "He's still alive!"

"Not for long," Mike informed him. "Throw him in the dead pile."

Kenney complied with Mike's command, dragging the mortally wounded soldier to an area about 20 meters from the CCP. After this brutal introduction to triage, Kenney went back for another casualty. Mike noticed dozens of less-seriously injured Kurds making their way toward his CCP. He quickly yelled to Gerry Kirk, "Gerry, you take charge of the walking wounded. Start an area over there out of the way—that area will be for the routine patients."

Capt. Wright came upon a man who was intact from the waist up but was missing legs and hips, with his intestines spread out on the pavement; he was still conscious and trying to sit up. For a brief moment Eric paused, remembering the scene from *Blackhawk Down* where a Delta operator had met a similar fate. Realizing there was nothing he could do to help him, Eric grabbed another casualty from a nearby burning vehicle and dragged him to Mike's CCP.

Mike was making life-and-death decisions, one after the other, deciding who had a chance to live and who would be allowed to die. It was part of his training and essential if any of the wounded were to be saved.

Eric and Nguyen also dragged casualties to Mike as the morbid process of sorting the casualties continued. When Kenney brought him another casualty, Mike said, "Ken, stay here—I need help!"

"Sure, what do you want me to do?"

"I need tourniquets on this guy's legs," Mike said, pointing to the BBC translator who lay on the ground and tossing Kenney a handful of triangular bandages that have a million uses.

Pointing to another casualty, he told Kenney, "When you get done with him, that guy needs one on his arm." Mike was busy putting on tourniquets as well, trying to stop the precious flow of blood from the severed limbs of what were now about a dozen wounded Kurds in his CCP. Mike applied nine tourniquets in about five minutes, saving the lives of more than half a dozen Kurds in the process.

Then Eric arrived with a "special" casualty being carried by several other Kurds. As they set him down beside Mike, they excitedly mulled around, talking on radios, yelling, and pointing at the casualty on the ground. Mike was unaware of what was going on around him as he concentrated on the casualty's wounds.

The Kurds seem to be getting more and more agitated about this one particular casualty. Eric asked what was going on, and a Kurd pointed at the wounded man and said, "Barzani." Eric immediately realized that the casualty was Wajih Barzani, the regional commander of the Kurds and the brother of Kurdistan Democratic Party (KDP) leader Masoud Barzani and a very important political figure.

As far as the Kurds were concerned, the number-two person in all of Kurdistan was fighting for his life at Mike's feet. Eric leaned over to Mike and offered a bit of advice, "Mike, this guy better not die—he's Barzani's brother."

Mike saw he had several wounds, including a serious head wound. He quickly dressed the wounds, and then turned to his aid bag to get a bag of IV fluid. When he turned back around, Barzani was gone, whisked away by his fellow Kurds to a waiting vehicle to be evacuated. Mike started treating another casualty.

Mike jumped from casualty to casualty, some of whom were still smoldering. The smell of burning diesel fuel and burning human flesh was now starting to become overpowering. For about twenty to thirty minutes, Mike Ray was the only fully qualified Special Forces medic on the scene. In front of him were close to fifteen seriously wounded Kurds; another two dozen less severely injured lay nearby. To his right were the bodies of another dozen Kurds who were already dead. About forty-five survivors owed their lives to his skill and valor in performing just as he had been trained.

THIRTEEN

JAVELIN ACE AND TANK KILL

B ack at the Alamo, we continued to trade rounds with the Iraqis in the intersection below. The Iraqi tankers knew they needed help and called in the heavy artillery from a battery of D-20 towed howitzers that were conveniently headquartered nearby. The first rounds began falling on us while Eric and his split team were dealing with the mass casualty problem back at Rock.

The D-20 is another standard weapon with its origin in the Soviet Union, exported primarily to Third World nations around globe. It fires 152mm projectiles weighing about 100 pounds each for a distance of up to about 10 miles. Howitzers are indirect-fire weapons. Unlike tank guns, they can shoot accurately at targets their gunners cannot see. In this case, we were the targets, and the gunners were shooting at us with the help of somebody down the hill, perhaps one of the tankers, who was adjusting their fire.

An HE (high-explosive) round arrived with the strange moaning sound made by large cylindrical objects moving through the air at high speed, then detonated about 300 meters down the hill and to our left flank. When the mortar team had dropped their first little 60mm rounds on us at about the same distance, we were not very worried, but this 152mm round with one hundred times the explosive force of the 60mms made an entirely different impression.

So far, every time we thought we had solved the enemy problem facing our teams, the Iraqis came up with some new wrinkle. Until now, we really were not worried about the tanks. They could shoot at us all day if they wanted, but their high-velocity guns were strictly line-of-sight weapons, and if we kept our heads down, we thought we would be safe. But the artillery fire changed the problem yet again.

Of course, they had the same idea. Behind the berm, we could not touch them because our Javelins were essentially line-of-sight weapons, too. Even though the missile was capable of a top-down attack, you needed to get a lock first, and the CLU required line of sight to get a missile lock. If the tank was not visible enough for the CLU to get a lock, you could not shoot the missile. While we tried to use close air support to get at them, they were trying to use tube artillery on us. So for a while, as the TACPs were sorting out what had just happened with the Tomcat pilots, the Iraqis were having more luck with their strategy than we were with ours.

The enemy battery's fire-direction center seemed to be quite professional. Their second round, also HE, dropped just 200 meters away with a ground-thumping crash. All of us understood that our life expectancy was suddenly quite short and getting shorter by the second. A third round landed, this time only about 50 meters from Marty. Instead of exploding with a boom, it went *pop* and began emitting clouds of white vapor.

"Time to move," Marty yelled.

"Amen, brother," I yelled back. "Load up the GMVs. Let's go! Let's go! Before we eat the next one!"

Before I could get on the IMBTR and relay to Nine-Two that we were moving, I could see them already loading their GMVs too. There's no way they could have heard me over the noise and the distance, but Capt. Saunders had come to the same conclusion and had already begun yelling the same orders to his guys. As fast as our GMVs would go, we pulled out of the little fortress we had called the Alamo.

Once again the enemy soldiers made a small mistake. It would not have seemed critical to them during training, but it permitted us to live a little longer and keep fighting in a real-world battle. Had that third artillery round been an HE, as it should have been, Marty and others would probably have been dead, our effectiveness as a fighting unit would have been severely impacted, if not destroyed, and the Iraqi tanks could have moved back up the hill to replug the Green Line. Instead, one of the junior members of a gun crew had selected the wrong projectile—he grabbed a smoke projectile instead of an HE—and that smoke round was exactly the small stroke of luck we needed at that moment.

Smoke is used to obscure the battlefield in order to screen movement, to prevent observation, and to allow attacks and withdrawals while the enemy is blind and unable to engage with his direct-fire weapons. It is handy when under attack by artillery to prevent a forward observer from correcting his battery's fire. At exactly the moment that the Iraqis had us at their dubious mercy, some young enemy private made a mistake that cost his force the battle. It was the worst possible event for his force and the best possible one for ours.

Under the cover of the enemy's own smoke, we withdrew under pressure for the second time, back to a defilade battle position that would soon be called Press Hill.

Back at Rock, Eric was running through the burning vehicles, working his way toward the back in search of more casualties, when he noticed a white Range Rover with the windows shattered. Instantly he realized it was one of the 10th Group vehicles, but empty. *Where are the occupants?* he thought to himself. He quickly looked for the characteristic "MICH" helmet of an American among the casualties. As he came around a vehicle that was turned on its side from the blast, he found them. They were treating wounded Kurds off to the side of the road.

Eric ran over and discovered Maj. Howard, commander of ODB-040, and two other members of his B-team. He also noticed that Maj. Howard was wounded.

"You okay, sir?" Eric asked.

"I'll be okay," Howard answered. "Don't worry about me—worry about the Kurds." Eric told him about the casualty collection point that Mike had set up on the far side of the bomb site.

"My medic is over there with a bunch of wounded. If you want, we can carry these guys over there," Eric said.

"Let's do it," Howard answered, and they carried more casualties over to Mike.

Just as they got to Mike's CCP, one of the fuel cans on the back of a burning vehicle exploded, sending a napalmlike wave of burning fuel onto the road. Eric, seeing that there were extra fuel cans on the backs of several other vehicles, realized that if one were to explode close to the CCP, it could literally shower everyone with fuel.

Eric called to Lihn and Rich, "You guys come with me! We've got to get those fuel cans away from those vehicles." Without hesitation Lihn and Rich followed their captain out into the wreckage, pulling fuel can after fuel can from the racks at the rear of the burning vehicles. At any moment one could have exploded, just like the one a few moments earlier. Some of the cans were very hot to the touch, but each of the guys was wearing Nomex flight gloves to protect his hands from burns. They quickly cut the straps holding the fuel cans in their racks with their knives and tossed them off to the side of the road, rendering them harmless.

As we pulled our vehicles to the side of the road after crossing over the top of Press Hill, I was able to see the destruction with my own eyes. It was far worse than I had thought. I ran over to Marty, who was beside Jake; both were setting up the SOFLAM laser designator for a close air support observer position.

Jake had received word that some F/A-18s were inbound with some Paveway laser-guided bombs (LGBs) for another try at the tanks. I asked Marty if he thought he could manage a few minutes without me while I ran to Rock to lend a hand.

"No problem," Marty answered. "I've got everything under control. Jake's about to start spanking the tanks with LGBs. They are not going anywhere—you go ahead and help the captain."

I ran to my vehicle to grab my aid bag from the back. Bobby asked where I was going. "Up to Rock," I said.

"I'm coming with you!" he yelled, scrambling for one of the Combat Lifesaver bags.

"I've got it, Bobby. You stay here."

"Nope," he countered. "I gotta take care of my 'Ranger buddy'!* Besides, I'm almost out of 40mm ammo, and I could get some off of Kenney's vehicle." Bobby was right; you never leave your "wingman." I told Steve to go help Marty and Jake, and to let Marty know I was taking Bobby with me. Bobby and I were running toward the mass of burning vehicles when Bobby once again showed remarkable wisdom for a rookie Green Beret.

"Frank, why don't we swing by Nine-Two and pick up Gino?"

"Good call, Bobby," I said, realizing that we could really use him. We ran over to Nine-Two's position, loaded down with first-aid gear.

When we got there, I found Ken Thompson.

"Ken, Bobby and I are going up to Rock to help with the casualties. Can you spare Gino?"

"Sure," Ken replied. "How many casualties do they have up there?"

"Thirty or forty," I answered.

"I'm coming too, then," said Ken. Jeff Adamec, who was listening to our conversation, then asked if he could go as well. Prior to becoming a weapons man, Jeff was a conventional infantry medic. Ken told him to grab an aid bag and follow us. We all started running.

The first casualty I encountered was a cameraman from the BBC. He was sitting by the side of the road, his face covered in blood from a shrapnel wound. "Where are you hit?" I asked.

"My face!" he said.

"Is that it?" I asked, quickly scanning him from head to toe for other wounds. "You're not hit anywhere else?"

"No, that's all," he said. I reached into my aid bag and grabbed a roll of Curlex, ripping it from its wrapper. "Hold this against the wound," I told him, and he did. I closed my aid bag and moved toward the area of the greatest damage, 50 meters farther on.

---

*A "Ranger Buddy" is the term for each soldier's backup or "partner" who goes everywhere with him. No individual US warrior goes anywhere on the battlefield alone.

As I got closer to the scene, I could not believe what I was seeing. It was obvious that Eric and the other guys had been fighting a different battle for the past half hour. The road was littered with bodies and parts of bodies and with puddles of blood and gore. I saw a foot without a boot on the pavement. Farther on there was a hand, then bits and pieces of formless tissue lying where they had splattered at the moment of explosion. Then, in the middle of the intersection, there was somebody's brain, perfectly intact and seemingly undamaged.

When we arrived at the CCP, Mike had eight or nine men laid out, at various stages of treatment. Some were yelling, others moaning. But most of the triage had been completed: the people on the dead pile had died, the people on the treatment pile were getting treated, and the Kurds were busy loading wounded onto the backs of trucks. When I saw the dead pile, I realized where the owners of those parts I'd stepped over ended up.

Gino teamed up with Mike, and both were now working on the most seriously wounded. Even though Bobby wasn't a medic, he wasn't fazed by the blood and gore. He jumped right in helping the other two medics.

"I'm going to sweep the objective for any remaining casualties," I told them, and walked off to search the area.

Over at the edge of the carnage was a white pickup truck with Tom Sandoval's company commander and the two other members of Four-Four. Maj. Howard still had not gotten his wounds treated and continued to insist he would do so only after all the other wounded were taken care of. He was coordinating the evacuation of the Kurd casualties and trying to keep the remaining uninjured Kurds under control. I walked over to the truck, where I found the two other injured members of Howard's headquarters element. One had a ruptured eardrum, the other a nosebleed, but they were otherwise unhurt. I found a few Kurds who had been injured slightly, but who had not been treated yet, and brought them over to the casualty collection point.

All the casualties had been pulled from within and around the burning vehicles. Mike Ray now had enough help to have things under control. Sixteen Kurds had been killed, forty-five wounded, some severely, but the death toll would have been far higher without the presence of Mike and so many other skilled SF soldiers. The severely wounded BBC translator would die a few hours later at the hospital in Irbil, bringing the death toll to seventeen.

When it was finally over, Mike stood up, covered with blood. He had gone through all the supplies in his own aid bag and the bags of several others. Bobby handed him a bottle of water, and Mike started walking back to his GMV along with the rest of his split team and went back to the fight.

Even with all the casualties evacuated, this was still a critical moment. If our guys were counterattacked by enemy reinforcements, they were vulnerable. They had been fighting for almost two hours; some of them had been fighting to save the lives of others. As the Kurds loaded the last of their dead and wounded on their trucks and headed back to Irbil, I could see some of my guys just wandering around. They had lost their focus on the battle, were dehydrated, and were physically and emotionally exhausted.

Matt Saunders, who had seen the tempo slowing from his position on Press Hill, ran over and told some of his guys, "Hey, we aren't done yet—let's get back to the fight." I started doing the same and went looking for Eric and the others who had been working on the Kurds. The sound of firing could be heard from the machine guns and Mk19s down the hill. It was time to get ready for another attack.

JASON BROWN, JAVELIN ACE

Press Hill was close enough to Rock that Jason also ran over to get more missile reloads from Eric's Humvee. As I saw him pulling the missile tubes out of the back, I grabbed Lihn, our other weapons guy, and said, "Come on, it's your turn to kill some armor." We both started running toward Jason.

As we reached the back of the captain's vehicle, Jason had just jumped from the bed of the vehicle onto the roadway. He was picking up the missiles he had leaned against the side of the vehicle when I interrupted him.

"Thanks, Jay—Lihn and I get these. You've already lobbed enough—time to let your 'junior' get in some licks." Jason gave me a tired look as we grabbed the two missiles out of his hands and headed to the top of Press Hill. So far Jason was three-out-of-four for the day—he had killed a truck and two APCs already, but he still could not resist the chance to shoot more. Although I had "stolen" two missiles from him, he knew that there were still two more in Gerry's vehicle about 50 meters farther back. While Lihn and I went off with our two Javelins, Jay quickly made a beeline for the other GMV. Since these were our last four missiles until the B-team could get us resupplied, we needed to make them count. Nine-Two probably had two or three left as well, and Four-Four only had one. There were still four T-55s down there without a scratch, and at least three more APCs. With about eight missiles left, we could only afford a single miss.

As Lihn and I made it to the top of Press Hill, I noticed that from this higher angle we could see more of the T-55s. "Lihn, see the tank just to the left of the roundabout?" I pointed to one of the tanks that were still shooting shells at us. "That one looks like the most exposed. See if you can get a lock and smoke it!"

"I got it," Lihn said, as he attached one of our two missiles to the CLU. Sitting down into a good firing position, Lihn went through the firing sequence as I watched. He searched through the CLU for the tank I had pointed out to him. As he sweetened up his track gates on his target, Lihn said, "I'm going to shoot!" with obvious excitement.

This was Lihn's first missile shot, and for a new 18B hot out of the Q course, it was the chance of a lifetime. As he squeezed the trigger, the missile left the tube with a pop and then a whoosh as it headed upward into the sky. I pulled my binos up to my eyes and trained them on the tank, at any moment expecting it to explode in a fireball.

I heard the missile explode as it hit the target, but for some reason I didn't see it. The tank was still there, next to the intersection. As I put the binos down and scanned the battlefield, I immediately saw where Lihn's missile had gone. The warhead scored a perfect and dramatic hit on the large concrete monument to Saddam in the traffic circle down at the intersection, blasting concrete chunks and dust in all directions. I heard cheers from the other guys on the hill as they sarcastically critiqued Lihn's missile shot.

"What the fuck, Lihn?" I said. "That's not a tank!"

He looked at me, puzzled. "Frank, I swear I locked on the tank—I don't know what happened."

"You shot a slab of concrete, that's what happened," I snapped at him, a little upset he had wasted a missile. "Give me the CLU—my turn," I told him.

Finally, I had a chance to shoot. Most of the team sergeant's job involves managing the work of the younger sergeants, keeping them pointed in the right direction and working as a team to execute the commander's intent. My job, on and off the battlefield, is more or less that of mid-level manager. But finally things had slowed down a little on Press Hill, and now I had a chance to use the Javelin myself.

I grabbed our remaining missile and mated it to the CLU and trained its sights on the same tank I pointed out to Lihn. As I fired the BCU and tried to get a good lock on the tanks, I realized how difficult a time Lihn had. Squeezing the left trigger several times trying to get a lock, time and time again I got an indication that the missile just couldn't see enough of the tank to get a good firing solution. According to the training from Jason, I only had about two minutes to get a lock and shoot before the missile would be useless. I dropped the CLU and missile into my lap and quickly scanned the battlefield for another target. Off to the right, actually on Nine-Two's side of the road, I saw an MTLB literally driving in a circle. At first I thought that someone might have gotten a lucky hit on the driver and that the vehicle was now a runaway, but then it would make occasional small turns left and right, as if it was avoiding something in the tall grass. It was obvious that it was still under human control. I raised the CLU, found the target easily, closed the track gates down, got a good lock, and fired.

The missile shot into the sky. Seconds later it impacted directly into the top of the Iraqi APC, with dramatic results. First, all the hatches blew open from the tremendous pressure created as the warhead penetrated the vehicle. Some of these hatches must have been unlocked because I saw some of the soldiers blown out, stunned but alive. If the hatches had been secured, the soldiers would have died instantly from the sudden rise in pressure. The survivors struggled to escape, but as they did, the ground around them erupted as the combined fire of four .50cal machine guns found the range and chopped them down.

Only an hour earlier, Jason had been begging me to let him shoot a Javelin. He was worried then that the war would be over before any of us had a chance to put all our training to work. He had whined that he would never get to actually launch a missile. In the hour since, Jason's world had become one missile shot after another, and we had been in continuous combat nearly all that time. After snagging the last two Javelins from Gerry's GMV, Jason ran up the steep slope to the crest of our new position and began searching for targets. He and the rest of us were really worried about the tanks. They were, so far, unscathed, but until they would expose themselves to our fire, Jason was willing to destroy any other mobile target with a juicy heat signature in the CLU.

One of the armored personnel carriers made the tactical error of dashing across the wheat field in what looked like an attempt to escape. Jason sent his fifth Javelin after it and was already reloading when the MTLB was smacked by the warhead. Almost immediately, Jason spotted another truck trying to bring reinforcements forward. He locked onto it with the CLU and sent his sixth Javelin downrange. About fifteen seconds later, the truck was engulfed by a fireball as the heat-seeking guidance system once again homed in on the vehicle's engine and punched its small projectile downward.

None of us gave this shot much thought at the time, although the continued success of the Javelin was a real revelation for most of the team. Jason had fired six of the missiles and scored kills with five of them, three on MTLBs and two on trucks, plus one that disappeared into the haze and missed. Later those five kills would make Jason somewhat famous as the first "Javelin ace."

Jason deserved the praise. Not only had he been a strong advocate for the weapon during training, he had validated the missile with his first, almost impossible kill of the troop truck. Without Jason's confidence in the missile, we might not have fought the battle in the way we did. He had a lot to do with our success in the fight.

Jake, Todd, and Saleem were not having much success against the tanks with the CAS. They tried to have the Navy drop a couple dumb bombs onto the tanks, but the bombs landed nearby and were ineffective. Unless hit directly, the tanks would continue to fire at us.

Even when F-18s showed up with the LGBs, we had trouble. Using the SOFLAM to laser-designate for the bombs seemed like a sure thing. Unfortunately, the tanks still didn't present much of a target because they were still in defilade, with only the top of the turret with its DShK machine gun and main gun exposed. When Jake would try to lase them, a lot of the laser energy would go over the tank and illuminate the grass 100 meters behind it. The bombs simply followed the laser beam, impacting harmlessly into the ground. When Jake would try to compensate for this and aim the laser a little lower, the bombs would impact on the road in front of the tanks. Jake made the call for some cluster munitions, hoping they would do the trick, but it would be some time before they got there.

ERIC STRIGOTTE'S TANK KILL

Up to this point, the enemy tankers had been fighting with the most skill and discipline of any Third World army we had ever encountered. As a result, the Iraqis had lost none of their T-55s and were able to call in artillery onto our little hiding places. Their gunnery, happily for us, was poor. But this platoon seemed to be commanded by a guy who kept his head even when all his nearby supporting infantry was getting hammered.

The tanks with their direct-fire guns, in combination with the enemy artillery providing support, were dangerous to our little force in two ways. They had the capability to destroy our probe into enemy territory and, in the long term, to plug the little hole we had found in the Green Line long enough to give the rest of the huge enemy forces nearby time to counterattack. One of Tom Sandoval's young sergeants, Eric Strigotte, happily changed that capability, and the stalemate we had reached with the tanks ended with the impact of a single round.

For a reason we will never know, one of the four tanks pulled out from behind the berm and began a dash across Highway 2. We had all been waiting for the T-55 platoon to make a move of some sort, or perhaps to surrender, but so far we had waited in vain. Eric put his third and last Javelin of the day in the air within moments after the T-55 pulled out.

The tank did not get far. We had all been impressed with the ability of the missile to inflict a lethal blow on the trucks and APCs, but had our doubts about how it would do against a main battle tank. Eric's shot fully converted us all. The warhead fired directly over the main gun tube, just in front of the turret, and cut a hole about an inch in diameter that penetrated the tube itself, detonating the 100mm HE projectile inside. The explosion blew out the tank gun's breechblock, venting the resultant gases into the turret and popping the hatches open.

The crew died instantly from the overpressure. The tank coasted to a stop. Even from our position about a mile away, we could hear ammunition in the hull begin to cook off with little popping sounds as components inside the turret caught fire. Within a minute or so, the main gun rounds ignited, and flames roared from the hatches with blowtorch intensity to 25 feet in the air.

Until now, every surviving enemy soldier on the battlefield, from the commander to the privates, could look at the tanks and have good reason for hope. We had not been able to touch them. The tanks had pushed us up the road, back the way we had come, and an enemy optimist might think that we were being destroyed. Now one brave, daring tanker had attempted to continue the counterattack and had been quickly killed for his valor. Eric Strigotte's missile shot was another tipping point in the fight, and the standoff was broken.

BAATH PARTY ENFORCERS

From the perspective of the enemy soldiers on the battlefield, this was what we call ENDEX, or "end of exercise." They were finished. Their will to fight, their discipline, and their courage had been good at the beginning and had held up fairly well during the battle. They had surprised us and pushed us back several times. If their gunnery had been as good as their tactics, we might easily have been destroyed.

The enemy commander had begun his counterattack at about 1040 hours local time with the imaginative ruse of hiding behind the troop trucks and approaching our roadblock on the intersection. At that time, he had a reinforced, company-size mechanized infantry task force with four tanks, eight APCs, three troop transports, and about 150 infantry soldiers. Now, at about 1215, we had killed seven of the MTLBs, all three trucks, and the only T-55 tank brave enough to maneuver against us. At least 50, and probably more, infantry soldiers lay dead in and around their trucks and APCs. The commander was probably killed in that tank because after Eric's shot, organized resistance ceased.

At 1245 hours, about 15 enemy soldiers appeared from a ravine, waving white pieces of paper, clearly surrendering. We immediately called a cease-fire, and a sudden silence descended on the battlefield. Mike Foss from Nine-Two carefully watched the group as they walked out of their positions and up the road in our direction. Because of the intel reports we had heard a day earlier describing the use of apparent surrenders to lure American units into ambushes, we kept our weapons trained on the group and motioned them to walk up the road to us.

We called a quick meeting of the team leadership and the Kurd commander. But as we were discussing how we were going to handle the surrender and how far we would let them come up the road before we sent the Kurds down to get them, an unimaginable chain of events took place.

With their hands in the air, and with the pieces of paper fluttering in the wind, the Iraqi soldiers all started to make their way up the road. They had not walked more than 20 meters before two white Toyota Land Cruiser SUVs came out of the haze and drove into the intersection.

While most of us were starting to relax a little and were still discussing how to handle the surrender, Mike Foss yelled over to us, "They're shooting them!" Mike watched in disbelief as half a dozen men dressed in long white robes and armed with AKs and pistols got out of the SUVs, then walked up to the soldiers in what was obviously some sort of confrontation. The soldiers, of course, were unarmed and defenseless. The leader of the men in white robes approached one of the soldiers and slapped him in the face. Then Mike saw him raise a pistol and shoot the man in the head. The rest of the group was then murdered before our eyes. Using their AKs, the remaining men systematically cut down the rest of the surrendering soldiers in several bursts of automatic gunfire. We all stood there in amazement in the same way we did when the armor had first appeared.

"What are we going to do?" Mike Foss demanded as we watched the men drop and heard the distant popping of the AKs. There was nothing we could do to stop the murders—we were too far away for that. Within just a few seconds, all the surrendering troops lay dead on the pavement. The guys in the white robes stood over them, talking.

Marty and Jake watched this evolve, and they quickly decided to impose some battlefield justice and deliver retribution on the enforcers. Jake made a call on his CAS net and almost immediately had an aircraft overhead with a laser-guided bomb. Jake quickly passed the laser code and gave the command "cleared hot!", while Marty lased one of the enforcers' SUVs on the highway with the SOFLAM laser designator.

The bomb struck dead center on the group with a tremendous flash and bang. When the smoke and dust cleared, the highway was clean and empty, and the murdered enemy soldiers, their assassins, and the SUVs were all gone. It was like someone had just taken a giant eraser and wiped them away.

The enforcers did have one effect. They motivated the remaining tankers and infantry to start fighting again. Within seconds, one of the remaining tanks lobbed a 100mm shell our way, letting us know this was far from over. With only three Javelins left, we decided to let Jake, Todd, and Saleem continue to try to kill the remaining tanks with CAS. Kenney Wilson and Bobby, as well as the guys from Nine-Two, got back behind their Mk19s and started lobbing a few 40mm rounds toward the enemy, letting them know we were still up on the hill and had no intention of leaving.

FOURTEEN

CHAOS ON ROCK

At this point, we had fired sixteen of the nineteen Javelin missiles that were included in our basic load when we left the MSS. Three-Nine-One and Four-Four had fired all of their missiles; Nine-Two still had three. Bobby, Andy, and the other gunners had burned through about two-thirds of our .50cal and 40mm ammunition. Considering the sort of forces that were supposedly still out there, somewhere in the valley, and based on the nature of the battle we just fought, we were in pretty bad shape, ammowise and missilewise. If another counterattack came, we'd be unable to duplicate what we had done earlier.

Just as I was telling my guys to hold off on expending any more ammo, I saw a Javelin missile leave, fired from the top of the ridge. I watched as the missile slammed into a mud hut next to one of the remaining tanks, converting its sun-baked walls into dust. Not knowing who had fired the missile, I ran down the ridge toward their position.

"Who the fuck fired that missile!" I yelled. As the group turned toward me, I could see the gunner sitting on the ground. As he lowered the CLU, I saw that it was Jeff Adamec. Jeff didn't belong to me, he was Ken's, but I had already committed myself by losing my temper, so I continued to let him have it.

"What the fuck, Jeff? Now we only have two missiles left. What do we do if more tanks come—throw rocks at them?"

Ken and Capt. Saunders probably thought I was out of line yelling at one of their teammates, and they were right. But no one knew how long we would have to wait for resupply, or worse yet, how long we would have to hold the hill.

"I'm sorry, Frank, I thought I could get him," Jeff answered.

"Okay, but from now on, let the TACPs try to kill them with some bombs," I told him, sounding a bit apologetic and hoping Ken and Capt. Saunders would let it slide. They did. We could occasionally see some AK fire, and every once in a while one of the tanks would lob a shell. Now we all found a front-row seat to watch the TACPs do their thing.

MORNING AT FORT BRAGG

Back at Fort Bragg North Carolina, it was about 5:30 A.M. Maj. Gen. Geoff Lambert, commander of Army Special Forces Command, was sitting at his breakfast table, drinking a cup of coffee and watching Fox News to see how things were going in Iraq. At the bottom of the screen, Fox would scroll news headlines while the anchor on the screen interviewed "experts" to get their take on what was happening.

What the general saw across the screen next made his heart sink. "BBC Reports twelve American Special Forces killed in apparent accidental bombing in northern Iraq." In the chaos, John Simpson had reported to the BBC that American Special Forces were among the casualties. Lambert began flipping through the news channels, trying to find out more. When he got to CNN, he saw the images of the burning Kurd vehicles and the T-55 tank that we had tagged earlier in the day, just off to the side. On the tank, he could clearly see "Roughneck 91."

Lambert knew it was the call sign of an ODA and thought the worst. Did he just lose a whole A-team? He quickly grabbed his secure phone and called the EOC, or Emergency Operations Center, located in the basement of the Headquarters for Army Special Operations Command. When the officer on the other end answered, Lambert inquired about the report. "Did we loose twelve guys this morning in

Iraq?" "Not that I'm aware of, sir," replied the officer on the other end. "The BBC is saying we lost some guys, and CNN is showing burning vehicles and saying dozens were killed and wounded," Lambert declared. "I need you to find out what happened; I'm on my way in."

Maj. Gen. Lambert lived on post and was only a few minutes' drive from USASOC headquarters.

The EOC immediately called the JSOTF in northern Iraq on the SATCOM. Within seconds, the JSOTF was calling for Eric Wright on his SATCOM in his GMV. Eric answered the radio. On the other end, the voice demanded to know if there were any American fatalities from the bombing. Eric answered with a simple "NEGATIVE, NEGATIVE, no fatalities."

By the time Maj. Gen. Lambert got to headquarters at USAOC, his answer was waiting. "Sir, the media got it wrong; we didn't lose anyone. Some teams from 3rd Group were close by, but the JSOTF confirms all of our guys are fine." Lambert's next thought was, *Oh my God, the wives! They'll all be getting up soon to get the kids ready for school, and they'll almost certainly be watching the news.* "Get me the 3rd Group duty officer," he ordered. "We need to get word to the wives that the report is bogus."

Within a few minutes, phone calls were going out through the Family Readiness Group (FRG), a network of wives set up to keep the spouses informed while their husbands were deployed. Lambert's preemptive strike on the rumor of American casualties had averted what was sure to be a hail of calls from wives demanding to know if their husbands were okay.

THE CAVALRY ARRIVES

About this time back in Iraq, early in the afternoon, the B-team rolled in with their big resupply trucks. It could not have been a better time. We saw the huge modified FMTVs of the B-team, aptly nicknamed "Mother" and "Mad Max" after their size and numerous modifications, which made them look like Mel Gibson should be driving them in a movie.

Kenney's suggestion to blow a route through the pile of dirt on the road behind us had resulted in one of the best decisions of the day, even if it did enable the media to reach our position. Opening the road had allowed rapid evacuation of the wounded Kurds, and now our support element was able to move up with fresh ammunition and missile reloads.

Jimmy Adams was with our company commander, Maj. X, as they drove through the carnage, which was still being cleaned up, and both of them were shocked by the blood and gore that littered the road and by the piles of shredded vehicles. Most of us in Special Forces have been conditioned to deal with death and dying. We try to recover quickly from such surprises and to get on with our missions, but sometimes even Green Berets find themselves stunned by unexpected disaster. Our commander seemed to be staggered by the extent of the death and injury at Rock. Members of the detachment noticed that Maj. X appeared deeply troubled by the disaster, even though it was being cleaned up by the time the B-team arrived.

For those of us in our battle positions 200 meters down the hill, worrying about the fratricide incident was a luxury that would have to wait. We still had a fight with tanks, artillery, and an unknown number of infantry. The Iraqis' organization and discipline appeared to be destroyed, but they were not retreating, and they were not surrendering. As long as they resisted, the route across the Green Line that Col. Cleveland needed in order to allow follow-on forces to use for their assault on Kirkuk was still plugged.

As Mad Max pulled up behind my GMV, I could see about eight Javelin tubes strapped to the back. Maj. X, Pat Rotsert, and Jimmy Adams pulled up in their GMV. Jimmy, manning the .50cal, casually asked, "I hear you guys have been having a little fun up here—can we play?"

"Yeah, you sure can . . . if you give up those Javelin missiles," I told him.

Jimmy perked up at the idea. "Why? Are there any tanks left?"

"Three, but we can't get them; they are hiding in defilade."

"Let me give it a shot," Jimmy said as he jumped out from behind his .50 cal.

"You're welcome to try, but we've already wasted two missiles on them," I told him.

While Jimmy dug out his CLU and a missile, I went looking for the B-team Ops sergeant, Keith Nann. "How many missiles do you guys have?"

"Just eight," he replied. "We resupplied Nine-Four and Nine-Five with a couple already. How many do you guys need?"

"Seventeen, minimum!"

"Damn Frank, that's a lot," Keith said.

"I know," I told him, "but we already fired those seventeen, and if these guys counterattack, we're gonna need them." Keith agreed, but told me he didn't think there were any more back at the FOB.

"I'm gonna let Jimmy shoot one; then I'll give you these seven. I'll try to go back to the FOB and find some more."

"Sounds fair," I replied. "How's the rest of the fight going?"

What Keith said amazed me. "Pretty much every team is engaged, all up and down the Green Line. The 10th Group guys are pushing toward Mosul. They just took Witch Mountain and are bombing the crap out of the Iraqis with B-52s." Witch Mountain was a key piece of terrain that the Iraqis covered with ADA (Air Defense Artillery) and communications equipment, and controlling it would be a significant accomplishment.

Jimmy Adams ran past us with his Javelin. We followed him to the crest of the hill. Amazed, we watched as the remaining MTLBs started moving again.

"Jimmy! That APC's moving! Take it out!" yelled one of the B-team guys. This was Jimmy's first time shooting the Javelin, but his training kicked in, and he set it up quickly.

Jimmy sat on the ground, energized the BCU on his missile, locked onto the MTLB, and let the missile fly. Just seconds earlier, the APC became a threat. Then Jimmy brought it to a stop with a resounding smack as his Javelin slammed into the top of the vehicle.

With the destruction of the final MTLB, the fight entered a new phase. Now we had two full A-teams, one B-team, and half of another A-team engaged with the remnants of the enemy task force. Behind us, the road was clear for resupply and reinforcement, and it was clear for the 173rd, if they wanted to use it. It was time to replace all the ammunition and fuel we'd expended, and the guys who were not firing up the enemy got to work hauling fresh ammo and diesel.

Jason oversaw the resupply, ensuring that all the ammo was cross-leveled among all four vehicles. We took four Javelins and gave two to Nine-Two, bringing their total to four as well. The one remaining went to Four-Four. Keith took off to look for more missiles with half the B-team in one of their FMTVs and a GMV, leaving the remainder of his team and their FMTV and GMV with us on Press Hill.

The team leadership and Maj. X gathered for a quick conference of war. Maj. X was quickly brought up to speed by Tom, Eric, and Capt. Saunders. We all knew what should be done. First, a couple of Javelin gunners needed to move forward and to the right in order to get flank shots at the tanks still hiding behind the highway, and Maj. X approved of this maneuver.

After the quick conference, we decided to move forward and spread out to reduce the target for Iraqi artillery and to cover our extreme right and left flanks. Nine-Two placed a pair of their GMVs about 500 meters down the road to Debecka to ensure that the enemy did not try to sneak up that way. The other two were moved about 100 meters forward of Press Hill to bring them on line with ours. Tom and his guys continued to deal with the Kurds, keeping them motivated to fight on, even after the tragedy that occurred at Rock.

At the same time, Sgt. Maj. Joe Ward was busy just behind Press Hill, setting up the 60mm mortar carried by the B-team. The mortar was the perfect weapon for engaging the enemy infantry, and Joe Ward was the perfect mortar gunner; he had trained on the weapon when he went through the Q course many moons ago. Over the years since, he had become an artist with it and could make the tube perform magic on command.

Eric's two GMVs were off to the right of the road and mine was on the left. A pipeline road offered the enemy a high-speed route for a flanking attack from the right, if they wanted to make one, so I peeled off my half of the team and sent them down the road to provide a bit of a buffer in an emergency.

ATTACK OF THE NEWS MEDIA

Then we had a sort of emergency, but one we were not expecting—hordes of media people. They started arriving in SUVs, six or seven vehicles, one after another, drawn in first by the false report of the Kurd capture of Debecka, then by the reports from John Simpson about the bomb strike.

By the time they arrived, the bomb strike mess was pretty well cleaned up, and we seemed to be the only entertainment available. They noticed our GMVs and moved down to swarm around us. The Arab-speaking reporters swarmed the Kurds, and the English-speaking reporters swarmed us, all of them wanting an interview. Most of them wore body armor, and some had bodyguards. One of them came over to introduce himself as an ex–British Special Air Service member and then asked if I would take time to be interviewed by the reporter he was protecting, Jane Arraf from CNN. I found it kind of funny that he tried the "secret handshake" with me, thinking his SOF (Special Operations Forces) background would somehow convince me to concede an interview.

"Look, my battalion commander explicitly told us not to talk to the media," I told him. "Besides, can't you see we're still a bit busy right now?"

"Two minutes is all she needs," he answered back.

"No, and that's it!" I said firmly in return.

Not more than thirty seconds later, I heard a female voice behind me. "What's going on?" Arraf asked.

"Look, I am not talking to you," I told her. "We're busy! Get away from me!"

She walked alongside me, insisting, "Just two minutes! Only two minutes!" She tried the same thing with other guys, with the same result. Most of the reporters were likewise, seemingly oblivious to the dangerous situation and to anything except their own requirements.

"Let's go forward again," I told my guys so we could get away from them. We moved again, this time about 400 meters down the slope from the spot we started calling Press Hill. Most of the reporters stayed on the hill, but not all. As I was positioning the vehicles, I heard a female voice and turned around to discover Arraf, her bodyguard, and her cameraman.

"Can you tell me what happened?" she asked.

There was something disarming about her—I wouldn't say she was a knockout beauty, but she was cute and seemed very tiny inside her body armor. Her hair was nicely done, and unlike the other reporters, she was not wearing a helmet. None of us had been around a Western woman for quite a while, and to be talking to one, complete with makeup, right on the battlefield, was extremely odd. Even so, I told her to get out of our position.

"Just two minutes," she pleaded again.

"*No!*" I told her again. There was still a fight going on.

While Eric Strigotte's tank kill had apparently ended any kind of organized resistance, the execution of the Iraqi soldiers on the road put a little backbone into the survivors. Most of them were pinned down behind the road. Occasionally one would make a dash for a new position. The remaining three T-55s continued to fire main gun rounds at us whenever we gave them a target.

We also received sporadic artillery fire, with most of the rounds flying well overhead or landing far off to our left. Tank rounds were exploding occasionally nearby, and my guys continued to engage any of the dismounted infantry who emerged from their cover and concealment. I ran about 100 meters over to the other side of the road, where Marty and his two GMVs were covering their sector.

As I was about to confer with Marty, I heard a voice behind me saying, "Can you please tell us what happened?" It was Jane Arraf again.

"Please leave me alone," I told her, but she kept pestering me for another five or ten minutes. Now I was getting mad, and I yelled at her, "Look! Get away from me! I am not talking to you!" Prior to this she had been doing a "stand-up" with the battlefield in the background and the camera set up on a tripod just to the rear of our battle position. Her cameraman got the idea that we did not want to talk, and he picked up his camera and tripod and began to move away.

I turned around and headed back to talk to Marty, thinking to myself, *Well, she's Marty's problem now.* I was wrong about that, though—she followed me again and kept asking the same damn question. I was able to deflect her again, and then she, her cameraman, and her bodyguard tried the same thing with Marty, Maj. X, and anybody else who would take any notice of her. They were more successful in avoiding her.

Finally, during a short lull I surrendered. "Okay, will you shut up and leave me alone if I tell you what happened?"

"Yes," she said. "Tell me what happened up there," meaning at the bomb site.

"No, I am not going to tell you anything about that, but I will tell you about the battle down here."

"Okay," she said. Her cameraman quickly set up, and she did a short interview with me showing the battlefield in the distance. I gave her a very quick summary of the battle—about shutting down the highway, our battle with the tanks, and what we had done with the Javelins, but with as little detail as possible.

"Can you tell us about what happened with the friendly bombing up on the hill?" she asked with the camera rolling, despite what I told her before the interview. This made me mad, but with the camera rolling I didn't think I should get too tough with her. I simply stated that I was busy with the tank fight and did not really know what happened.

When I was done with the summary, she asked, "What's your name?"

"I can't tell you," I said, and got back to work. Up and down the skirmish line, other guys were being pestered by reporters in similar ways. We could deal with the enemy, but somehow we didn't have a way to repel an assault by these reporters.

Marty and I looked across the battlefield, littered with burning vehicles and dead Iraqis. I knew there were probably another fifty to seventy-five Iraqis down there somewhere, and it bothered me.

"Marty, there are still a lot of them hiding down there; we need to clear that intersection and those tanks before it gets dark."

"I know. I'd hate to see it get dark and have them escape," Marty added.

"Not just that," I said. "I'd hate to see them get reinforced and try to hit us again after dark. What do you think we should do?"

"I know what we need to do," Marty stated. "We need to take out those tanks."

I used my IMBTR radio, turning it to the company battle frequency to call over to Nine-Two, who were across the road. Rob Parker answered, and I said, "Can you guys come over here? We're going to do a real quick leadership meeting. We need to talk about going down the hill and clearing the objective."

Maj. X overheard the call to Rob on his IMBTR and didn't like what he had heard. "Wait a minute," he responded. "What do you mean, you're going to clear the objective? You said you were just going to take out those tanks."

"Yes, sir," I replied. "We're going to go get that armor, and then we will sweep the objective."

"Wait a minute," he said. "Everybody come back to my position." We complied, with Eric, Marty, and me getting to the major first. I waited until the guys from Nine-Two showed up before saying anything more. They arrived quickly—Matt Saunders, Rob Parker, and Ken Thompson. Sgt. Maj. Ward also joined in on the huddle while the other guys fired an occasional burst from their battle positions. We were concerned that the media people were listening in over our shoulders—an extremely odd situation for folks in our business.

Matt came over and asked Eric, "What are you guys going to do?"

"We're going to go down there and take the objective," Capt. Wright answered.

Before Capt. Saunders could respond, Maj. X said, "Wait a minute. Nobody is going down there, and nobody is taking any objective!"

We couldn't believe this. "What do you mean, sir, 'Nobody is taking any objective'?" Marty asked.

"Hold on a minute—we're not done yet."

"I know we're not done, sir. We're going to soften them up some more, drop more bombs on them, and get the tanks from a better position," I told him. "But eventually we have to go down there and clear the objective."

This was a seriously strange conversation. It got stranger, and here is the reason. The US Army conducts combat operations in ways that are formalized and almost ritualistic and that are codified in our doctrine. Everything US Army units do during real-world combat is driven by our basic doctrine, and every soldier begins studying this doctrine in Basic Training. The doctrine keeps everybody pretty much on the same proverbial sheet of music no matter what is happening in a battle. Commanders at all levels are permitted some flexibility, but always with the goal of completing an assigned mission while preserving "combat power." Our mission, assigned by our battalion commander, was to find a way for the 173rd Airborne Brigade to cross the Green Line. We had almost, but not quite, completed that mission.

Army doctrine is explicit about the way Army units conduct battle, and we had followed that doctrine by using our mobility and our firepower to engage and destroy a far superior enemy by what the Army calls "attrition"—the gradual grinding process that takes out the enemy's combat power, one bite at a time. ODA-391 had been training for this mission and studying the Army doctrine that made it possible since the team was reformed nine months earlier.

The discussions we had with Lt. Col. Binford and Col. Cleveland about how we would conduct ourselves in battle were in the context of doctrine. Those discussions concerned "actions on contact," or how we would react when an enemy force was initially encountered. We had not discussed how we would finish a fight, but we were arguing about that now, and with our own company commander.

Until Maj. X arrived, Eric and Matt were the tactical commanders and had the authority and responsibility for the conduct of the fight. Although they consulted their warrant officers and team sergeants on what we were doing (and we'd give them our opinions even if they didn't ask for them), their heads would have rolled, not ours, if the enemy had prevailed in our fight. But Maj. X was now clearly the tactical commander, and Matt and Eric, along with the rest of us, were required to defer to his judgment and follow his orders. In essence, standard Army doctrine specified that we had some chores to do now that we had been resupplied and reinforced. It was the local tactical commander's responsibility to insure completion of the mission by destroying the enemy, either by killing them or by their surrender. Until the enemy forces were either dead or disarmed, they remained a threat to not only us but to the entire force and the Northern Safari mission. There are basically five phases for attacking a strong point: *recon* the objective and develop the concept of the operation; *move* to the objective; *isolate* the objective and select a breach site; *attack* and secure a foothold; and lastly, *exploit* the penetration and *clear the objective*.

Everything we had ever been taught told us that now was the time to finish them off, sweep the objective, consolidate it, and get ready for the follow-on forces coming behind us. We knew there were many wounded enemy down there who were suffering and who could be treated once surrender was accomplished. We knew that there were survivors down there who could be interrogated for information about enemy forces and enemy intentions. We knew there were surely maps and documents that could be used to identify the locations and intentions of enemy forces.

We also knew that now was the time for the tactical commander to drive on, and for some mysterious reason, that was not happening. Maj. X seemed to think that this sporadic exchange of fire was far more dangerous than the rest of us did. After the intensity of combat in the morning, this sort of exchange seemed almost peaceful and quiet from our perspective. Perhaps because of seeing the carnage or perhaps by nature, Maj. X seemed to be having trouble deciding what we should do.

"Hold on! Don't go anywhere," the major ordered. The enemy tanks continued to fire occasional main gun rounds at us, their artillery continued to drop 152mm rounds on us, and we continued to return fire to keep their heads down with our .50cal machine guns and Mk19s. But the stalemate continued. As long we were standing around, we were at risk of being overrun and defeated by a counterattack. We were also at risk that a lucky round would find us.

"Sir," I said, "the sergeant major has the mortar set up, and he can cover the intersection. He has plenty of range with the mortar and can cover our movement easily. We have two full A-teams, half of another, and the full B-team—forty-five Americans, and about forty Kurds, too. Let's get a plan together so we can go down there to finish those guys off before they get reorganized and reinforced."

"Don't go anywhere," the major demanded. He and the other officers conferred while the rest of us fumed.

Ken Thompson and I moved off to one side. "Kenney, we can't leave those tanks down there—we have to do something before it gets dark, or they will be shooting at us all night long. Let's get the sergeant major to lay down a good volley of mortar fire on the armor—that will let us get around to their flanks with the missiles and get some Javelin shots on the tanks!"

"Hold on," the major said to this idea. "Let's call the FOB."

"The FOB?" I asked. "What's the FOB going to do for us? They are 40 miles away. This is our call. We don't need anything from them."

The argument continued for forty-five minutes. It reminded most of us of the same sort of conflicts we had with the major back at Fort Bragg over the same kinds of issues. Then the argument was about training; now it was about war. Both of the A-teams and the B-team guys, too, were in disbelief that we were being restrained from finishing the fight, and the captains continued to discuss the problem with the major.

"Alright," I finally told Eric, "we're going back to our positions down the hill. At least we can keep shooting at them, and if we can get the TACPs to keep dropping bombs on their positions, then we'll be ready to go when the major changes his mind." Jake Chandler was waiting, working his radios out of our GMV.

"Jake, I don't care what kind of aircraft or bombs you can get, start dropping anything and everything on those tanks. We have to chase those guys away from that armor. The major is not going to let us do it on our own."

This was just what Jake wanted to hear. The Air Force arrived with all kinds of ordnance, and he and Ali began calling them in on the remaining tanks. Jake jumped from the GMV and moved forward to set up the SOFLAM at a place where he had a clear view of the entire battlefield.

I turned away for a moment, and when I looked at Jake again, there was Jane Arraf. She was ten feet from him, sitting on the ground, doing a live on-camera report while he was talking on the radio. Although she was not actually interviewing anybody, she was just getting in the way, and whether she knew it or not her microphone was picking up the secret laser codes and call signs that Jake was calling in to the planes. Arraf had showed up again, out of nowhere and against our request, and again she had inserted herself into our fight.

Perhaps emboldened by Jane Arraf's behavior, another female reporter now also came down the hill with her crew and began doing on-camera reports from within just a few feet of where our guys were fighting. I looked over at Marty and said, "I know what's going to happen—one by one, they are all going to come down here."

We had moved forward to get away from the media and not out of tactical necessity. As long as the reporters stayed back up on the hill behind us, the media people were not much of a problem. But down here, mixed in with the military, they were creating a hazard, both to themselves and to us. And sure enough, several more of them began slowly moving in on top of us again.

By now it was early afternoon. The Air Force tactical air controllers had taken over the bulk of the fight. Jake was happy and doing what he did best. Todd Gannon, the TACP from Nine-Two, Saleem Ali from Four-Four, and Jake Chandler were all working together. While Saleem managed the aircraft overhead, Todd was working the SOFLAM, keeping the laser on the target, and Jake was calling in the "nine-line" request for bomb delivery.

Finally the survivors had enough. We could see the tank crews bailing out of their turrets, and the infantry jumped up, and all of them started to run. We could see them trying to escape through the wheat field, heading on foot in the direction from which they had come earlier in the day.

Before, the Iraqis had displayed excellent order and tactical discipline. Now, the remainder was in panic. They attempted to escape back toward Makhmur, and this was another mistake. As long as they stayed hidden, we could not do much to them with our direct-fire weapons. The TACPs must have killed some with the submunitions, but at least fifty to sixty of them had survived until now.

When they ran, they were out in the open instead of under the cover of the berm. Our gunners suddenly had lots of targets, running as fast as they could go, probably trying to get away from the bombs. Now, our .50cal machine guns and the Mk19s began cutting the enemy down. All eight of the big guns were pouring fire onto the enemy soldiers, knocking some down, while others dove for cover in the wheat.

Suddenly, I became aware of one of the other reporters who had moved down to our vehicle. This woman, with her long blond hair and her blue body armor, was an alien being in our midst. She was clearly agitated and began shouting at us. "What are you doing?" she yelled, over and over. "They're running away—why are you still shooting at them?" she kept demanding of all of us. "Why are you men shooting them in the back?"

I ran over to her immediately. She was disrupting the fight and distracting everybody, and I had visions of her sending out reports about us that made us look like war criminals.

"Look," I said. "Let me explain the Law of Land Warfare to you. They are not running away—they are withdrawing. The rules are simple: They can either surrender, or they can die. Those are their choices. If they surrender, we will immediately stop shooting. But as long as they are armed and still on the battlefield, those guys are legitimate targets. If we let them escape, they would be free to regroup and then counterattack us. Even if they didn't attack us themselves, they could tell other units where we are and how to attack us. We cannot let them do that. We cannot permit a single enemy soldier to get back to his force. That's why we are still shooting."

The woman was clearly not happy with what I had told her, but she had an answer to her question. She said nothing more, but stood off to one side while her camera operator continued to record the fight. I went back to work, taking care of the guys and making sure they had ammunition. But I was concerned that she would broadcast a report that just showed us shooting the enemy in the back without providing the context I had given her. We did our best to get all of the enemy, but a few dozen got away. When they were out of range, the shooting slowed and then stopped.

Ordinarily, this is the time we climb in our GMVs and go down to clear the objective while it is apparently abandoned. Maj. X had prohibited that until now, so it was time to try to change his mind again. Marty, Eric, and I went back up the hill. Matt Saunders from Nine-Two was headed the same way, with the same idea.

"Anybody left on your side of the road?" Matt asked.

"Nope," Eric said, "we don't see anybody left—they all ran on our side, too."

"What do you guys think we should do now?" Matt asked.

"We need to go down there and clear the objective," Marty answered.

Maj. X was standing nearby and said, "Wait. You guys hold on a minute."

"But, sir, why should we hold on? They're gone, or wounded, or dead. We need to take care of their wounded and to clear the objective," I told him.

"You've been dropping cluster bombs down there. There could be unexploded bombs, and I don't want you going down to the objective," Maj. X snapped back. We were all incredulous. "You guys have done great work up till now, and I would hate to have it ruined by having somebody step on a cluster munition," he continued.

We found this was to be an unbelievable and unacceptable directive. Our doctrine doesn't tell us to avoid clearing an objective that may still be dangerous—we work in a dangerous business and know how to keep risks to a practical minimum.

"Sir," I told him, "we will watch where we put our feet."

"But there are still burning vehicles down there—a tank might explode. There might be a sniper out there."

All of us had a sinking feeling of disbelief at this guidance. It was time for the local commander to exploit all our advantage in the fight, before the enemy had a chance to turn it around. Our doctrine demanded it, and our training had prepared us for this moment, but now we were being restrained. I told him, "We will take our time, sir, we'll work our way down there, and we will clear the objective."

Maj. X looked directly at me and said, "No, you're not!"

Marty added, "Sir, we have got to clear the objective. There is no Special Forces school that I have attended that let's you get away without finishing the job. There is intel down there."

"Look. We are not going down there until I call the colonel and he tells me what he wants us to do."

"Great, sir," I said, "give him a call. But we are going to go down there and finish what we started."

"No! Sgt. Antenori, you will not!" He turned to Capt. Wright and ordered, "Eric, you guys stand by. Don't you dare go down there!"

Capt. Saunders took over, but he was more diplomatic about it than

I was. "Maj. X, we need to go down and clear the objective." He went through all the same arguments I had made, but in a more reasonable tone of voice. It still did not work. Maj. X just shook his head. I was so angry that I had to walk away, but I could still hear the discussion. Then Matt walked away in disgust, and I waded in to try again.

"Sir, what is your one reason for keeping us from finishing this? What is bothering you so much about it?"

"I think you guys want to go down there to gawk. I think you all want to go down there to count bodies and see how many guys you killed."

"Of course we want to see what kind of damage we inflicted on the enemy. That's part of our mission, but all of us have been taught to clear the objective at the end of a battle. We are required to pass through the objective once the enemy has been defeated. We have not done that," I answered.

"Well, I am not going to let you go down there to fulfill your need to see what kind of damage you've done."

We argued back and forth about this for a while, and Maj. X wouldn't budge. Finally, I walked back to the team, fuming mad, and Eric and Marty were as angry as I was.

"What's up, Frank?" they wanted to know. "When are we going down to the objective?"

"We're not going. The major doesn't want us to do anything. He's afraid to move. He's afraid we're going to blow a foot off on an unexploded cluster bomb. He said we did a great job, but that he's worried we'll ruin it all by kicking a bomb or getting smoked by a sniper. He is also concerned that we might get hurt if a tank blows up, so he wants us to stay here until it is safe or Lt. Col. Binford tells him to go ahead."

The guys, of course, could not believe it. "No way," Bobby said.

But Eric and Marty confirmed what I had told them. "Yeah," Eric said, "Maj. X doesn't want us to leave—he's worried that somebody will get hurt."

"He doesn't want anybody to get hurt?" Bobby yelled. "What the fuck—I thought we were Special Forces. If I wanted a job where there was no risk of being hurt, I would have joined the fucking band!"

"We're staying here for now," I told them, "so just get out the sniper rifles and the spotting scopes. If you see anything moving down there, kill it," I said, giving them something to do while we waited for the major to release us.

The guys found a few targets over the next few hours but nothing too exciting, just an occasional pickup truck on the highway. Putting one of the .50cal rounds into the engine block brought each truck to a stop without hurting anybody, and it kept the highway closed.

Artillery rounds continued to fall around our position. Without an observer to correct their fire, the enemy shells detonated harmlessly at random distances. A lucky shot was still a possibility, though, and as long as the enemy was still shooting at us, the battle was not over. Like the rest of the team, I was still steaming mad.

"Eric," I said, "if we had gone down the hill, cleared that objective, and chased those guys, we could have rolled them all up. They are running scared now! Just the sight of our GMVs with our big American flags would have produced a surrender of all of the rest of that unit."

I went back up the hill to try to reason with Maj. X one more time. "What did the colonel have to say, sir?" I asked him.

"I haven't talked to him," he replied, and apparently he had not tried. Darkness was falling, and we had very little time to make a sweep of the enemy battle positions before night.

"Do you want me to call Binford?"

"No! You are not going to call him!" Now he was mad, too, because he could see that I was trying to go around him.

"Sir, we are going to watch that objective all night. When the sun comes up in the morning, my guys and I are going down there to clear the objective."

"No, Sgt. Antenori, you are not to go down to that objective!"

"Sir, why are you afraid to have us finish this fight and clear the objective?"

"I am not afraid!"

"Something is stopping you from doing what we are supposed to be doing, and we all want to know what it is."

"I do not want to ruin a good thing. You guys have done a good job; don't ruin it by getting somebody hurt or killed."

"We know how to be careful and when to take calculated risks. This is not a business for anybody who is afraid of getting hurt, sir." This debate continued for a while longer, but he would not move. I told him once again that in the morning Nine-One was going down the hill. He told me once again that we were not.

Despite everything that had happened since we pulled out of the MSS at Pir Da Ud earlier that day, we could not get much rest during the night. Enemy artillery continued exploding every twenty minutes or so, and the threat of an enemy counterattack remained a tremendous concern. Just before it got dark, Keith Nann returned from his supply run to the FOB for more missiles.

"How many did you get?" I asked.

"Thirty-six!" he yelled with joy.

"Thirty-six? How the hell did you manage that?" I inquired.

"You wouldn't believe me if I told you," Keith said.

"Hey, we're not going anywhere anyway. Fill us in on where you found all those missiles."

What Keith relayed was a tribute to the resourcefulness of the Special Forces NCO. When Keith had made it back to the FOB, he found out that all the Javelins had been issued out to the teams. However, someone reminded him that the 173rd Airborne was sitting at the airfield in Irbil, still trying to get its act together, and that they might have some spare missiles. Keith drove off to the airfield. Once there, he asked the young sergeant who was guarding the gate to the location of the ammunition supply point (ASP). The young NCO did not know how to answer the burly SF NCO. Directing total strangers to the ASP was not something you were supposed to do.

Seeing hesitation in the young soldier, Keith pulled rank. "Listen here, Buck Sergeant; I'm a master sergeant with the 3rd Special Forces. Right now there are A-teams in heavy fighting on the other side of that ridge. If you don't tell me where the ASP is, a lot of them will die. Where's the ASP?" The young sergeant, faced with a dilemma, made the right choice. He told Keith where to find the ASP.

Seeing the success using rank had with the guy on the gate, Keith thought he would keep it going with the guys in the ASP.

"Gentlemen, my name is Master Sgt. Keith Nann, and I'm with the

3rd Special Forces Group. Right now, my battalion is fighting a division of tanks on the other side of that hill. I just came from the JSOTF, and I need every Javelin you have, now!"

A young second lieutenant, seeing the monstrous-looking FMTV, looking at his face, and hearing the magic letters *JSOTF* (Joint Special Operations Task Force), wasted no time telling his soldiers to give Keith the missiles. Keith said they even loaded them on the FMTV while he waited. He returned to Rock triumphantly, as he should have.

We now had plenty of missiles. Both Nine-Two and Three-Nine-One took on another twelve missiles each, bringing our "new and improved" basic load to three per truck, or twelve per team. Keith gave Four-Four three more, bringing their total to four, and kept the remaining nine for the B-team. We were armed to the teeth once again.

HERE COME THE TANKS

Around midnight Jake got a call from a B-52 crew high overhead that brought everybody wide awake. While returning from another mission, the "BUFF" (an acronym standing for Big Ugly Fat Fellow, and used as slang for B-52) was using the "Litening Targeting Pod" under its wing to scan the Iraqi countryside for "targets of opportunity." The Litening Pod is essentially an infrared TV camera. As the B-52 flew by our position, the radar-navigator saw something on his screen. "We see armor headed toward your position on the road, from the northwest," Jake heard. "Looks like seven or eight armored vehicles and about a dozen or so light trucks."

This was just what we were afraid of, a counterattack. Marty called Nine-Two: "Jake just got a report that more enemy vehicles are apparently moving down the highway. We are going to push forward and set up an ambush position on the ridgeline."

"Roger that," came the reply.

All of us jumped into the vehicles and headed over toward the high ground on the right, still a good position and less than 600 meters from the highway. At the same time, Nine-Two moved down the hill and set up a blocking position across the road just to make sure no enemy units leaked back toward Rock.

"We've got your back," Matt called on the radio.

Within a few minutes, our team had a good ambush position about 600 meters from the road and about 700 meters to the right (west) and forward (south) of our previous location near the Alamo.

"Here's what we're going to do," Marty radioed back. "We're going to engage with all our Javelins, then pull back. When we do, that's your cue to engage with your Javelins. Then we are going to pull back up to Press Hill." This was essentially volley-fire of the sort that worked so well earlier in the day. All the CLUs were out of their cases and mated to missiles, and nobody was thinking much about sleep.

Then Eric reported back to the B-team and Maj. X, "We're moving forward."

"How far?" Maj. X demanded.

"Far enough to cover the road; our view is blocked from here." It didn't take long to get into position and set up. All the weapons were locked and loaded. We were all ready to rock and roll.

The radio came alive again with the commander's voice: "What are your grid coordinates?" Eric answered and supplied the information from our GPS.

"Roger," the major called, "out." But he radioed back again in a few minutes, asking for our position again.

"I gave you the coordinates," Eric answered. "Don't you have a map?"

"Right, I can figure out that position on the map, but I want to get a feel for where you are on the battlefield. Can you turn on an IR [infrared] strobe light?" At this point, all the guys had their IMBTRs scanning both our team internal and the company battle frequency, so everybody heard this bizarre transmission.

Ordinarily our radio communications are somewhat private. Each team has its own frequency, somewhat like an intercom, that lets us talk informally. We did this primarily on our IMBTR radios, with a specially selected frequency. The IMBTRs were generally low power and not good for transmissions of more than a few miles. Our radio traffic with the B-team and Maj. X had been on a frequency specified in the SOI (Signal Operating Instructions) passed out by the JSOTF before we left Romania. Because the B-Team was usually several miles away, we usually used SINGARS radios mounted in the GMVs because they had more power. Until Maj. X's arrival on the hill, most of the guys never bothered to program the company frequency into their IMBTRs. Now they all wanted to be in the know.

A similar phenomenon had occurred with Maj. X before he arrived at Rock, the major had been too far away to hear the radio transmissions among us, Nine-Two, and Four-Four, so he had heard none of the actual battle communications.

Now he could monitor everything on the battle frequency used by both of his ODAs, and he seemed to be getting nervous. Perhaps that was because Matt and Eric were maneuvering on their own, without his guidance. But now there was nothing private at all about this exchange. Although he could now monitor our conversation, everybody could also hear his ludicrous request, and I heard guys laughing from all the vehicles.

What happened next was a rarity; Marty lost his temper. "Give me the mike! Give me the damn mike! Let me talk to him!" Marty barked as he tried to wrestle the hand mike away from Eric. "We're not turning on any fucking strobes!" When Marty was a Q-course instructor, his specialty was small unit tactics. He was responsible for evaluating the patrolling and tactical skills of young officers and NCOs as they tried to become Green Berets. "How the hell did this guy make it through the Q-course?"

Turning on an IR strobe would have been holding up a sign for the enemy that said, *Here we are—aim at this spot.* The abandoned Iraqi tank we found earlier in the day was equipped with night vision capability. We had found several pairs of Soviet NVGs (night vision goggles) on the POWs as well, so we all knew the Iraqis would have been able to see an IR strobe from miles away. Instead of complying with the insane request, Eric keyed his radio and relayed Marty's comments. "I am not turning on a strobe light. We're set up in an ambush line."

"I need to see where you are," the major insisted. "Can you face toward me and blink the illuminator on your PVS-7s a couple of times?"

"Is this guy fucking serious!" Marty said again. "For a guy that's awful worried about us getting hurt, he's trying awful hard to get our asses killed!" The IR illuminator on the PVS-7s was small and intended for use inside buildings where there is little to no starlight, a condition known as true darkness. It was also easy to see with night vision goggles since it was the equivalent of turning on an IR flashlight. While the major must have thought directing the light back in his direction might limit the ability of the enemy to see it, he apparently didn't consider that light would "splash" off of the vehicles and surrounding terrain, again giving away our position.

Eric then did the smart thing. While still sitting inside his GMV, he waited a few seconds without doing anything, and then called the major on his radio: "Okay, I am blinking the illuminator—can you see where we are?"

"No, nothing."

"Too bad—must be terrain in the way," said Eric as he threw the radio aside in disgust. Actually he was furious.

"They're getting closer," came the word from the B-52 crew. All of us intently scanned the road and surrounding area with every night vision system we owned—the thermal sights on the weapons as well as our PVS-7 and NVGs (14 helmet mounted). Even the CLUs were scanning for the enemy.

"Anybody see the vehicles?" Eric called on the radio. None of us had.

The B-52 crew reported, "I have your team spotted. We still see a bunch of tanks coming down the road straight for you."

"Put a JDAM on them," Jake suggested.

"Roger," he said. Then a moment later came the order: "Bomb away."

Jake warned everybody, "Inbound. Fifteen seconds!" We all took cover. That 2000-pound bomb hit about 600 meters away, just down the hill from our ambush site. The blast was so strong that I thought it was going to suck the shirt right off me. It lit up the night in a huge flash, whiting out our NVGs for a few seconds.

The bomb shook us up in two ways—physically and tactically. The bomber crew was apparently seeing something that we could not see. And if the tanks were that close, we were in deep trouble. Were the enemy vehicles hiding in the draws and wadis that blocked our view? How were they getting right on top of us? Everybody was expecting to have the enemy tanks pop up out of the terrain at close range at any second, but we were ready for them this time.

"We ought to be able to hear them," Marty yelled on the radio, and he was right—at 600 meters, the sound of tank engines and the squeaking, clanking tracks should have been clearly audible in the still night air.

MAJ. X PULLS BACK

The radio came alive again, this time with more bad news from Tom.

"The Kurds back up the hill are in a firefight with dismounted Iraqis." That meant that the enemy had us between a hammer and an anvil—the infantry behind blocking any escape and the tanks to our front preparing to finish the job their buddies had begun.

What a jam! Everybody's "pucker-factor" was off the scale with the news that we had apparently been flanked and surrounded.

"What are you guys doing down there?" Maj. X called, perhaps wondering why we were dropping bombs right in front of us.

"Getting ready to engage the tanks," Eric answered.

"Okay, okay," he said. "I'm leaving."

"What do you mean, you're leaving?" Eric was incredulous again.

"You guys have this under control, right? I am going to take the B-team and pull back to secure the pass," the major said over the radio.

This decision made no sense to us. The pass was about 3 kilometers to the rear, far from the threats being reported on the radio. Losing the B-team meant that a third of our local combat power would be gone, just when we expected to have the enemy in our face at close range and hitting us with armor as well as infantry. It also meant that no one would be guarding the road from Debecka that intersected the road to Irbil at Rock. Maj. X climbed into his Humvee and led his team away from the anticipated fight, leaving Nine-One and Nine-Two to absorb the expected attack alone.

It took a few minutes for the significance of this decision to sink in with us all, but then Keith Nann, the company Operations sergeant, spoke up. Keith was at the end of the B-team convoy as it wound back up the hill toward relative safety. Normally, Keith's job is not to make tactical decisions for the company, but he made one now.

"Sir! What the fuck are you doing?" Keith radioed on the company frequency. "We have two A-teams down there—we're supposed to be watching their backs! We need to get back down there—this is fucked up, sir! TURN THE FUCKING TRUCKS AROUND!" Keith ordered. Even though he was an E-8 master sergeant, he was countermanding the order of an O-4 major.

Jimmy Adams, the other senior NCO on the B-team, backed Keith up. "We can't leave those two A-teams down there alone," Jimmy told the major. The trucks turned around, and the B-team resumed blocking the road behind us from attack. That was a huge relief.

Long minutes ticked by while we scanned for the enemy attack. It never came. Then the radio came to life with a report from Tom Sandoval. One of the Kurds apparently started shooting at a ghost, and so the rest of them opened up, too. There was no firefight, just a false alarm.

Matt called Eric on the radio, "Eric, do your guys see any vehicles?" "Negative, we don't see or hear anything," Eric replied. Matt then got a hold of Tom on the radio and asked him if he saw anything from his position at our original Alamo. "Nothing," replied Tom. "Something's not right Eric," Matt relayed, "I'm going to pull my guys back to Press Hill to try and sort this out." "Roger that, we'll meet you there," Eric replied.

When we all made it to Press Hill, it only took a few minutes to figure out what was happening. There were no tanks. We never figured out what the B-52 pilots were seeing, but there was not an enemy vehicle still alive on the battlefield in front of us. Perhaps the destroyed vehicles from earlier in the day got the pilots excited. Even though the tanks were destroyed and abandoned, smoldering fires inside would provide a heat signature for the IR sensors. We had a good view of the road. The range with our NVGs and CLUs extended about 8 miles, and there was nothing moving on it.

Disgusted with the episode, relieved that we were not engaging tanks at 500 meters, and annoyed by the issues of battle command and control, Eric and Matt decided to pull their teams back to our original locations astride the road. Then, as we all relaxed a bit, the idea of shooting at ghosts started to seem funny. Marty and I laughed about it, tremendously relieved.

Then Keith came down to talk to us. We had only heard part of his conversation and were too busy getting ready to kill phantom tanks to pay a lot of attention to anything the B-team was doing.

"That fucking guy ran!" Keith told us. We were appalled. "Yeah, the fucking major jumped in the fucking truck and picked up the whole fucking B-team and started running back toward fucking Irbil! He was going to leave your two teams out here, hanging! We turned him around and brought him back."

After that, the members of the teams shunned Maj. X. Nobody would talk to him unless it was necessary. In my opinion, this officer might have been excellent in a staff position. He was personable, a nice guy, a good planner and organizer, but it didn't seem to me and the guys on the team that he had what is needed in a combat commander. We expect a Special Forces officer to lead from the front, to be aggressively loyal to his men, and to especially show both moral and physical courage in the face of the enemy. To the disgust of the men of the whole company, this officer seemed incapable of these things. We thought he had no business on the battlefield.

For all of us on Nine-One, this looked like another downhill ride on the black-sheep roller coaster. We were thinking, *Now what? We are still stuck here on this damn hill, we still cannot clear the objective, and we have a company commander who seems to be excessively cautious and ran away from the battlefield, leaving us to face tanks by ourselves—how do we function as a part of this company from here on out?* After talking to Eric and Marty and the other guys, we decided to stay put, ride the night out, and see what could be done in the morning.

The Iraqi artillery might not have been very good at hitting us, but they were great at keeping everybody awake. Every twenty minutes or so another round would land in the general area with a thump that kept us on edge. I was exhausted. Finally Eric came over and said, "Frank, you need to go to sleep. You've been going all day. All the other guys have been able to grab at least a two-hour 'power nap.' We're at 50 percent security, there's no need for both of us to be up, and I'll take it for a while—go get some sleep." I was dead tired and decided to give it a shot.

A VERY RUDE AWAKENING

I walked over to my GMV. I took off my MICH helmet and set it in the passenger seat. I leaned my M4 carbine against the side of the GMV so both it and the helmet were within arm's reach. I took off my pistol belt and holster and used them for a pillow. I rolled up in a poncho liner, lay on the ground next to the GMV, and quickly drifted off to sleep. I was asleep less than fifteen minutes when a bloodcurdling scream jolted me and everybody else wide awake.

"FRAAAAANK! MMMMIIIIIKKKEE! Help!" My first thought was that we were under attack and that the enemy was already on top of us. The whole team must have had the same idea. My NVGs were on my helmet; I was literally blind in the darkness and couldn't see jack.

My heart jumped into my throat, and I thought, *Somebody fell asleep, and the Iraqis snuck into our perimeter and have overrun our position. We are getting our throats cut!*

Another scream: "AAAHHHHHHH!!!! HHHEEELPP!!!!" Now I recognized the voice: it was Rich—calling for help. I scrambled for my helmet and M4, got the helmet on, flipped down the NODs (Night Observation Device), grabbed my carbine, and lay in the prone position, ready to fight.

Only then did I get a good look at what was happening to Rich. He was rolling around on the ground, flailing madly, next to his Humvee. Suddenly, in the NODs, I could see all the lasers from the PEQ-4 aiming systems on our carbines sweeping the area around Rich—all the other guys were ready to start shooting with their personal weapons. While Rich was wrestling with something, the other guys and I immediately started scanning the area with our NODs and lasers, certain that the shooting would begin any second.

Finally, one of the other guys went over to help Rich and found him entangled in his poncho liner, which he had zipped into a lightweight sleeping bag.

"Rich! What is it?" I heard Mike say.

"A SNAKE!!! Get it off, get it off! It's biting me!" Rich continued to scream.

Mike quickly separated Rich from his poncho liner, but found nothing. Rich had been having a mefloquine dream—a reaction to the weekly antimalaria drug we were all required to take. The drug prevents malaria, but sometimes it induces extremely vivid dreams, and that was what had happened with Rich. He was asleep on the hood of his Humvee when the dream began, and he was sure that a snake that had managed to get in the bag with him was attacking him. He rolled off the hood and dropped to the ground. Mefloquine nightmares were one of the drug's cruel side effects. To the guy having the dream it was completely real, so as far as Rich was concerned, he really did have a snake biting him.

Although it might have seemed trivial, that episode scared me more than any other incident of the previous two days. I was not really frightened by the attacking armor or the artillery rounds that landed nearby or even the prospect of enemy tanks popping up out of the night. I could deal with an enemy 500 or 600 meters away, even an enemy tank. But waking up from a dead sleep to the prospect of hand-to-hand combat was a profoundly frightening experience. For several very long moments, I had thought for sure that we were all about to die. It was a while before I could sleep again.

DOGS AND DEATH

Throughout the remainder of the night, we could hear the distant sound of many dogs barking and growling. It was continuous throughout the night. Some dogs were visible in our night vision systems. We could see them walking around on the road, but could not quite make out what they were doing at that distance. But with daylight, we could see the dogs through our powerful spotting scopes—dozens of them, feeding on the bodies of the dead infantry.

The dogs were fighting over these corpses, ripping body parts off. Eric looked through his binos, he couldn't believe what he saw. A dog was running down the road with what looked like a human arm in it's mouth. "Bobby, is that dog carrying an arm?" Bobby was looking through a sniper's spotting scope, it had a much higher magnification than the binos, and he could clearly see what Eric was looking at. "Yes, Eric, that dog is definitely walking away with someone's arm." Dogs

feeding on bodies is probably one of the most gruesome things a soldier can see in combat, but it has probably occurred hundreds of times
during centuries of warfare.

An old farmer walked down the road and began to run the dogs off,
kicking them and hitting them with sticks. He left, and then returned
with four or five other people, some of them women, and a cart. They
collected some of the dead Iraqi soldiers and removed them from the
battlefield, presumably for burial. The entire time, Kenney and Jason
watched them through the scopes of their sniper rifles, hoping the
civilians would not be stupid enough to pick up an AK-47 and become
a combatant. None did, and we let them bury their countrymen.

MORNING, 7 APRIL

That long, ghost-filled night finally ended. The phantom tanks down
the hill were mysteriously gone, along with the phantom infantry that
had scared the Kurds. Rich recovered from his phantom snake attack.
Only twenty-four hours had elapsed since we began our attack toward
Objective Rock, but that one day had been filled with more action-
packed adventure than any other in my entire career. The following
day would also be eventful.

LAST TANK ENGAGEMENT

We were scanning the battlefield with high-power optics, looking for infantrymen trying to sneak up on us, when Lihn Nguyen saw what
looked like a small dust cloud coming from behind a village about
3 miles to our southwest. He focused in, but could not quite see what it
was. As he continued to watch, another T-55 tank appeared from
behind a wall that surrounded the village. Two Iraqi soldiers were riding
on the tank. Most likely they were infantrymen, hitching a ride.

Lihn let out a yell. "Tank! On the hill, over there," he said, pointing
in the general direction of the village.

"Where, Lihn?" Bobby asked. I wanted to know too, and I squinted
to see, but could not see a thing.

Lihn was looking though a high-powered spotting scope and could easily see the tan-painted tank. To the rest of us, the tank was invisible with the naked eye at that distance.

Bobby peeked in Lihn's scope. Then he yelled, "I see it! I see it!"

"Which way is it going?" I asked.

"It looks like it's making its way toward the highway," Bobby answered, "but it's not coming this way."

"It doesn't have to. All he has to do is get across Highway 2, and we have a problem."

Lihn then asked, "Frank, can I try to take it out with a Javelin?"

"Man, that's far away," I told him. "I don't know, Lihn."

"Jason took out that truck at about three clicks," he reminded me, "and that APC he shot had to be just as far. What's the worst that could happen—the missile falls short?"

"Okay. Since you saw it, you can shoot it. Go ahead and grab a missile," I told Lihn. Then I said to Jake, "Get on the horn and get us some CAS, Jake. I don't think Lihn's going to hit that tank from here."

"Already on the way," Jake answered. While we were discussing the tank, Jake had taken the initiative of putting in a call for anything close by. "We have a B-52, on its way back from another mission, that still has two bombs. He'll be here in fifteen minutes."

Lihn sat down with the Javelin and CLU. Bobby sat next to him, looking through the spotting scope, and told us the tank was still moving slowly toward the highway. The rest of us still could not see it.

"Are you sure you can hit it, Lihn?" I asked him again, but there was no way Lihn was going to surrender an opportunity for a tank kill.

"Yeah, I'll get him." We all watched while Lihn stabilized himself for the long shot.

Lihn looked through the day sight of the CLU, which is simply a 4x monocular, less powerful than a standard pair of binos. He had difficulty finding the tank. After about thirty seconds of searching, he asked Bobby to "talk him in on" the tank. Bobby quickly began talking him on, using simple directions.

"You see the wall closest to us?"

"Yeah."

"Go about 500 meters to the right, following the top of the ridgeline."

"Okay."

"Now come straight down about 200 meters, and that's your tank."

"Got it!"

Lihn switched to the narrow-field-of-view thermal sight, which at 9x has a bit more magnification. He now could see the heat signature of the tank in his viewer. It was little bigger than a speck, but he thought he could get a lock. Lihn initiated the BCU, beginning the process to spool up the gyro and cool down the seeker. Now he was committed to shooting. He brought the track gates down to their smallest possible setting and tried to get a lock on the tank. Time and time again he squeezed the left trigger of the CLU, which locks the missile's seeker onto the image of the tank.

"Damn it!" Lihn yelled. "I can't get a lock." Realizing we were running out of time on the BCU, I sat down beside Lihn and told him to pass me the missile. I looked through the CLU and could not see the tank, so I switched back to the day sight.

"Bobby, talk me on!" Once again, Bobby went through the drill of getting me into the area the tank was in. Finally, I could see the tiny image of the T-55. I switched to the thermal sight setting, confirming the target by seeing the heat signature against a cool background. With the BCU already initiated, I simply switched to the "seeker-view" and started trying to bring the track gates down on the thermal image of the tank.

With the track gates on the lowest setting, I tried to get a lock, going through the same routine as Lihn. Like Lihn, I had no luck. With time running out, knowing that I was about to lose power from the BCU and have a worthless missile on my shoulder, I made the decision to fire anyway. Switching back to the day sight, I lined the tank up in the notch at the bottom of the field of view. My intent was to simply line up the shot and lob the missile.

Since I had never gone through formal training on the Javelin, I did not know that the notch at the bottom was only for ranging. Jason did not cover that in the quick class he had given. I had gotten the idea to use the notch from firing the Stinger Missile. The Stinger had a similar sight, and when you fired a Stinger, you had to place the target in that notch at the bottom before you squeezed the trigger to fire the missile.

With the tank lined up inside the notch, I squeezed the right trigger, knowing that there was little chance of hitting the tank but that the missile would be worthless soon anyway, and fired. The missile left the tube on its long journey toward the tank. I got up, dropped the spent tube from the launcher, and handed the CLU back to Lihn.

"Go get another missile—that one's going to miss," I told him. As Lihn and I walked back toward the GMV for another missile, Bobby continued to follow the T-55 in his spotting scope. After what seemed like a good thirty seconds, Bobby let out a yell.

"Whoa! You hit it! You hit it!"

"What? No way in hell I hit that tank, Bobby."

"Frank, I'm telling you, you hit it. I saw the missile smack it."

"Bob, there's no way I hit that tank. I never got a lock."

"Frank, I'm telling you that you got it," Bobby insisted. "I saw the missile impact the tank, and when the smoke cleared, the two guys that were on it were gone." I looked through the spotting scope myself in disbelief. I saw the tank, now sitting motionless, on the dirt road that led from the village out to Highway 2. The two riders were gone, but I did not see any smoke like we saw with Eric Strigotte's tank shot.

"I think I missed, Bob. The guys probably jumped off when the missile exploded close by."

"Frank, I'm telling you, you hit that damn tank." Bobby was firm, but I was extremely doubtful. It would be almost two weeks before we found out that the missile actually did strike the target.

Five minutes after I had fired the Javelin, Jake had the B-52 drop a pair of 2000-pounders near the village to put the exclamation point on another skirmish with the Iraqis. We saw no more tanks from that point on.

A little later in the day, a full-size pickup truck slowly drove down Highway 2 from the direction of Mosul. We watched and determined that the occupants were not military. We let the truck go, allowing it to slowly drive through the intersection and continue on toward Kirkuk.

The vehicle slowed down as it cautiously drove through the carnage. *Probably somebody rubbernecking,* I thought to myself. After going about 500 meters past the intersection, the truck stopped. Slowly, it turned around and headed back toward the intersection. Just before it got to the intersection, it stopped again. Two men in civilian clothes got out and started looking around.

"One of these dummies is going to pick up an AK—who wants to bet?" I commented. Nobody took me up on it. They should have, because they didn't go for the AKs. Instead, one of the guys pulled out a cellular phone; the other retrieved a pair of binos from the truck and started scanning the ridgeline we were sitting on.

"Son of a bitch, they are looking for us," Eric called out. "Fire their ass up." Kenney let loose first, sending a burst of 40mm from his Mk19, followed by Jason firing a burst of .50cal. Kenney's first volley landed just 20 meters in front of the truck; Jason's rounds skipped off the asphalt just behind it. Both men dove for a ditch on the side of the road, disappearing from sight.

"Anybody see them?" Eric asks.

"They're in that ditch," answered Jason. Kenney lobbed a few more 40mm, trying to flush them, but they did not move. Since the 40mm rounds explode on impact, someone lying in the ditch was relatively safe unless a round landed directly on top of him. We could not get them, but they could not move, either. Then Marty got a great idea.

"What about the 60mm? We could have the sergeant major put some prox [airburst] rounds on top of them."

"Do it," Eric said.

Marty got on the radio and contacted Joe Ward. Joe was more than willing to lend a hand. He already had the mortar set up and lobbed the first round downrange. Looking through his binos that had a special reticle specifically designed for adjusting indirect fire, Eric called off the impact location of the first round and fed the corrections to Marty, who relayed them to Joe via radio, in order to get him closer to the guys in the ditch. Joe made the adjustments and fired the second round. It landed just short of the ditch. Eric gave one more correction, then told Marty to give him fire for effect. Marty called out on the radio, "Six rounds HE prox, fire for effect!"

Joe cut loose with a barrage of airburst mortar shells. We watched as each of the six rounds burst at two-second intervals above the suspected hiding position of the two men. You could see the ground below them jump as shards of shrapnel dug into the dirt. Joe Ward lived up to his hype; his mortar skills were superb. Luckily for us, the Iraqi mortar men that fired on us the previous day did not have any experts like Joe Ward with them, or we would never have made it out of the intersection.

THE TAXI

Later in the day, a taxi almost repeated the behavior of the pickup truck. First the taxi approached the intersection. Seeing the destruction, the driver wisely turned around and headed back in the direction he came from. Then he foolishly turned around again and attempted to travel down Highway 2 and pass the intersection. Since it was clearly a civilian vehicle, we had no intention of harming the passengers or driver. At the same time, it could not be permitted to drive back and forth, potentially reconning the terrain for another counterattack.

If we had been down on the road, we could have stopped it, searched it, questioned the occupants, and then turned it around. Instead, we fired single a .50cal bullet from the Barrett into the road in front of the taxi. Wisely, the taxi driver stopped, and four people emerged with their hands up, not knowing quite what had happened but certain that they had a problem.

So did we. I called up the B-team on the radio and said, "We've stopped a taxi by shooting a warning shot. Four passengers are standing on the road with their hands up. I am sending two vehicles down there to talk to them. Over."

The B-team Ops sergeant, Keith, replied, "Roger that. Frank, send them down there!"

Gerry and Marty took their vehicles down the hill while the rest of us provided overwatch, just in case. They verified that the people were innocent civilians struggling with the decision of whether or not to drive through the intersection. There were no weapons or radios in the taxi, so Marty let them go. They drove off, continuing toward Kirkuk.

Before they returned to our position, Gerry and Marty's guys took the opportunity to do a hasty inspection of the battlefield. Gerry did a quick count of thirty-two bodies of enemy soldiers that were visible, scattered around the intersection. Lacking the major's authorization to stay longer, they then got back in their GMVs and drove back up the hill.

Both ODAs managed to endure the rest of the day, but we were bitching about the way we were being used during the whole time. The reason we were all so annoyed was that our commander was using us in a weak and dangerous way that was completely outside doctrine.

Special Forces had a history going back forty years of sometimes being used as conventional infantry, with disastrous consequence.

We are misused partly because there are so few of us—one company of Special Forces soldiers is only about one-third the size of a regular, full-up infantry company. We do not have all the organic support of an infantry unit, either. We are excellent at sneaking into places, making a mess of things, and then getting away safely. We are lousy at digging foxholes and guarding intersections.

If we had been cut loose from our static positions, we could have gone after the artillery battery down the road, or gone up and down Highway 2 to secure the flanks for the 173rd Airborne's long-delayed advance behind us. We would not have become a target for the enemy that was still, on Day 2, trying to kill us all.

Everybody was dead tired, grimy, sweaty, and disgusted with what appeared to be a lack of intestinal fortitude on the part of our commander. We clearly had a leadership crisis on this battlefield, and it was driving us nuts. Another 152mm artillery shell roared overhead, impacting a few hundred meters behind us on our right flank.

None of us really wanted to have anything further to do with the major after he seemingly ran from a fight, but the constant drone of enemy artillery flying over our position, was getting to me. So I went up the hill to the B-team to find the major anyway. "What's going on?" I demanded. There's another old saying that goes: "Eventually, even a blind squirrel finds a nut." The Iraqis were firing their shells blindly at us, but Murphy's Law of "Anything that can go wrong will go wrong" told us that sooner or later, they'd get lucky.

"We're waiting to see what the colonel . . ." He got out before I interrupted him.

"I don't want to hear 'We're waiting to see,' sir! I am not going to sit here another day, taking artillery fire. Those gunners are going to get lucky sooner or later and hit us, and I am not going to eat a 152mm artillery shell while you try to figure out what the hell is going on!"

"Sgt. Antenori! The FOB is trying to figure out what's going on, and as soon as the colonel tells me, I will pass it on to you," he snapped back.

"Sir, the FOB isn't here. They're 40 miles away. They can't possibly comprehend our situation. Somebody has to make a fucking decision around here," I said, trying once again to get him to make a decision on his own.

"I explained the situation to Lt. Col. Binford. We're simply going to wait for guidance from him on our next move," he answered. That was it. I'd had enough with Maj. X's indecisiveness.

In the grand tradition of the role of Special Forces team sergeants, I confronted Maj. X in a way that would seem mutinous anywhere else, and said, "Here's the deal, sir—I am going to give you until midnight tonight, and if we are still here, I am pulling my ODA out of here, and we are going back to Irbil. I will not allow my guys to ride out another night of artillery on this frigging mountain."

If it seems like an odd thing for a sergeant to be giving ultimatums to a major, it is. I would not have tried—or gotten away with such speech—with any other SF commander. Our tradition in Special Forces is to take rank somewhat less seriously than in other communities. Team sergeants in Special Forces are never very bashful, but this was an extreme response to what seemed to me an extreme failure of command.

An officer like Lt. Col. Binford would not have tolerated a sergeant speaking to him that way for a minute. Binford would have said—and properly, too—"Sgt. Antenori, stand at ease! I'm the commander, and you're the team sergeant. Shut up and let me do my job while you do yours! Get your ass back down that hill." But that is not what our commander said.

"Okay, okay, I'll contact the colonel," he meekly replied.

"Midnight tonight. We're leaving, one way or another."

Eric backed me up by adding in a nonemotional tone, "Sir, We will leave." With almost any other officer, this sort of conduct would be worth serious career problems. I was out of my lane again, but sometimes a team sergeant can say things more effectively than a team commander. "Oooh, shit, Frank," Eric said, "you really know how to charm senior officers, don't you?"

"This is bullshit, Eric," I said. "We're a ground mobility team—we aren't supposed to sit here and dig in; that's what the regular Army is for. We are supposed to be constantly moving. This is crap. If he doesn't have the balls to get on the radio and tell the Old Man to make a decision, we'll make a decision for him."

ROCKET BARRAGE

Around 1900 hours local time, just before dark, another civilian pickup truck slowly approached the roundabout and stopped in front of our position. The truck driver stepped out and displayed a small white flag and appeared to be completely innocent. Tom Sandoval's guys took some Kurds and drove down the hill to meet the driver.

He told them that he was a Kurd himself, trapped on the wrong side of the Green Line with his family for years, and that the Iraqi authorities would not permit him to return to their home in the north. He asked if it would be possible for him to return the next day with his family and drive across the Green Line and go back to Irbil.

"Sure," they told him. He got in his truck and drove back the way he had come.

About twenty minutes later, Andy was sitting in his vehicle, watching the battlefield to our front, now apparently vacant. He saw some streaks of light in the distance and said, "Look, somebody is firing tracers over there!" I looked and knew that they were way too big to be tracers, but I could not quite figure out what they were. They burned out after a few seconds.

"What the hell was that?" somebody asked. A few seconds later, we would find out. Large airburst explosions began to detonate along the ridgeline right behind the B-team and Four-Four. They were obviously the warheads from some kind of rocket. As we watched each explosion detonate in a linear pattern along the ridge, we concluded that we were being attacked by a heavy barrage of 122mm rockets. The flashes must have come from a BM-21 launch vehicle, and the streaks of light must have been the rocket motors.

We concluded that the story given to us by the truck driver was a ruse and that the man had a chance to pinpoint the exact location of our battle positions while talking to Tom and the Kurds. He took this information back to the enemy, who then engaged us with the rockets.

Fortunately for us, these rockets are not targeted individually to hit point targets like our individual vehicles, while they would have been ideal for area targets like large numbers of troops in the open. The Iraqis seemed to have unloaded a whole launcher's worth of the weapons at us—twenty-one rockets. None of them scored a hit.

Following the barrage, we were ordered to pull back to join the B-team. On arrival, we got word that we were going back to Irbil and the FOB. We did not know if the rockets had convinced the major to insist on the FOB retasking us.

Before leaving, all of us from Nine-One and Nine-Two drove over to say good-bye to Tom Sandoval and his faithful companions, Eric, Dirk, Kris, and the STS guy, Saleem. They were not glad to see us pull out.

"What do you mean, 'Good-bye'?" they said. "We're not going any-where."

"We're going back to Irbil. We aren't going to sit here; that's not our mission."

It was a long drive back to Irbil in the dark.

We did not roll into the FOB compound until about 0300 local time. But when the guys at the FOB met us, they were very pleased to have us back. They had heard a lot of the radio traffic and thought we had done a good job.

Lt. Col. Binford was waiting, too. "Hey, Sgt. Antenori—I heard about your Javelin-fest. How many missiles did you shoot?"

"I shot two, sir," I told him.

"How many did you hit?"

"I know I hit one, but I think I missed the second one, a tank," I an-swered, not knowing then that the second was a kill, too.

"Well, in that case, I guess we'll just have to take that $75,000 out of your paycheck for wasting government property," he teased.

"Fine, sir," I joked back at him. "Just write the statement of charges up when we get back, and I'll be glad to sign it."

"Good job out there," he said then, serious and sincere. He was pleased, and properly so, but the war was not yet over.

"What's next for Nine-One, sir? And I hope it isn't something that requires us to sit on a hill and take artillery fire all night long."

"We're getting ready to take Kirkuk," he said. That was just what I wanted to hear.

FIFTEEN

STAND-DOWN

Our next mission, the liberation of Kirkuk, came quickly, but Baghdad was captured on April 9, and the war fizzled out soon thereafter—once again we were "men without jobs," but this time without complaint.

ODA-391 and our brother teams were notified to prepare to return to Fort Bragg. After the usual ritual inspections and paperwork, we loaded our GMVs on Air Force C-17 transports and were soon back in North Carolina among our friends, families, and the Special Forces community.

When we got off the plane at Green Ramp, Pope Air Force Base, our most senior commanders, Maj. Gen. Lambert and Lt. Gen. Kensinger were waiting to welcome us. Both had been briefed on our fight and its amazing outcome. Ordinarily, when general officers meet the troops returning from a deployment, everybody suffers in the hot sun while long speeches are made. Not this time—both officers merely gave us a quick "Well done, and welcome home," and released us to our families. We were grateful for both the sentiments and for the consideration.

Later Maj. Gen. Lambert asked Eric to make an appointment with his secretary for an informal briefing on the tank fight and to bring me and Marty along. The three of us put together a quick briefing, complete with photos, and showed up in Lambert's office a few days later. Normally, generals are pressed for time and you'd be lucky to get fifteen minutes with them, but Gen. Lambert was sincere and told us to give him all the details, no matter how long it took. For the next hour and a half Eric, Marty, and I relayed to him all the details of the battle at Debecka. We talked about the train-up, the great support, and the great equipment that included the Javelin and the GMVs.

During the briefing, Gen. Lambert sat there like a proud father. When we concluded Gen. Lambert sat there in silence for a few minutes, then looked across the table at Eric, Marty, and me. "Do you guys go to church?" he asked us. "Well, if you don't, you had darn better start." Then he turned to his chief of staff, Col. Nye and said, "We need to get this story out to the public." He then turned back to us. "Gentlemen, what you did, along with the accomplishments of the ODAs in Afghanistan, have brought Special Forces back to the forefront of the Special Operations Community. We are again in our glory days, much like Vietnam." Then he handed the three of us coins shaped like dog tags. "I usually only give these to guys that were wounded when I visit them at Walter Reed, but as of today, I'm giving them out to guys who've kicked some ass as well." He then thanked us again for what we all did that day.

I didn't know it at the time, but because of that briefing, when Gen. Lambert mentioned getting the story out into the public, he volunteered me to help him do it. For practically the entire year before I retired, I would give that same briefing dozens of times to VIPs and other groups. The story would also be featured in *The New York Times* and *Army Times*.

In the rush to get the teams back from Iraq, some administrative corners were cut. Much to my disappointment, the awards process was not properly followed, and some of the guys who demonstrated valor at Debecka received quite minor decorations. Mike Ray and the guys who helped him save dozens of Kurds, braving exploding gas tanks and RPG rounds, got very minor awards for their valor. Bobby and Andy were also denied the awards I felt they deserved that day, both received minor decorations in comparison to some of the other medals that were handed out.

In August of 2005, after more than twenty years in the Army, I retired.

Despite what we expected, our SF AOB commander, although temporarily sidelined, did not suffer any consequences for his less than courageous performance on the battlefield on 6–7 April. He has recently been selected "below the zone," or ahead of his peers, for promotion to lieutenant colonel, and he will almost certainly be given command of a Special Forces battalion.

With operations still being conducted throughout the world in support of the Global War on Terror, he'll more than likely command Special Forces soldiers in combat again.

SIXTEEN

AFTER-ACTION REVIEW

After every major event, in training or in actual combat operations, US Army units conduct a discussion we call an "after-action review," or AAR. These sessions give all the players a chance to look at what we were supposed to do, what we actually did, and what we learned from the event. From these AARs, we gather "lessons learned" that can be applied to the next mission, and this process has been a major factor in the tactical successes of the US Army in recent history. Here is what we learned from the Battle of Debecka Pass.

First, the fight at Debecka was a larger lesson than just the destruction of an enemy mechanized infantry task force by a small number of lightly armed soldiers. Our engagement forced the enemy forces in the northern part of Iraq to stay in position and prevented them from moving to the south, where they could have engaged the coalition assault on Baghdad. This was the most important part of our mission—much more important than the destruction of the enemy's combat power. To the enemy, Col. Cleveland's forces in the north looked big and threatening, and they could not be ignored.

This was accomplished by very small numbers of Special Forces soldiers with very light weapons and equipped as light infantry—another important lesson. Our twelve man team carried the same firepower as an infantry company, yet we were able to perform a broader set of missions and act as force multipliers by leveraging the use of indigenous forces. Since the First Gulf War, the armed forces of the United States have been redesigned to be lighter, much more agile, and far more effective than before. Nowhere has this concept of lighter, faster, and more lethal been better implemented than within the United States Special Operations Command (USSOCOM). Policy decisions made almost two decades ago, by men and leaders with vision, paid off big in the recent battles fought by Special Operations Forces in Iraq and Afghanistan.

Confidence and trust: Although it is not always apparent in my story, one of the keys to our success was the tremendous confidence that was invested in us, as individuals, as teams, as unconventional warriors. That confidence is new, and it paid off in many ways. In previous conflicts, the conventional army and its commanders tended to use Special Forces only when absolutely necessary, and when they had to, they did so with skepticism. Col. Cleveland set up his overall goal and campaign plan. He then allowed his battalion commanders, Lt. Cols. Tovo, Waltemeyer, and Binford, to develop their own battle plans to meet those goals. While Col. Cleveland was involved with every aspect of our operations in Iraq, I never once saw him micromanage his battalion commanders, his team leaders, or his soldiers. We wish all commanders would emulate him.

Equipment: The equipment itself generally performed superbly. Our radios, weapons, and GMVs all worked as advertised.

The GMVs: Despite having to bear huge loads, these vehicles gave us the perfect combination of agility and firepower. They are the perfect platform for ODAs with a "direct action" or "deep reconnaissance" specialty. Because of modifications made at Anniston Army Depot by US-ASOC, and the additional ones we were able to make on our own, we had the weapon platforms we needed to defeat a much larger force, and we had the fuel and water and MREs to take our show on the road for days at a time. The GMVs' off-road performance let us fight from places where conventional vehicles just could not go. And when we needed to scoot from our exposed battle position at the traffic circle to a protected one up the hill, the GMVs were faster than the enemy gunners.

Command and control: Despite my frustration about the way ODA-391 was sometimes employed, such issues are common when a big organization like the Army tries to do big things in a hurry. We had a few problems with a few individuals, but overall, the Special Forces part of the show functioned like clockwork. Recent advances in satellite communications literally allow generals to pick up the phone and speak to a guy on the ground thousands of miles away. The potential downside of that capability is that now every ODA "downrange" can be commanded by somebody in the Pentagon giving orders by SATCOM radio, but that didn't happen—another example of trust. Our orders were brilliantly simple and elegant, and they allowed us the tactical flexibility to adapt to changing circumstances without constantly asking for permission.

We did have one serious problem with one of our AOB commanders, but again, that was with an individual; the cause was not an institutional flaw. Combat has odd effects on people, sometimes good and sometimes not, and the carnage at Objective Rock upset a lot of people. A Special Forces AOB commander, though, is supposed to rise above the confusion of the battlefield and execute his unit's mission; lives depend on it, and the larger mission depends on it too.

Conflict and cooperation between 3rd and 10th Groups: Since each Special Forces Group has its own special areas of responsibilities, it is inevitable that each also has its own corporate culture. When you marry two groups, as was done with us and the 10th Group teams, you get the vices and the virtues of both. Tom Sandoval and his guys brought with them all the virtues of the "unconventional warfare" mission—the ability to work with the local populace, to adapt to the local culture, to get help with the fighting from the indigenous population. At the same time, Tom and his guys were very lightly equipped and armed, and their tactical perspective was consequently different than ours. Even though it took a bit of negotiation, we were able to sort out our differences and accomplish our mission successfully together.

Awards and decorations: This has always been an issue in Special Forces, beginning with the first teams sent to Vietnam and continuing today. The tradition in SF is that uncommon valor is a job requirement. The standards for awards are consequently far higher than those in the rest of the Army, and that tradition has been maintained for the ODAs who fought at Debecka. Eric, Gerry, Mike, Lihn, Kenney, Rich, and the other guys who risked their lives to rescue the Kurds, pulling dozens from burning vehicles while fuel and ammunition were exploding, showed incredible heroism. It is still my opinion that they deserve the Soldier's Medal that was submitted for them. They deserved much better than the Army Commendation Medal they ended up with.

Andy and Bobby fought with unmatched valor and ferocity, while constantly exposed to enemy fire. Both were deservedly recommended for Silver Stars, but these decorations were downgraded all the way to—once again—Army Commendation Medals (at least these had "V" for valor devices). Andy and Bobby deserved much better.

The ODA concept: The US Army has been using the same basic design for a Special Forces A-team for more than forty years, with virtually no significant change. The wisdom of this unit structure has paid off in combat over and over again. When that bomb fell among the Kurds, Eric was able to split the team down the middle and do two things effectively at once—fight the battle and treat the casualties. The idea that everybody on the team should be cross-trained in the skills of the other guys and be a medic in an emergency paid off, too.

The whole Special Forces system is, in fact, based on four fundamental ideas that most civilians don't typically associate with a military organization:

- First, we all understand that our soldiers are more important than our hardware.

- Second, it is the quality of these soldiers—their maturity, courage, technical skills, cultural sensitivity, and language proficiency, and their ability to lead and to follow—that is the foundation of our effectiveness.
- Third, the process of producing good Special Forces soldiers is a long, slow, expensive one. Over the years we have experimented with lower standards and faster training, with poor results.
- Fourth, the process of minting competent Green Berets can't be accelerated. Every time the United States goes to war, there is a push to somehow create more of us in a hurry. It just can't be done.

During the last election, there were several presidential candidates that touted they would "double" the number of Special Forces during their first term of office (four years). These politicians are completely ignorant of the process required to produce these types of warriors. Not only will it require decades of time, but it would most likely have a damaging effect by lowering the standard required for recruitment, training, and duration of completion of Special Forces training. While there is some room for growth, slow, well-resourced, and careful monitoring of quality are the keys to increasing the numbers of Special Forces.

NINE-ONE'S LUCK

In some ways, Nine-One was phenomenally lucky. First was the way that the guys on the team gelled and became a true unit. An ODA, for better or worse, is like a family, and it has many of the normal family conflicts. Nine-One became, as a result of our tank fight, one of the most famous ODAs in recent Special Forces history, and that could be a problem for guys in our business. But instead of disintegrating under the pressure of huge egos, they became more cohesive, and better soldiers.

It was Nine-One's luck to be alongside two great SF A-teams, Nine-Two and Four-Four, when that enemy task force materialized out of the haze in 2003. They outnumbered us at least five to one, outgunned us with their tanks and artillery, and caught us all flat-footed in the open. According to all the rules of probability, we should have had our clock cleaned, but the history of warfare is full of odd little incidents like that, where a big Goliath gets slain by a little David, where the quality of the warrior is more important than his numbers or weapons. Even in the era of smart bombs and cruise missiles, the intangible personal qualities of courage, skill with weapons, teamwork, imagination, discipline, and audacity are able to defeat vastly superior forces.

Tom Sandoval and the guys from Four-Four, Matt Saunders and his guys from Nine-Two, along with Saleem, Jake, and Todd, our tactical air controllers, and our brave volunteer drivers, Steve Brunk and Ed Bromley, did something important on that hill. We've all been told over and over again that we were just lucky, but I think it was the kind of luck that you manufacture yourself.

We were lucky, if you want to call it that, because the US Army Special Operations Command has maintained very high standards for the selection and training of Special Forces soldiers in the Q course. We were lucky, I guess, that our commanders—mostly—treated their soldiers as responsible adults able to think for themselves before, during, and after the battle.

We were lucky that somebody in the food chain ensured that we had enough ammunition to be good with our weapons—and that the commander of little Fort Pickett, instead of offering us some risk-averse, excessively constrained-by-safety, micromanaged range, made sure we fired all that ammunition in a way suited to a real-world battlefield. We were lucky to be American Special Forces soldiers.

ODA-391

Nine-One, at this writing, is still mostly together. Eric has moved off to another assignment. Gerry and I have retired. Marty is still the XO (Executive officer, or second in command), and most of the other guys are still on the team. They've been back to Iraq and Afghanistan twice and will probably go again.

Before the war, my little team of guys had a reputation as black sheep—loud, abrasive, overconfident, pushy misfits. The reputation was well deserved because we somehow developed that magical warrior quality of audacity that can't be bought and can't be taught.

When those tanks came rolling out of the haze to confront us, it was just what we had been training for over the past weeks and months. We had been challenged over and over about just such an event, and we had always said that we could take on such an opponent and win. Somehow or other—and it really was not just luck—when the time and the challenge came, Nine-One, Nine-Two, and Four-Four were the right guys in the right place with the right skills and the right weapons. We piled them up, and we didn't run.

"ROUGHNECK NINE-ONE, OUT."

SPECIAL FORCES KILLED IN ACTION

Master Sgt. Jefferson Donald "JD" Davis, ODA-574
KIA (killed in action) 5 December 2001 in Afghanistan, north of Kandahar

Sgt. 1st Class Daniel Henry "Dano" Petithory, ODA-574
KIA 5 December 2001 in Afghanistan, north of Kandahar

Sgt. 1st Class Nathan Ross Chapman, ODA-194
KIA 4 January 2002 in Afghanistan, in the Gardez area west of Khost

Chief Warrant Officer Stanley L. Harriman, ODA-372
KIA 2 March 2002 as a result of gunfire from an Air Force AC-130 gunship that mistook his convoy for enemy forces

Sgt. 1st Class Daniel Aaron Romero, B-5-19SFG
KIA 15 April 2002 in Afghanistan when rockets he was attempting to dismantle exploded

Sgt. 1st Class Peter P. Tycz II, ODA-365
KIA 12 June 2002 as senior medic aboard US military plane that crashed in Afghanistan

Sgt. 1st Class Christopher J. Speer, HQ USASOC
WIA (wounded in action) 27 July 2002 in Afghanistan, near the village of Ab Khail. He was evacuated to Germany, where he died 6 August 2002.

Sgt. 1st Class Mark Wayne Jackson, ODA-145
KIA 2 October 2002 near the city of Zamboanga in the Philippines

Sgt. Orlando Morales, A-2-7SFG
KIA 29 March 2003 when his mounted reconnaissance unit was ambushed near Geresk, Afghanistan

Sgt. 1st Class Mitchell A. Lane, ODA-365
KIA 29 August 2003 when he fell 25 feet while conducting a fast rope infiltration into a known enemy cave complex in Afghanistan

Master Sgt. Kevin N. Morehead, B-3-5SFG
KIA 12 September 2003 during a firefight in a predawn raid in the town of Ar Ramadi, Iraq

Sgt. 1st Class William M. Bennett, B-3-5SFG
KIA 12 September 2003 during a firefight in a predawn raid in the town of Ar Ramadi, Iraq

Staff Sgt. Paul A. Sweeney, A-3-3SFG
KIA 30 October 2003 during an ambush near Musa, Qalax, Afghanistan

Sgt. Roy A. Wood, ODA-2092
Fatally injured 9 January 2004 in a vehicle accident near Kabul, Afghanistan

Master Sgt. Kelly L. Hornbeck, C-3-10SFG
WIA 16 January 2004 when an improvised explosive device hit his vehicle, DOW (died of wounds) two days later on 18 January 2004

Master Sgt. Richard L. Ferguson, C-2-10SFG
Fatally injured 30 March 2004 after the Humvee he was riding in flipped over

Sgt. Maj. Michael B. Stack, C-2-5SFG
KIA 11 April 2004 when his convoy was ambushed near Baghdad, Iraq

Chief Warrant Officer Bruce E. Price, 1-3SFG
KIA 15 May 2004 when his detachment was ambushed while on combat patrol near Kajaki in southern Afghanistan

Capt. Daniel W. Eggers, A-1-3SFG
KIA 29 May 2004 in Kandahar, Afghanistan, when his vehicle hit an improvised explosive device

Sgt. 1st Class Robert J. Mogensen, A-1-3SFG
KIA 29 May 2004 in Kandahar, Afghanistan, when his vehicle hit an improvised explosive device

Maj. Paul R. Syverson III, HQ 5SFG
KIA 16 June 2004 during a rocket attack on Logistical Support Area Anaconda, Balad, Iraq

Staff Sgt. Robert K. McGee, ODA-155
Died 1 July 2004 in Manila, Philippines, of non-combat-related injuries

Staff Sgt. Paul C. Mardis, ODA-585
WIA 20 May 2004 in Mosul, Iraq, when an improvised explosive device struck his vehicle, DOW 15 July 2004 at Walter Reed Medical Center

Capt. Michael Yury Tarlavsky, A-1-5SFG
KIA 12 August 2004 near Najaf, Iraq, when his unit came under small-arms fire and grenade attack

Staff Sgt. Aaron N. Holleyman, ODA-531
KIA 30 August 2004 near Khutayiah, Iraq, when an explosive device detonated near his Humvee

Staff Sgt. Tony B. Olaes, A-2-3SFG
KIA 20 September 2004 when his vehicle came under fire during a combat patrol near the town of Shkin in Afghanistan's Paktika Province

Staff Sgt. Robert S. Goodwin, A-2-3SFG
KIA 20 September 2004 when his vehicle came under fire during a combat patrol near the town of Shkin in Afghanistan's Paktika Province

Sgt. 1st Class Pedro Munoz, 1-7SFG

KIA 2 January 2005 during offensive combat operations in Afghanistan's Herat Province

Sgt. Jeremy R. Wright, 2-1SFG

KIA 3 January 2005 when an enemy IED exploded near his Ground Mobility Vehicle during operations in Afghanistan's Konar Province

Sgt. 1st Class Allen C. Johnson, 1-7SFG

KIA 26 April 2005 in Khanaqin, Afghanistan, when he was attacked by enemy fire during a combat patrol

Sergeant 1st Class Steven M. Langmack

KIA 31 May 2005 near Al Qaim, Iraq, after he was attacked by enemy small-arms fire during combat operations

Staff Sgt. Leroy E. Alexander, 1-7SFG

KIA 3 June 2005 in the vicinity of Orgun-e, Afghanistan, when an enemy improvised explosive device exploded near his Ground Mobility Vehicle

Capt. Charles D. Robinson, 1-7SFG

KIA 3 June 2005 in the vicinity of Orgun-e, Afghanistan, when an enemy improvised explosive device exploded near his Ground Mobility Vehicle

Staff Sgt. Christopher N. Piper, 1-7SFG

WIA 3 June 2005 near Orgun-e, Afghanistan, when an enemy improvised explosive device exploded near his Ground Mobility Vehicle, DOW 16 June 2005 at Brooke Army Medical Center

Sgt. 1st Class Victor H. Cervantes, 1-7SFG

KIA 10 June 2005 near Orgun-e, Afghanistan, during combat operations

Master Sgt. Robert M. Horrigan, 1-7SFG

KIA 17 June 2005 in western Iraq when his unit was attacked with enemy small-arms fire during combat operations

Sgt. Jason T. Palmerton, 1-3SFG

KIA 23 July 2005 near Kandahar, Afghanistan, during combat operations while on patrol near Qal'eh-Ye Gaz

Sgt. 1st Class Brett Eugene Walden, 1-5SFG
Died 5 August 2005 near Rabi'ah, Iraq, when his Humvee and a fuel truck collided

Staff Sgt. Christopher M. Falkel, 1-5SFG
KIA during combat operations near Deh Afghan, Afghanistan

Capt. Jeremy A. Chandler, A-1-3SFG
Died 11 August 2005 from non-battle-related injuries while he was conducting training operations at Tarin Khowt, Afghanistan

Sgt. 1st Class Trevor John Diesing, HQ USASOC
KIA 25 August 2005 when an improvised explosive device detonated near his position in Husaybah, Iraq

Master Sgt. Ivica Jerak, HQ USASOC
KIA 25 August 2005 when an improvised explosive device detonated near his position while he was conducting combat operations in Iraq

Sgt. 1st Class Obediah J. Kolath, HQ USASOC
WIA 25 August 2005 in Husaybah, Iraq, when an improvised explosive device detonated near his position, DOW 28 August 2005 at the Landstuhl Regional Medical Center

Staff Sgt. Gary R. Harper Jr., 2-5SFG
KIA 9 October 2005 when his reconnaissance mission was attacked by enemy forces near Baghdad, Iraq

Staff Sgt. Matthew A. Kimmell, 3-5SFG
KIA 11 October 2005 in Muqdadiyah, Diyala Province, Iraq, when an improvised explosive device detonated near his Humvee

Capt. Jeffrey P. Toczylowski, 1-10SFG
Died 3 November 2005 from injuries suffered during a combat mission in Al Anbar Province, Iraq

GLOSSARY

AAR
: after-action review, a sort of postmission discussion of what happened, how, and why, and what lessons may be learned and applied in the future

Alamo
: an informal term for a defensive battle position, normally a natural terrain feature providing cover and concealment—a rallying point from which a unit must fight

APC
: armored personnel carrier, a tanklike vehicle without a large cannon and with the ability to deliver infantry near an objective with safety from rifle and machine gun fire

ASP
: ammunition supply point

A-team, or ODA
: Twelve men operating as a unit—one captain commanding, a warrant officer functioning as second in command, with "slots" for two weapons specialists, two communications specialists, two medics, two

engineers, and two Operations/Intel sergeants. An A-team can be split into two subunits, each with a full complement of skills, for short-duration missions.

BCU   battery coolant unit, the Javelin missile component that provides electrical power to the weapon's subsystems

BMP   Bronevaya Maschina Piekhota, a very popular armored personnel carrier design originally from the Soviet Union and now in service with many nations

B-team   The headquarters element of a Special Forces company, comprising eleven men. The B-team includes the company commander, administrative staff, logistics support element, and other specialists. It has the same skills and weapons as a standard A-team and can fight as one when required.

CAS   close air support

CLU   command launch unit, the sighting system for missiles like the Javelin

CSM   command sergeant major, the senior enlisted member of units of battalion size and above

defilade   a natural depression in the terrain that can be used for protection against direct-fire weapons like rifles or tank cannon

ENDEX   slang for "end of exercise"

FMTV   a large type of cargo truck collectively known as the "family of medium tactical vehicles"

FOB   forward operating base, the headquarters that commands and controls teams in the field

FTX   field training exercise

IMBTR   a fairly new and very well-regarded squad radio used by the Army and Marine Corps

JDAM   Joint Direct Attack Munition—a tail kit that turns a dumb bomb into a smart one by adding a GPS-based navigational computer and control fins

JRTC   Joint Readiness Training Center, a facility at Fort Polk, Louisiana, where US Army units participate in large-scale realistic exercises

JSOTF   Joint Special Operations Task Force

M2   .50cal heavy machine gun in use by the Army for eighty-five years, affectionately known as "Ma Deuce"

M240   7.62 mm medium machine gun

M4   the carbine variant of the M16 rifle, the standard US Army individual weapon for the past forty years

M107 Barrett   .50cal sniper rifle, capable of first-shot kills on individual soldiers at nearly a mile

MICH   Modular Integrated Communications Helmet, a varia-
(Pronounced   tion on the standard Kevlar "brain bucket" used by
mitch) Helmet soldiers and Marines

Mk19   40 mm grenade-launcher that functions somewhat like a machine gun

MSS   mission support site, a temporary base of operations close to the objective

MTLB   Maschina Transportnaya Legkaya Boyevaya, a fast, low, tracked APC of Soviet design with a crew of two and room for ten cramped infantry soldiers and their gear

NCO	noncommissioned officer, normally a sergeant in pay grades E-5 ("buck" sergeant) through E-9 (sergeant major). NCOs are organizationally subordinate to all commissioned officers (second lieutenant and above), although such distinctions are sometimes not apparent to observers.
NODs	night observation devices—night vision goggles and sight systems, also known as NVGs
ODA	Alternate name for A-team
ODB	Alternate name for B-team
OPCON	operational control, it is common for units to be "married up" or "chopped" to other units for short periods and missions, as ODA-391 was when it was under the OPCON of 10th Group before crossing the Green Line.
PEQ-4	a small rectangular device often mounted on M4 carbines, the PEQ-4 includes both a laser beam that can be used to engage targets at night and an infrared area light source that functions somewhat like a flashlight, both invisible except with NODs.
Q course	qualification course, the program that trains soldiers to be members of Special Forces teams
RTB	return to base
SOFLAM	Special Operations Forces Laser Marker, a pointing device used to designate targets or other objects of interest on the battlefield
TACP	tactical air controller party (usually two men but only one during the events at Debecka)
TTPs	tactics, techniques, and procedures